Praise for *The Positive Shift*

"The research is clear: Your mindset is one of the greatest predictors of your success and well-being. With practical strategies and stories, Catherine Sanderson shows you how to apply this research at work, with your family, and in your own life."

—Shawn Achor, *New York Times* bestselling author of *Before Happiness* and *The Happiness Advantage*

"A smart and engaging exploration of the science of happiness and how we can use it on our own lives."

—Daniel Gilbert, author of *Stumbling on Happiness* and professor of psychology at Harvard University

"As someone who in the past has suffered from anxiety and depression, I only wish this book had been available in those dark days. It is chock full of evidence-based strategies of how to convert the Eeyores of this world like me into Tiggers. And we really can change into more kittens and rainbows sorts of people! Professor Sanderson shares in her warm and conversational voice what really makes a difference to our mental health, from using money to save time, to planning a trip (even better than going on one), and why we should give gifts to everyone. I was electrified to read the data and evidence for lots of stuff I naturally have learned to do in my own efforts to become calm and well. But I discovered a whole lot of new ideas, too: try saying 'I don't do something' rather than 'I can't.' Above all, this is a book that gives hope. We can change our mindset, and in doing so we really can become happier and healthier, and even live longer. Here's to making *The Positive Shift*."

—Rachel Kelly, bestselling author of *Walking on Sunshine: 52 Small Steps to Happiness*

"*The Positive Shift* offers a rare and valuable combination by offering deeply practical advice about what can seem an impossibly abstract problem: How can we use our big brains to increase our well-being?"

—**Michael Norton, professor at Harvard Business School and coauthor of *Happy Money***

"Everyone seeking to live a long and successful life needs *The Positive Shift*! Catherine Sanderson's mantra that our mindsets have powerful influences on our performance—good and bad—gives us an incredible set of tools to make important changes at any stage of life."

—**Marc E. Agronin, MD, author of *The End of Old Age: Living a Longer, More Purposeful Life***

"Dr. Catherine Sanderson, nationally recognized as a fabulous teacher, researcher, corporate speaker, and consultant, has gifted us with a gold-mine of information to reduce stress and improve our life. Using only empirically significant research findings, case histories, personal anecdotes and foibles, and self-quizzes, Professor Sanderson provides clear and compelling take-home instructions for adopting a positive mindset. Her warm and accessible writing style will definitely enable you to become happier, healthier, and wiser and live longer. Who could ask for anything more!"

—**Dr. James B. Maas, Weiss Presidential Fellow and former professor and chair of psychology at Cornell University and CEO of Sleep for Success***

"The Positive Shift is a lucid work, drawing upon the latest scientific findings, that will enable readers to enhance their health and well-being in daily life. I especially liked Dr. Sanderson's ability to weave events from her own life into this tapestry designed to help others."

—**Edward Hoffman, PhD, author of *Paths to Happiness: 50 Ways to Add Joy to Your Life Every Day***

The
POSITIVE
Shift

The POSITIVE *Shift*

Mastering Mindset to Improve Happiness, Health, and Longevity

Catherine A. Sanderson

BenBella Books, Inc.
Dallas, TX

BENBELLA
BenBella Books, Inc.
10440 N. Central Expressway, Suite 800 | Dallas, TX 75231
www.benbellabooks.com | Send feedback to feedback@benbellabooks.com

Printed in the United States of America
10 9 8 7 6 5 4 3 2 1

Library of Congress Cataloging-in-Publication Data
Names: Sanderson, Catherine Ashley, 1968- author.
Title: The positive shift : mastering mindset to improve happiness, health, and longevity / by Catherine A. Sanderson.
Description: Dallas, TX : BenBella Books, [2019] | Includes bibliographical references and index.
Identifiers: LCCN 2018036996 (print) | LCCN 2018041331 (ebook) | ISBN 9781946885715 (electronic) | ISBN 9781946885449 (trade paper : alk. paper)
Subjects: LCSH: Self-actualization (Psychology) | Self-care, Health. | Longevity. | Interpersonal relations.
Classification: LCC BF637.S4 (ebook) | LCC BF637.S4 S256 2019 (print) | DDC 158.1—dc23
LC record available at https://lccn.loc.gov/2018036996

Copyediting by Miki Alexandra Caputo
Proofreading by Jenny Bridges and Chris Gage
Indexing by Amy Murphy Indexing & Editorial

Text design and composition by Silver Feather Design
Cover design by Oceana Garceau
Cover photo © iStock
Printed by Lake Book Manufacturing

Distributed to the trade by Two Rivers Distribution, an Ingram brand
www.tworiversdistribution.com

Special discounts for bulk sales (minimum of 25 copies) are available.
Please contact bulkorders@benbellabooks.com.

To Bart,
for his ability to change a flat tire
but also so much more.

Contents

Introduction

I gave a talk a few years ago on the science of happiness at a large financial services convention in which attendees had the option to sit in on one of several presentations on different topics. At the end of my lecture, a woman came up to me to tell me how much she enjoyed it. And then she said, "To be honest, I almost didn't come to your session, because I figured that I would really hate you."

Her comment was—let's just say—unexpected. So, I thanked her for her unusual compliment and then asked her why she had such a negative expectation.

She responded, "I just figured that anyone who talked about happiness for an hour would be all about rainbows and kittens and that by the end of the hour I would want to strangle you."

I open this book with that story to illustrate a key principle that I'll return to repeatedly in the pages ahead. There are indeed some people who are naturally happy and who do consistently see the world in an overwhelmingly positive way; these are the "kittens and rainbows" people. If you are one of those people, congratulations . . . and truly, you don't really need this book because you are already probably doing the right things to find happiness and good health.

Unfortunately, I am not one of these people. I worry about far too many things. Is this traffic jam going to make me miss my plane? Is that pain in my stomach a sign of cancer? Is my son with mediocre grades ever going to get into college? My natural tendency is quite honestly one of doom and gloom—pretty much the opposite of the kittens-and-rainbows perspective.

So, how did I manage to write a book on strategies for finding happiness? Good question!

For the past twenty years, I've taught classes and conducted research on various topics within psychology. As part of my job, I regularly read scientific studies to stay up to date on the latest findings in my field. Over the last five or so years, some of the most interesting and exciting research has come from an emerging field called positive psychology, which examines the factors predicting psychological and physical well-being. Here are just some of the fascinating findings from researchers in this field:

- Spending time on Facebook makes us feel sad and lonely.[1]
- Expensive brand-name medicines provide better pain relief than the generic stuff, even if they share the same ingredients.[2]
- Placing a cell phone on a table reduces the quality of a conversation.[3]
- Patients in a hospital room with a view of nature recover faster from surgery than those without.[4]
- People with positive expectations about aging live on average *seven and a half years longer* than those without.[5]

As I took in the assorted research and tried to synthesize it to share with my students, I became more and more convinced that these seemingly disparate findings actually illustrate a really simple point: Our happiness in daily life, the state of our physical health, and even how long we live are largely determined not by external events, but rather by the way we *think* about ourselves and the world around us.

Why does spending time on Facebook make us feel bad? Because we compare our lives to other people's lives, and most people post only the good parts of their lives on social media. This leads us to think that other people consistently experience great events—successful kids, fabulous vacations, impressive careers, and so on. Our own lives can't seem to measure up.

Why do expensive brand-name medicines work better than the low-cost generic ones? Because we think that costly medicines will work better than their cheap counterparts, and this belief causes us to act in ways that lead us to physically feel better. For example, if you are about to undergo a medical procedure and are worried about the pain, receiving a drug that you believe will reduce this pain will substantially lower your anxiety. And in turn, this decrease in anxiety will help reduce the pain you feel.

As I read all this research on how our beliefs affect how we feel, I started trying to use this information to change my own thoughts and behavior to try to find greater happiness. So, instead of mindlessly surfing the internet as I lay in bed, I made a point of finding a great book to read. Even when I felt too busy to exercise, I chose to take a twenty-minute walk at lunch.

For some people, adopting a positive mindset comes naturally. These people find the silver lining in every cloud and are happier and healthier as a result. For others, including myself, adopting this type of optimistic worldview takes time, energy, and effort. These people have to shift their pessimistic general predisposition to find that mysterious silver lining, and they have to work diligently to engage in behaviors that make them feel better, not worse—like going for a brisk walk in nature to cope with sadness, rather than looking for happiness at the bottom of a pint of Ben & Jerry's ice cream.

But here's the good news for those who struggle to feel happy: no matter our natural tendency, we can all achieve greater happiness and better health by making relatively small changes in how we think about ourselves and the world. As author Elizabeth Gilbert writes in her 2006 memoir *Eat Pray Love*:

> Happiness is the consequence of personal effort. You fight for it, strive for it, insist upon it, and sometimes even travel around the world looking for it. You have to participate relentlessly in the manifestations of your own blessings. And once you have achieved a state of happiness, you must never become lax about maintaining it. You must make a mighty effort to keep swimming upward into that happiness forever, to stay afloat on top of it.

Positive, optimistic thoughts don't come easily to me; I have to work for my happiness. For the last few years, I've deliberately shifted my mentality to be more in line with what the research shows makes people happier. Instead of wallowing in other people's glowing social media posts and comparing my own fortune (or lack thereof) to theirs, I shift my thinking to stop these negative thoughts and instead focus on the very real things I have that are good. My kid's not going to be valedictorian, but he's got a great group of friends. My family's not spending two weeks in Tahiti, but we really enjoy our one week in a rental house on the Jersey Shore.

My natural inclination is clearly not to find the silver lining, but with time and energy and effort, I find it easier all the time to shift my thinking in ways that do make me happier. My goal in writing this book is to give others who also struggle to feel happy specific, science-based strategies they can use to improve the quality—and longevity—of their lives. So, congratulations on taking the first step by picking up this book, and I very much hope *The Positive Shift* will help you find the happiness you deserve.

PART 1

DISCOVERING MINDSET

Chapter 1

Mindset Matters

On May 1, 2015, forty-seven-year-old Dave Goldberg, a highly successful Silicon Valley executive and spouse of Facebook's chief operating officer, Sheryl Sandberg, died suddenly of a heart attack. In an instant, Sandberg became a widow and single parent to two young children—a ten-year-old son and an eight-year-old daughter.

Thirty days later, Sandberg shared a tribute to her husband about what she had learned from this loss, saying, "When tragedy occurs, it presents a choice. You can give in to the void, the emptiness that fills your heart, your lungs, constricts your ability to think or even breathe. Or you can try to find meaning."

This book is about what it takes to make that choice: both when dealing with the small irritations of daily life—traffic jams, job interviews, car trouble, and so on—as well as when facing the devastation of immense loss—a divorce, a serious illness or injury, or even the death of a loved one.

Inconveniences and hardships, minor obstacles and major roadblocks, are part of life. We can't avoid stress or prevent bad things from happening to us or our loved ones. But we do have control over how we *think* about the bad things and whether we have the wherewithal to find some good in terribly difficult circumstances. And most important, learning how to adopt a positive mindset, no matter what, can have lasting effects on our happiness, health, and even how long we live.

THE POWER OF MENTAL SHORTCUTS

As we go about our daily lives, we are bombarded with information. We read newspapers, watch television, and scour the internet. We interact with people in our communities, pass billboards, listen to the radio. And we attempt to organize and make sense of all the different information we receive from these different sources.

Because it's simply impossible to thoughtfully and thoroughly sort through all this information, we take shortcuts in our thinking, often without conscious awareness. For example, people rate a wine sample they are told costs ninety dollars a bottle as much better than a wine sample they are told costs ten dollars a bottle, even when in reality the wine is exactly the same.[1]

We also use mental shortcuts to form expectations about people we meet. When we encounter a medical professional in a hospital setting, we tend to assume that person is a doctor if he is male and a nurse if she is female.

This process of taking shortcuts to make sense of the world is based on stereotypes we've formed from our experiences. We assume more expensive wine tastes better, because we expect higher quality to command a higher price. We assume men are more likely than women to be doctors, and that women are more likely than men to be nurses, because that has typically been our experience.

The images we see and hear in the media reinforce these stereotypes. For example, media messages often portray pretty dismal images about aging. In movies, TV shows, advertisements, and especially infomercials, older adults are presented as developing memory problems, struggling with various physical limitations and the like. Repeated exposure to these images can create negative expectations about the aging process.

Most important, the mental shortcuts we develop influence how we think about ourselves and can influence our behavior in fundamental ways. According to one study, midlife adults who hold negative beliefs about aging report having less interest in and less enjoyment of sexual behavior.[2] Older adults who *feel* older—regardless of their actual chronological age—are especially likely to report having such negative beliefs about sex.

Although this example illustrates the downside of holding negative expectations, holding positive expectations can lead to beneficial outcomes. For example, people who are told they are given a "lucky" golf ball drain 35 percent more putts than those who are given a "regular" golf ball.[3] Moreover, people who perceive some type of "upside" to a painful activity or procedure can feel less intense pain, which helps explain why many people voluntarily undergo some types of pain (e.g., navel piercing, tattooing, climbing Mount Everest). People also remember such pain later on as less intense than it actually was at the time. With practice, we can learn to use mental tricks to influence our behavior in positive ways.

HOW EXPECTATIONS CREATE REALITY

Imagine you are a teenager with a new learner's permit and you are driving for the first time with your grandparents. You are aware of the stereotype of "bad teenage drivers," so you are worried about making any mistakes while driving. This anxiety about potentially making a mistake—and reinforcing that stereotype in front of your grandparents—distracts you from your focus on careful driving and leads you to make errors you might not have made otherwise.

This is a simple illustration of how the stereotypes we hold can have an impact on our behavior. Psychologists call this process *stereotype threat*, which describes the situation in which concern about confirming a negative stereotype about one's group disrupts the ability to focus on a particular task. In turn, this lack of focus leads, ironically, to worse performance on that task, leading people to unwittingly demonstrate the negative stereotypes about their group they were worried about proving.

The initial studies on stereotype threat examined the impact of negative stereotypes about African Americans on their academic performance. In one study, social psychologist Claude Steele and his colleagues at Stanford University brought in both African American and white college students and asked them to take a test of verbal skills—a test in which there is a stereotype that African Americans do less well than whites.[4] To test whether inducing this stereotype would influence performance, half of the students were told that the test they would be taking evaluated "intellectual ability" to activate that stereotype. The other half of the students were simply told that they would be taking a "problem-solving task unrelated to ability," in which case the stereotype wasn't activated. Although all students took the same test, African American students who were specifically told that the test measured intellectual ability performed substantially worse than whites. In contrast, there were no differences on test scores between African Americans and whites for those who weren't deliberately reminded of the negative stereotype about their ethnic group's verbal abilities.

Subsequent research has demonstrated the powerful effects of stereotypes on many different types of behavior in many different groups of people. As described in his 2010 book, *Whistling Vivaldi: How Stereotypes Affect Us and What We Can Do*, Claude Steele found that women who are reminded of the stereotype that "women aren't good at math" perform worse on a subsequent math test than those who aren't reminded of such a stereotype.[5] Similarly, white athletes who are told a golf putting test measures "natural athletic ability" perform worse on this task than those who are not told, presumably owing to fear of confirming the well-known stereotype that their ethnic group is not so athletic.

These studies all illustrate the power stereotypes have to influence our behavior, sometimes in significant ways.

THE BIG IMPACT
OF SUBTLE TRIGGERS

The last section described the influence of blatant reminders about stereotypes on people's behavior. In many cases, however, stereotypes affect us in much subtler ways.

Researchers in one study gave young girls, ages four to seven, a doll to play with for five minutes.[6] Some of the girls were given a Doctor Barbie doll while others were given a Mrs. Potato Head doll. Although both these types of dolls are marketed to young girls, they differ substantially in appearance, with the Barbie dolls portraying a much more physically attractive and sexualized appearance than the Potato Head ones. The girls were then shown ten photographs portraying different types of occupations and were asked which of these jobs they, and boys, could do when they grew up. It turns out that girls who played with a Barbie doll—even when the doll was dressed as a doctor—saw fewer career options available for them compared to boys. In contrast, there was no difference in perceived career options available for them compared to boys for girls who played with the Mrs. Potato Head doll. This study suggests that playing with a highly sexualized toy influenced young girls' beliefs about what type of work they could do.

Similarly, women in college express less interest in the field of computer science after seeing pictures of a stereotypical computer science classroom (featuring *Star Trek* posters, technology magazines, science fiction books, etc.) than after seeing photos of a more neutral classroom (featuring nature posters, general magazines, plants, etc.).[7] Both these studies show how subtle triggers in the environment influence how people think about themselves and can have substantial consequences.

What's particularly remarkable is that even subtle reminders of stereotypes that apply to other people influence our own behavior. In one clever study, researchers at New York University brought in college students to participate in a test that supposedly measured language proficiency.[8] They were given various sets of words and were told to use those words—and only those words—to form a grammatically correct sentence. Half the students received a set of words that cued old age, such as *retired*, *old*, and *wrinkled*. The other students received a set of neutral words, such as *private*, *clean*, and *thirsty*.

After finishing this task, students were told that the study was over, and they were free to leave. But unbeknownst to them, this is the part of the study the researchers were most interested in examining. As students left the room, the researcher started a stopwatch and timed how long it took students to walk down the hall to the elevator. Just as they predicted, students took significantly longer to walk down the hall after they had been exposed to the "old" words than those who saw the neutral words. This study shows that stereotypes can and do influence our own behavior, even when those stereotypes don't directly apply to us! After all, the students in this study aren't elderly, yet being exposed to stereotypes about older people still led them to behave in line with such generalizations.

UNDERSTANDING MINDSET

In addition to navigating stereotypes, our behavior is also influenced by the particular mindsets, or mental frames, we adopt about ourselves and the world. Our mindsets—which include thoughts, beliefs, and expectations—determine how we perceive and respond to events in our lives. They also include expectations we hold about our abilities, traits, and characteristics. Are we optimistic or pessimistic? Good at math or terrible with numbers? A people person or a shy introvert? Our distinct attributes, after all, are what define us as individuals.

Another fundamental aspect of mindset is our beliefs about the potential for these attributes to shift over time. Carol Dweck, a psychology professor at Stanford University, has conducted extensive research showing that people vary considerably in such beliefs. Some people believe that basic qualities, such as intelligence and personality, are fixed and stable—this is a *fixed mindset*. Other people believe these qualities are malleable and can and do change over time with effort—this is a *growth mindset*.[9] Whether we have a fixed or growth mindset influences how we approach different situations, how we respond to mistakes and failures, and how we see and respond to challenges.

Here's a simple example of how the mindsets we hold exert a strong and lasting impact on our behavior: Many well-meaning parents and teachers praise children's strong academic performance by labeling them smart. On the surface, this label seems like a nice compliment, and surely one we'd all like to hear about our own intellectual ability.

Yet considerable evidence now points to the hazards of this label for children's enjoyment, persistence, and achievement in academic settings. What's the drawback to hearing you are "smart"? This label leads children to believe that intelligence represents a fixed characteristic, meaning some people are innately, and permanently, smart, whereas others are not. A child who is told that he or she is smart often adopts a fixed mindset about the nature of intelligence and becomes deeply concerned about the possibility of disconfirming this label. If in the future this child performs poorly on a test, this single negative performance would be highly informative—and devastating: "I did poorly on this test, so maybe I'm not so smart after all."

Children may respond to their concerns about failing to live up to this expectation by underperforming; they try only problems they are certain they can solve (thereby depriving themselves of the opportunity to challenge themselves and grow). As Robert Sternberg, dean of the School of Arts and Sciences at Tufts University, notes, "If you're afraid of making mistakes, you'll never learn on the job, and your whole approach becomes defensive: 'I have to make sure I don't screw up.'"[10]

On the other hand, people who adopt a growth mindset, and see their abilities and characteristics as able to change through effort and practice, experience substantial benefits. Mistakes are seen as opportunities to learn and grow, and thus people are motivated to pursue challenging tasks in order to develop such strengths. For example, seventh graders who hold a belief that intelligence can develop show increases in grades during the first two years of junior high school, when schoolwork becomes more challenging and grading standards become more rigorous, whereas those without such beliefs show no such improvements.[11] Similarly, athletes who adopt a growth mindset understand that talent alone is insufficient, and that serious effort and rigorous training are the keys to success, achieve at higher levels. One recent study even found that giving teenagers (who were all already experiencing mental health problems) a thirty-minute lesson about growth mindset, and our ability to change and improve over time, led to lower levels of anxiety and depression as long as nine months later.[12] In sum, adopting a mindset focused on the power and potential for change results in substantial benefits.

MINDSET REALLY MATTERS

Our beliefs about whether our fundamental personal qualities can change influence virtually all aspects of our lives. For example, people who believe their levels of anxiety and depression can't be changed, no matter how hard they try, show more symptoms of anxiety and depression than those without such beliefs.[13] People with such beliefs report higher levels of worry and sadness and even physical symptoms of anxiety such as sweaty hands and panic attacks.

Similarly, the mindset we hold about aging influences both cognitive performance and physical health. According to one study, adults ages sixty-one to eighty-seven who believe that the aging process is fixed and inevitable show lower scores on a memory test and higher blood pressure after they are reminded about negative stereotypes about aging.[14] In contrast, those who believe that the aging process can be changed don't show such reactions; they don't buy into the inevitability of such stereotypes and therefore don't suffer these negative consequences.

Our mindsets also influence how we relate to and interact with others in fundamental ways. Researchers in one study examined people's beliefs about whether empathy is malleable, meaning whether the ability to put oneself in someone else's shoes can change with effort.[15] Study participants rated whether they believed a person's level of empathy is something very basic about them, and it can't be changed, or whether they believed a person can change how empathic they are. The researchers then measured people's willingness to try to empathize with someone who disagreed about a personally important social or political issue.

As the researchers predicted, people who held more malleable beliefs about empathy showed a greater willingness to listen respectfully and try to understand the other person's views. Such effort can lead to better interpersonal relationships and lower levels of conflict.

It's no surprise, then, that our mindsets influence our willingness to work through problems in close relationships. People with a soul-mate mindset believe that having a good relationship is mostly about picking the right person. They see relationships in an all-or-nothing way.[16] Unfortunately, this belief leads to two types of dysfunctional behavior: ignoring problems—since any problems would mean the relationship is bad—or giving up. Studies of college student romantic couples show that those with a soul-mate theory spend less time trying to work things out when facing a stressful relationship event—they basically withdraw effort and give up. Those with a work-it-out mindset, on the other hand, see acknowledging and working through problems in an open and constructive way as an essential part of building strong relationships. When facing stressful events, they work hard to fix things and try to reframe such problems in a positive way.

Researchers in one study examined people's beliefs about sexual satisfaction and, in particular, whether sexual satisfaction is found through finding the "right" partner (a fixed mindset) or whether it develops through effort and hard work (a growth mindset).[17] Those with growth beliefs about sexual satisfaction show higher levels of sexual satisfaction and relationship satisfaction. Their partners also report higher levels of sexual satisfaction, indicating that believing good sex takes time and effort benefits both people in a relationship.

These examples illustrate how beliefs about whether our particular attributes are fixed or changeable have significant consequences for the quality and longevity of our interpersonal relationships as well as our psychological and physical well-being.

UNDERSTANDING
YOUR FAILURE MINDSET

Perhaps the most important step in understanding mindset is acknowledging that people vary in how they think about the causes of disappointments and failures in their own lives.[18] Some people blame negative events on themselves and on their flaws and inadequacies. They obsess and ruminate about these bad outcomes and beat themselves up. Other people adopt a much more positive mindset in the face of failures and disappointments. They recognize that difficulties happen to everyone and try to keep things in perspective.

As you can probably imagine, people who show self-compassion in the face of negative events experience better outcomes. They have lower levels of anxiety and depression and feel happier and more optimistic overall about the future. For example, first-year college students who have more self-compassion during this difficult life transition show greater engagement and motivation in college life.[19]

Here's a simple test you can take to figure out how you think about yourself: Created by Dr. Kristin Neff, the Self-Compassion Scale[20] allows you to assess, for example, whether you beat yourself up when things don't go well or give yourself a break. To compute your score, check the number that reflects how much you agree or disagree with each of the following sets of five statements.

The first five items measure whether you are pretty hard on yourself; the next five measure whether you practice self-compassion. For those with relatively low scores on the first items and high scores on the second set of items, congratulations! People with this score pattern are doing a good job of adopting a positive mindset in the face of disappointment. But for those with high scores on the first five items, coupled with low scores on the next set of items, you need to develop skills and strategies for treating yourself better. Don't worry—you'll learn about such approaches in subsequent chapters of this book.

	STRONGLY DISAGREE	DISAGREE	MIXED	AGREE	STRONGLY AGREE
1. I'm disapproving and judgmental about my own flaws and inadequacies.	1	2	3	4	5
2. When I'm feeling down, I tend to obsess and fixate on everything that's wrong.	1	2	3	4	5
3. When I fail at something important to me, I become consumed by feelings of inadequacy.	1	2	3	4	5
4. When times are really difficult, I tend to be tough on myself.	1	2	3	4	5
5. When I see aspects of myself that I don't like, I get down on myself.	1	2	3	4	5

TOTAL SCORE:

	STRONGLY DISAGREE	DISAGREE	MIXED	AGREE	STRONGLY AGREE
1. When things are going badly for me, I see the difficulties as part of life that everyone goes through.	1	2	3	4	5
2. When something upsets me, I try to keep my emotions in balance.	1	2	3	4	5
3. When something painful happens, I try to keep a balanced view of the situation.	1	2	3	4	5
4. When I fail at something important to me, I try to keep things in perspective.	1	2	3	4	5
5. I'm tolerant of my own flaws and inadequacies.	1	2	3	4	5

TOTAL SCORE:

WHAT'S THE TAKE-HOME POINT?

The evidence is clear: the mindset we bring to how we see ourselves and the world exerts a strong impact on virtually all aspects of our lives, including how fast we walk, how well we remember, and how we interact with romantic partners.

But here's the most important news: Our mindsets can change. So, even if our natural tendency is to see things in an all-or-nothing way, with time, energy, and effort, we can shift to a growth mindset and adopt a more positive frame on virtually all aspects of our lives, from how we improve our relationships to how we age. We can all learn to think about something in a new way, and experience happier, healthier lives as a result.

Below are some examples of how subtle changes in mindset can have not-so-subtle influences.

Adopt a New Label

Even small shifts in the environment can shift our mindsets and have a real impact on outcomes. For example, Kevin Dougherty, a professor of sociology at Baylor University, was determined to change students' mindsets about taking exams, which are typically anxiety provoking.[21] He used a variety of strategies to shift these negative expectations. First, he labeled exam days "learning celebrations" to create a positive expectation about how students would perform. Second, he brought in balloons, streamers, and treats on these days to create a festive classroom environment. His goal was to "create an ambience for assessment that enhances learning and joy." In other words, he wanted to shift students' mindsets about exams from dread and fear to joy and celebration. And his efforts paid off. These strategies led to improved test scores.

We can all use this simple strategy of changing how we think about our own feelings to experience better outcomes. Are you anxious about hosting a party, speaking up in a meeting, or giving a toast at a wedding? Reframe your anxiety as energizing arousal that's keeping you alert and on your toes. That's precisely what professional athletes, actors, and musicians do to perform their best in high-stakes situations. Adopting a new mindset takes time, but with practice we can all learn to change maladaptive thought patterns and experience better outcomes.

Take a Chance

Many people—perhaps even most—go through life feeling scared to take risks, because taking a risk raises the possibility of failure. So we stay with jobs we don't find rewarding and in relationships that don't make us happy. Most of us have a risk-averse mindset that encourages us to settle for safety instead of venturing boldly into the unknown.

As I was working on this book, a great story appeared on social media about a young woman, Noelle Hancock, who lost her job as a journalist in New York City when her employer's company shut down. Although she could have looked for other employment opportunities closer to home, she made the decision to move to Saint John, one of the Virgin Islands in the Caribbean Sea. She found a job scooping ice cream on the island and now lives a dramatically different life.

Many people read about a dramatic life decision like this and fantasize about taking a similar risk in their own lives . . . but then feel too nervous. However, research shows that we experience more regret over things we choose *not* to do than things we choose to do. In one study, people were asked what they would do differently if they could live life over again.[22] More than half of the regrets had to do with inaction—should have attended or completed college, should have pursued a particular career, should have tried harder in social relationships or marriages. In contrast, only 12 percent were regrets of action—shouldn't have smoked, shouldn't have gotten married so early, shouldn't have worked so hard. (Another 34 percent were indeterminate.) This study shows that we tend to regret inaction more than action.

So think about shedding your risk-averse mindset and take an action that may feel scary. Quit a job that doesn't make you happy. Find a new relationship—or take action to make your current relationship more satisfying. Take a trip around the world instead of staying in your easy and familiar environment. As author H. Jackson Brown Jr. said, "Twenty years from now you will be more disappointed by the things that you didn't do than by the ones you did do. So throw off the bowlines. Sail away from the safe harbor. Catch the trade winds in your sails. Explore. Dream. Discover."[23]

Believe in Change

Earlier in this chapter I described how people vary in their beliefs about whether particular attributes are fixed or changeable. But no matter where we naturally fall on this continuum, adopting a growth mindset can lead to substantial benefits. For example, teaching high school students to adopt a growth mindset about intelligence and personality leads to higher grades and lower levels of stress and physical illness.[24]

Shifts in mindset can also change how we relate to other people in really important ways. In one of the most profound demonstrations of the benefits of creating a growth mindset, researchers gave people one of two articles to read about empathy.[25]

Half the participants read an article that described how empathy was malleable over time. This article states, "People learn and grow throughout life. Empathy is no different. It too can change. It is not always easy, but if they want to, people can shape how much empathy they feel for others. No one's empathy is hard like a rock."

The other half read an article that describes how empathy is largely fixed and thus would not change. This article states, "In most of us, by a very young age, our empathy profile has set like plaster and cannot soften again. Even if we want to change our empathy and shape how much empathy we feel for others, we are not usually successful. Empathy becomes pretty hard, like a rock."

All study participants then had the opportunity to contribute in some way to a campus drive to help prevent cancer. Some methods of donating were relatively easy, such as donating money or passing out information books at a campus booth. Other methods required greater levels of empathy, such as volunteering to listen to cancer patients share their stories.

Can you predict the researchers' findings? There were no differences as a function of which article participants read in terms of the "easy" ways of helping, including donating money, participating in a walkathon, or distributing information booklets. However, those who read an article describing how empathy can change indicated they would volunteer more than twice as many hours at a cancer social support group—the most empathically demanding of the methods of providing help.

These findings provide powerful evidence that adopting a growth mindset has real and substantial benefits across multiple domains, including academic performance, physical health, and altruism.

Chapter 2

Why Zebras Don't Get Ulcers: Mindset Affects Health

T hink about the last time you felt stressed—heart racing, stomach queasy, muscles tensed. What caused that feeling of stress? For most of us, the daily events that cause stress are, in the scheme of things, pretty minor. Maybe you have an important work presentation, or you are stuck in traffic, or you feel overwhelmed by all the things you have to do or the bills you have to pay. Of course, these are all real stressors and people's bodies react accordingly.

Physiological stress reactions are designed to help humans (and animals) respond to extreme, life-threatening situations—say, when you are chased by a large barking dog or when you are in combat during war. These physiological reactions may also be adaptive during other seemingly "high-pressure" situations, such as during a job interview or on a first date.

The truth is we often show a physiological stress reaction even in situations that are not actually life threatening in any way. Unfortunately, this tendency to show a stress response even in these non-life-threatening situations can have a negative impact on our physical health. This ongoing activation of the stress response in our daily lives may help explain the high rate of stress-related illnesses, including headaches, ulcers, and coronary heart disease. As Stanford University neuroscientist Robert Sapolsky writes, "Stress-related disease emerges, predominantly, out of the fact that we so often activate a physiological system that has evolved for responding to acute physical emergencies, but we turn it on for months on end, worrying about mortgages, relationships, and promotions."[1] This may be why, as Sapolsky cleverly notes, "zebras don't get ulcers," but humans often do.

Although most of us, fortunately, don't face true life-or-death stressors on a regular (or even irregular) basis, we often overreact psychologically to small stressors and cause ourselves tremendous anxiety and anguish. And, at least in some cases, this reaction can in turn have life-threatening consequences.

In this chapter, I'll describe how your mindset can have real and lasting effects on your physical health. But don't stress! At the end, I'll describe specific strategies you can use to manage stress in a better way—to be more like the zebra.

THE POWER OF PLACEBOS

Imagine you're walking through a drugstore desperate to buy a medication that will relieve your horribly unpleasant cold symptoms—nagging cough, sore throat, stuffy nose. And then you are faced with a choice: buy the cheaper generic version or spring for the expensive brand-name option. Although intellectually you understand that these two medications are exactly the same, you make the choice to buy the higher-priced item. Why? Because you, like most of us, believe it will work better.

It might surprise you that this belief is accurate; expensive brand-name medications *do* work better. But here's the irony: these medications work better only *because* we believe they do. And that belief is what leads to greater symptom relief. Placebo medicines and treatments can produce very real and even lasting effects on virtually every organ system in the body and many maladies, including chest pain, arthritis, hay fever, headaches, ulcers, hypertension, postoperative pain, seasickness, and symptoms of the common cold.

Let me share an illustration of how our expectations about a medication actually influence its effectiveness. In one study, people who reported having frequent headaches were given tablets labeled "Nurofen" (a brand name) or "Generic Ibuprofen." In reality, half the tablets were active ibuprofen and half were placebos. The results? People who received placebo pills labeled with a brand name reported greater headache relief than those who received the exact same pills with a generic label.[2]

This study provides powerful evidence that the label really does matter. Participants who took the brand-name labeled medication reported similar levels of pain relief regardless of whether they received actual ibuprofen or the placebo. But for those who received the generic label, those who received actual medication reported greater pain relief than those who received the placebo.

Our expectation that a medicine will work better has a tangible effect on our experience of pain.

It's not just brand names that create expectations—even believing a drug costs more, which we associate with higher quality, increases its effectiveness. People who believe a newly approved painkiller costs $2.50 per dose report experiencing greater pain relief than those who are told the drug had been marked down and only cost ten cents. In both cases, the drug was a pill containing no actual medicine.[3]

Now, a really important question is whether these findings about the greater effectiveness of drugs people *believe* are expensive hold true not just in lab-based experiments but in real-world conditions. The answer is yes—that is precisely what is seen in studies testing all sorts of drugs treating a variety of conditions. For example, patients with Parkinson's disease who believed they were receiving an injection with a drug (though it was actually just a saline solution) costing $1,500 per dose reported that it worked more than twice as well as those who received a drug they believed cost only $100 per dose.[4]

UNDERSTANDING
THE PLACEBO EFFECT

So the placebo effect—that is, a beneficial outcome caused simply by the anticipation that some type of intervention (such as a pill, procedure, or injection) will be helpful—is clearly very powerful. But how exactly does creating expectations about pain relief lead us to feel better?

One explanation is that people's beliefs about a treatment have an impact on their behavior. Specifically, when we expect a particular drug will be effective, we may change our behavior in ways that actually lead to beneficial effects. Imagine having a splitting headache and then taking a pill that you are certain will take away this pain. This expectation that the pain will soon disappear may lead you to relax, which in turn helps reduce the headache.

One of the most vivid examples of the power of a positive mindset in improving health outcomes was found by Bruce Moseley, an orthopedic surgeon at the Houston Veterans Affairs Medical Center.[5] In this study, researchers randomly assigned men with osteoarthritis of the knee to one of three groups:

- Men in the first group underwent standard arthroscopic surgery.
- Men in the second group underwent a rinsing of the knee joint, but it was not scraped as occurs during standard surgery.
- Men in the third group did not receive the actual medical procedure—their knees were merely cut open with the scalpel to create a scar.

All participants were told they were taking part in a research study—and agreed—though they were not told which type of procedure they would receive. All patients were then assessed regularly over two years to determine whether "actual surgery" was indeed better than "placebo surgery." Researchers asked these men questions about how much pain they were experiencing and whether they had increased function for engaging in daily life tasks, such as walking and climbing stairs.

The findings were remarkable. There were no differences in degree of pain or function among patients in the three groups at any point during the follow-ups.

Although the researchers couldn't tell exactly what led to the equivalent improvement for men in all three groups, one possibility is that simply believing they had received surgery that would improve their functioning changed their behavior. Men in all three groups may have diligently followed recovery instructions, such as getting regular exercise to increase movement and working with a physical therapist. Their behavior, in turn, may have led to reduced pain and improved functioning.

Other studies have revealed similar findings about the effectiveness of "placebo surgery." For example, patients with spinal fractures who receive a fake procedure report reductions in pain and even improvements in physical functioning, and patients with Parkinson's disease who receive placebo surgery show significant improvement in motor function.[6]

Some research indicates that placebos can actually bring about physiological changes in the body, which in turn inhibit the experience of pain. For example, the belief that a drug will help reduce pain may activate the endorphin system, which acts naturally in the body to provide pain relief. In line with this view, people who believe they are receiving a pain-reducing drug show decreased activity in areas of the brain and spinal cord that respond to pain.[7] Moreover, people who receive a pain medication in an expensive-looking box, with fancy lettering and a brand-name label, show similar responses in the brain, whereas those who receive the same medication in a plain box with a generic label do not.[8] These studies suggest that the placebo effect reduces pain at least in part by changing how the brain responds to pain.

HOW MINDSETS INFLUENCE HORMONES, HUNGER, AND HEALTH

The placebo effect clearly demonstrates that our expectations about the effects of drugs physically alter how our bodies—and brains—respond. In this way, our mindsets about drugs' effectiveness actually lead us to feel better. But this is just one of the ways in which our mindset influences our bodies' physiological response.

In a powerful demonstration of the impact of mindset, researchers asked participants to taste two different French vanilla milkshakes.[9] Some of them were told that their first milkshake was a diet drink called Sensi-Shake; they were told it contained no fat and no added sugar and was only 140 calories. The rest of the participants were told that this drink was a type of dessert called Indulgence; they were told it was high in fat and sugar and contained 620 calories. One week later, all participants returned and tasted what they were told was the other milkshake.

In reality, of course, the two drinks were identical.

After the participants finished the drink, researchers measured the level of ghrelin in their bodies. Ghrelin triggers hunger, meaning that as hormone levels rise, so does hunger. So, after we've eaten a big meal, our ghrelin levels drop, which tells the body, "You've had enough to eat."

The Sensi-Shake image describes the drink as healthy and low calorie; the Indulgence image describes the same drink as a high calorie dessert.

Crum, A. J., Corbin, W. R., Brownell, K. D., & Salovey, P., Mind over milkshakes: Mindsets, not just nutrients, determine ghrelin response. *Health Psychology*, 30(4), 424-429, 2011, APA, reprinted with permission.

As the researchers predicted, people who believed they had consumed the high-caloric drink showed a substantial drop in ghrelin levels—about three times more than when they believed they had consumed the diet drink. Simply believing they'd consumed more calories led to changes in the body's physiological response—and a substantial drop in hunger.

Now, this milkshake study only tested the short-term effects of one's mindset. But other research shows that our mindset can lead to significant and lasting physiological changes in our bodies. For example, researchers asked women who had jobs cleaning hotel rooms to participate in a study on the benefits of exercise.[10] All the women were given information about the importance of engaging in regular physical activity in order to stay healthy. Next, half the women were also told that the work they were doing cleaning hotel rooms was already enough exercise to meet the surgeon general's daily requirements. They were told, for example, that changing linen for fifteen minutes burns approximately forty calories, and that vacuuming for fifteen minutes burns about fifty calories.

People in the other group were not given this information.

The researchers then returned to the hotel four weeks later to measure any changes in the women's health, including weight, body fat, and blood pressure. The study found that simply telling people that they were engaging in physical activity actually led to improved health outcomes. Specifically, compared to the women who received no information, those who had been told that their cleaning activity counted toward the recommended daily physical activity showed a decrease in weight, blood pressure, body fat, waist-to-hip ratio, and body mass index (BMI).

How? The researchers aren't exactly sure. Did women who were told their cleaning activity counted as physical activity engage more vigorously in such activities? Did their newfound confidence that they were in fact meeting recommended daily physical activity guidelines lead them to make other changes in their eating and exercise behaviors? Although the precise mechanisms explaining the improved benefits aren't known, these findings suggest that simply changing people's mindsets about their activity can lead to healthier outcomes. As Ellen Langer, a psychology professor at Harvard University and the author of this study, notes, "I think this study reveals that we potentially have far more control over our psychological and physical functioning than most of us realize."

WHY POSITIVE PEOPLE EXPERIENCE LESS STRESS AND BETTER HEALTH

As described at the start of this chapter, the way we think about stress has a major impact on physical health. People who think about stress as detrimental and debilitating show higher levels of cortisol, a stress hormone, in response to challenging situations. Over time, this physiological response can lead to bad health outcomes, including higher blood pressure and cardiovascular disease.

But it isn't just the experience of stress that affects health— the very *perception* that stress affects health also does! In one study, researchers asked nearly twenty-nine thousand people to rate their overall level of stress over the last year and how much they believed that stress affected their health—a little, a moderate amount, or a lot.[11] People who reported having experienced a lot of stress and who also believed that stress had a large impact on their health were 43 percent more likely to die over the next eight years. In contrast, people who experienced a lot of stress but did not feel stress had a major impact on health were no more likely to die than those who had experienced little or moderate levels of stress.

This finding indicates that it isn't necessarily the experience of high levels of stress that increases the risk of mortality but rather a high level of stress *coupled with* the belief that stress leads to negative health outcomes. In fact, people who believe that stress affects health "a lot or extremely" are more than twice as likely to die from a heart attack compared to those without such beliefs.[12]

On the other hand, people who go through life with a positive outlook not only feel happier, they also experience better physical well-being across virtually all dimensions.[13] They have fewer physical symptoms, such as coughing, fatigue, and sore throats, and recover from surgery faster and with less pain. They have lower rates of both major and minor illnesses, including asthma, flu, ulcers, hypertension, diabetes, and even strokes and coronary heart disease. Perhaps most remarkable, one study even shows that among patients receiving chemotherapy for ovarian cancer, those who are high in optimism show a greater decline in cancer markers.[14]

People who go through life with a positive outlook have better health in part because they experience less stress. When they face difficult life circumstances, they use adaptive coping mechanisms—tackling problems head-on, seeking out social support, finding the silver lining, and so on. Proactive approaches to stress minimize its effects and its wear and tear on the body.[15] As a consequence, people who are in the habit of practicing such approaches and seeing the glass as half full have stronger immune systems and are thus better able to fight off minor infections.

In one study, researchers measured happiness in 193 healthy adults, and then—with the participants' permission—dripped a solution containing a cold virus into their nostrils.[16] (Remember, colds aren't life-threatening in healthy people.) Then, for the next four weeks, the participants reported on their cold-related symptoms, such as coughing, sneezing, runny nose, and so on. Although all participants were directly exposed to the cold virus, not all of them ever developed a cold. In fact, people with an overall more positive outlook reported fewer cold symptoms and were less likely to develop a cold at all. These findings held true even when researchers took into account other variables that could affect susceptibility to illness, such as age, sex, body mass, and overall health.

THE POWER OF REFRAMING STRESS

When I was in my early twenties, my boyfriend, Bart, and I got a flat tire while driving on a freeway near downtown Atlanta. I immediately panicked—this was long before everyone had cell phones. I worried we would be stranded for hours. I worried that I'd either have to walk alone and get help or stay alone with the car. I worried that our whole day would be ruined by this car trouble.

As Bart pulled to the side of the road, I shared my many concerns. He looked questioningly at me and said, "I'm just going to change the tire—it will take a couple of minutes."

What for me was a major problem Bart saw as a minor inconvenience. He changed the tire, and we were on our way in about fifteen minutes. (This was also when I decided I should marry this guy; he is now my husband.)

Here's another personal example of how mindset matters. The popular press has devoted countless articles to the increasing pressure children feel when taking high-stakes standardized tests, and many teachers and parents complain about these tests. In some districts, parents even pull their kids from school on testing days. So, when my son Robert was heading to school for the first day of such testing, I asked him how he was feeling. He smiled and said, "Oh, I love testing—this is the best day of the year!" (Clearly his father's son.)

When I asked Robert why this was such a good day, he reported, "It is so quiet. Everyone just writes and no one talks. And you get candy."

Many people can, and often do, think about standardized testing as stressful and anxiety-provoking. But for Robert, an introvert, the testing provides a very welcome break from the loud chaos of school. Everyone is quiet, reading, and filling in bubbles on Scantron forms. And, as he said, there's candy at the end. What's not for him to like?

These anecdotes support what considerable scientific research tells us: different people react to the same thing in different ways.

Many people think about stress as a negative and something to be avoided because it leads to poor outcomes—low test scores in children, career burnout in executives, and "choking" in athletes. Unfortunately, seeing stress in a negative way increases anxiety, disrupts performance, and becomes a self-fulfilling prophecy, precisely *because* of this mindset.

However, people who view stress as a normal part of daily life and with a positive mindset experience stress as exhilarating and invigorating and as giving the body extra energy to respond effectively to various challenges. As you might predict, people with this type of mindset often end up with better outcomes. These are the folks who do their best work under pressure and when stakes are high.

EVALUATING YOUR STRESS MINDSET

I'm sure you are now wondering about yourself. Well, you're in luck because researchers Alia J. Crum, Peter Salovey, and Shawn Achor have developed a self-test to assess one's stress mindset.[17] To compute your score, check the number that reflects how much you agree or disagree with each of the following eight statements.

	STRONGLY DISAGREE	DISAGREE	MIXED	AGREE	STRONGLY AGREE
1. The effects of stress are negative and should be avoided.	1	2	3	4	5
2. Experiencing stress depletes my health and vitality.	1	2	3	4	5
3. Experiencing stress inhibits my learning and growth.	1	2	3	4	5
4. Experiencing stress debilitates my performance and productivity.	1	2	3	4	5

TOTAL SCORE:

	STRONGLY DISAGREE	DISAGREE	MIXED	AGREE	STRONGLY AGREE
1. Experiencing stress facilitates my learning and growth.	1	2	3	4	5
2. Experiencing stress enhances my performance and productivity.	1	2	3	4	5
3. The effects of stress are positive and should be utilized.	1	2	3	4	5
4. Experiencing stress improves my health and vitality.	1	2	3	4	5

TOTAL SCORE:

Add up your ratings separately for each set of four. The higher the total score on the first four items, the more negative your stress mindset. The higher the total score on the second set of four items, the more positive your mindset about stress.

Now that you have a sense of how you think about stress, know that, regardless of your score, you *can* shift your mindset, for better or for worse. Understanding the role of mindset in influencing how you think about stress is the first step in learning how to think about, or reframe, it in a new, more positive way.

WHAT'S THE TAKE-HOME POINT?

Stress is unavoidable. We all experience irritating daily hassles, like having to wait in a long line, dealing with irritating coworkers, and feeling overwhelmed by an endless to do list. We can't eliminate all stress from our lives. But we do have a lot of control over how we think about, or frame, the challenges we face. Here are some strategies you can try to handle this stress in better ways and reduce its negative effects on the body.

Relax

Stress leads to bad health outcomes precisely because it creates physiological arousal, which, over time, exerts wear and tear on the body. But learning to counteract the body's natural response to challenges can help reduce arousal, and thereby prevent, or at least reduce, the negative effects of stress. Learning techniques for relaxing your mind and body can go a long way toward reducing the negative effects of stress on blood pressure, heart rate, and muscle tension.[18]

Deep-breathing techniques are a simple relaxation approach designed to help people return their bodies to a state of rest and relaxation. During times of stress, our breathing rate naturally becomes more rapid and shallow. Deliberately focusing on taking deep breaths and filling the lungs with oxygen helps the entire body relax, thus lowering arousal. Soldiers who return from serving in war and experiencing combat trauma show lower levels of anxiety even after just one week of intensive breathing practice.[19]

Using the *progressive muscle relaxation* technique, people focus on consciously tensing and then releasing each part of their body (hands, shoulders, legs, etc.) one at a time. This helps people learn to distinguish between a state of tension and a state of relaxation and is very useful in remaining physically calm in virtually any stressful situation.

Guided imagery is a specific type of relaxation technique that pairs deep muscle relaxation with a specific pleasant image. This approach is designed to help people physically relax and to focus their minds on something other than the specific causes of their stress.

Training in relaxation techniques may even help people manage the stress caused by very serious, even life-threatening, stressors. For example, women with breast cancer who receive relaxation training report reduced levels of depression, and patients with coronary heart disease who receive relaxation training are less likely to experience a subsequent cardiac event.[20]

If you find yourself constantly feeling stressed about the minor or major events of your life, learn strategies to help calm your body—and mind. Many techniques for practicing relaxation are found on the internet. Moreover, in chapter 8, "Change Your Behavior and Your Mindset Will Follow," I'll describe meditation, a particular strategy for relaxation that leads to better psychological and physical well-being.

Change Your Stress Mindset

The negative consequences of stress on our physical and psychological well-being are constantly portrayed in our society. But we don't have to buy into these messages. Instead, we can choose to reframe how we think about challenges we face, and adopt a new, more positive mindset about stress.

People who go through life with a positive outlook, no matter what irritations life brings, do this type of reappraisal naturally, which is a pretty good mechanism for reducing the negative physiological effects of such experiences.[21] It also helps explain why they are less likely to develop depression following crises in their own lives.[22]

But merely changing how you *think* about stress can have a big impact. People who learn strategies for thinking about stress in a more adaptive way—as energizing and inspiring, not just exhausting and debilitating—show better psychological and physical well-being. For example, college students who learn about the benefits of stress, including how stress increases arousal and thereby leads to improved academic performance, show lower levels of math anxiety and better math scores.[23] This type of reframing reduces cardiovascular stress and its overall wear and tear on the body.

Here's a simple example about the practical benefits of changing our stress mindset. Researchers in one study assigned employees at a large financial institution to watch one of two videos.[24] One group of people watched a stress-is-debilitating video; this video described various harmful aspects of stress, including its role in leading to poor performance at work and negative health outcomes. The other group watched a stress-is-enhancing video; this video described the benefits of stress for improving creativity, productivity, and the immune system.

As the researchers predicted, people who watched the stress-is-enhancing video showed substantial benefits. They reported better work performance, as well as lower levels of anxiety and depression.

We can't control what life throws at us, but we can all practice reframing difficult events as challenges, not threats. And this shift in mindset has substantial benefits for our psychological and physical health.

Practice Self-Compassion

One of the easiest ways we can help manage stress, while minimizing the negative effects of stress on health, is to simply give ourselves a break. As I described in chapter 1, "Mindset Matters," people who have high levels of self-compassion, meaning a tendency to treat oneself with kindness and compassion, think about negative events in less dire terms.[25] They also are less likely to blame themselves when bad things happen, which in turn reduces the experience of stress.

People who cut themselves some slack when bad things happen are also better able to fight off minor and major illnesses. To test the benefits of practicing self-compassion on health outcomes in one study, researchers asked people to assess their own acceptance of aspects of their flaws and inadequacies and then take a stress test.[26] They then measured participants' levels of inflammation, a physiological marker of stress linked with cardiovascular disease, cancer, and Alzheimer's.

Their findings revealed that people who were lower in self-compassion had higher levels of inflammation even before taking the stress test, indicating that these people basically go through life experiencing more stress. People who were low in self-compassion also showed even higher inflammation after the stress test, indicating that they react in adverse ways to normal daily life stressors. Over time, their lack of self-compassion could take its toll on their health and even their longevity.

So here's an easy way to feel happier and be healthier: cut yourself some slack. Forgive yourself, be kind to yourself, and treat yourself with care and compassion.

Chapter 3

Older Adults Are Wise, Not Forgetful: Mindset Affects Memory

John Goodenough, a professor of mechanical engineering and materials science at the University of Texas at Austin, has received many accolades for his work developing batteries. In 2014 he received the Charles Stark Draper Prize for his contributions to developing the lithium-ion battery. In 2017 Professor Goodenough filed a patent application for a new kind of battery. He is also regularly seen as someone who may win the Nobel Prize in Chemistry.

But what's perhaps most surprising about Professor Goodenough is his age. He is ninety-five. Goodenough believes he has done most of his best work during his older years. As he says,

"Some of us are turtles; we crawl and struggle along, and we haven't maybe figured it out by the time we're thirty. But the turtles have to keep on walking."[1] This perspective has led him to keep working on various physics problems in his seventies, eighties, and even nineties. He also notes that one real advantage of his age is the freedom it provides to explore new ideas. Goodenough says, "You no longer worry about keeping your job."

Now, think about the beliefs you hold about growing older. What comes to mind? For many Americans, young and old alike, stereotypes about the aging process are pretty negative. We think of advanced age as a time in which people are less active, experience health problems, and develop memory problems. We even have a distinct term for forgetfulness in older adults: "senior moments."

Do older adults experience some declines in cognitive processes, such as problem-solving, reaction time, and memory, with age? Yes.

But these declines are far, far less severe than we commonly assume. People do show some signs of decline in *fluid intelligence*, which measures problem-solving and reasoning skills, with age. However, older adults actually score even higher than younger adults on *crystallized intelligence*, which measures the ability to use skills, knowledge, and experience.[2] This finding makes sense; after all, older adults have had a lot more time to acquire such abilities.

Researchers in one study asked both younger adults (ages eighteen to twenty-nine) and older adults (ages sixty to eighty-two) a series of questions assessing financial literacy, such as interest rates, debt contracts, and economic decision-making.[3] Older adults scored as well or better than the younger participants on all their measures. So although younger people have advantages when it comes to the ease of learning new information, the knowledge that older adults have acquired over a lifetime more than makes up for their decline in the ability to gain new information.

A "SENIOR MOMENT"? NOT EXACTLY

A few years ago, I was headed to a meeting in Princeton, New Jersey, which is about a four-hour drive from my home in Massachusetts. I'd had a long day—teaching classes, attending meetings, doing laundry before my departure, and so on. I finally left my house at 9 PM—later than I intended to leave—and clearly at that point was in a rush to get on my way.

I was making pretty good time on the drive, thanks to relatively little traffic in the late evening, and at 11 PM was on the Tappan Zee Bridge (marking the halfway point of my drive) when my husband, Bart, called with a question. "Did you mean to leave your suitcase on the bed?" he asked.

Ummm, no, I definitely had not intended to leave the suitcase on the bed. This was particularly bad news since there was no way at that hour I could turn around and drive back to get it. It was also especially unfortunate that I had chosen to do my late-night drive in sweatpants and a tattered T-shirt—and was due at the meeting at 8 AM.

I asked Bart to check online and see what stores would open in the Princeton area before 8 AM, realizing that I was not going to be able to attend the meeting in my current outfit. You can probably guess what he found out: the only option for getting new clothes before 8 AM was Walmart. (This is a good example of beggars can't be choosers.)

I arrived at the hotel shortly after 1 AM and asked for a 6 AM wake-up call. I drove to Walmart and within thirty minutes had purchased a complete outfit for the day, courtesy of the Miley Cyrus collection (a change from my typical attire).

When I shared this embarrassing story with my colleagues at lunch—after begging out of our last meeting of the day so that I could head to a mall to buy more clothes for the next few days of meetings—my colleagues couldn't contain their laughter (and now ask me at all subsequent meetings whether I have remembered my suitcase). But I was in my forties when this event happened, so everyone attributed my forgetfulness to being overworked, tired, and having too much on my plate.

Let's say that event had happened when I was in my sixties or seventies or eighties. Can you imagine the explanations that would be made? This is just a simple example of how we can interpret the same event in different ways to fit the stereotypes we hold. Our mindset of a busy working mom tells us that forgetful behavior is caused by juggling too many different roles. Similarly, when college students lose their ID cards, keys, or cell phones (all of which happen with great regularity), no one assumes they are truly experiencing memory loss. In contrast, our mindset of forgetful behavior by an older adult assumes it is caused by dementia.

As you'll learn in this chapter, these stereotypes not only affect how we see and interpret such behavior but can also have substantial effects on older adults' own memory. In fact, simply reminding older adults about ageist stereotypes, such as the supposed decline in memory with age, can lead to lower performance on memory tests, which of course confirms such stereotypes. This self-fulfilling process is caused by stereotype threat, as described in chapter 1, "Mindset Matters."

THE HAZARDS OF NEGATIVE AGE-RELATED STEREOTYPES

Given the constant references to "senior moments" in our daily lives, including messages from magazines and television shows and movies, it makes sense that older people are worried about their own memory performance. The media bombards us daily with negative images of aging, leading us to think that aging means becoming more forgetful, less attractive, less active, and closer to death. But just as research on stereotype threat has already been shown with other negative stereotypes, explicitly reminding older adults about the supposed memory loss that occurs with age actually impairs memory performance.

To test the impact of hearing about age-related stereotypes on memory, researchers in one study asked older adults, ages sixty-two to eighty-four, and younger adults, ages eighteen to thirty, to read one of three fake newspaper articles.[4] One of these articles emphasized the typical age-related decline in memory and suggested that older adults needed to rely on other people for help. For example, this article states:

> Although findings such as these only reinforce our most negative conceptions of aging on mental abilities, these researchers note that this does not necessarily imply that older adults are

unable to function in everyday life. They suggest, however, that in order to maintain adequate levels of functioning, older adults may have to increasingly depend upon the help of memory tools as well as friends and family.

Another article emphasized more positive findings about the memory-age link, such as:

Findings such as these continue to damage our mostly negative conceptions of the effects of aging on mental abilities. Rather than supporting the view that biological changes lead to inevitable losses, these findings suggest that the degree of memory loss is to a certain extent under control of the environment and the individual.

A third, neutral article contained no specific information about the memory-age link.

All participants then completed a standard memory task in which they studied a list of thirty words for two minutes and then had to write down as many words as they remembered.

The researchers found that young adults performed at a relatively high level regardless of which newspaper article they had read. They remembered on average 60 percent of the words, and performance did not differ at all based on the particular article they had read.

But can you guess what the researchers found with the older adults? As you might have already predicted, older adults performed worse on the memory test if they had read the article emphasizing negative effects of aging on memory. Specifically, older adults who read the neutral or positive articles recalled 57 percent of the words, whereas those who read the negative article recalled only 44 percent of the words.

This study illustrates the impact that reading a single article on memory has on older adults' performance on a subsequent simple task. Can you imagine what the real-world effects are of hearing about such stereotypes constantly? And see how such stereotypes can themselves lead to lower memory performance in older adults? This is a vivid example of the power of our mindset.

WHY TEST FRAMING MATTERS

Other research reveals that even subtle wording changes can lead to memory problems in older adults. In another study, researchers compared performance on a trivia test in younger adults (ages seventeen to twenty-four) and older adults (ages sixty to seventy-five).[5] All participants were given a list of sixty random trivia statements to learn, such as "About four hours are required to boil an ostrich egg" and "James Garfield had the largest shoe size of any US president." They were told to study these lists of facts, which had been randomly chosen to make sure participants would need to memorize these in order to perform well, and that they would later take a test on these items.

However, the researchers actually gave different groups of people slightly different information about the nature of this test—the key factor that varied in this study.

One group of people, which included younger and older adults, were told they would be taking a memory test and that participants should "remember" as many statements from the list as possible. Specifically, people in this memory group were told, "In this experiment, we are interested in how good your *memory* is," and "You will be tested on your *memory* of this information in phase two."

In contrast, people in the other group were told that they should "learn" as many statements from the list as possible, but the word "memory" was not used. People in this learning group were told, "In this experiment, we are interested in your ability to learn facts," and "You will be tested on this information in phase two."

Next, all participants were given the same test, in which they had to read a list of trivia statements and rate whether each was true or false. The researchers had made changes to some of the original statements to make them false, such as "About six hours are required to boil an ostrich egg." The researchers then computed performance on this test for both younger and older people in the two different groups.

As the researchers predicted, the type of instructions people were given about the test led to substantial differences in performance. When researchers described the test as measuring *learning*, there were no differences in performance between older adults and younger adults. But when researchers framed the test as focusing on *memory*, older adults performed substantially worse than younger adults. These findings demonstrate that older adults do not necessarily perform worse on memory tests than younger adults. In fact, older adults only show worse performance when they are concerned about confirming the age-related stereotype of lower memory skills in their age group.

This study shows relatively minor, though important, effects of test framing on memory performance in a short-term memory test in a psychology experiment.

But other findings reveal that even more subtle changes in test framing can have clinically significant effects. For example, researchers in one study with adults ages sixty to seventy told half of these participants that they were at the "older end" of the age spectrum they were testing (describing an age range of forty to seventy), whereas others were told they were at the "younger end" (describing an age range of sixty to seventy).[6]

Half of the participants in each of these two groups were given a fake article entitled "Memory and the Older Person." This article described information about the common memory failures that older people experience, such as failing to remember appointments, forgetting where they left common items (keys, glasses, etc.), and needing regular reminders and lists in calendars and notebooks to help cope with their memory problems. The other participants were also given an article to read—"General Abilities and the Older Person," which focused more generally on cognitive declines with age but did not mention memory at all. Finally, researchers gave all participants a standard memory test used to diagnose dementia.

Their findings illustrate the tremendous power of expectations on disrupting memory performance. Specifically, 70 percent of the people who believed they were on the "older end" of the spectrum of participants and who read an article describing the memory problems associated with aging met the clinical criteria for dementia. In contrast, only 14 percent of those in the other three groups met the diagnostic criteria for dementia, including those who believed they were at the "older end" of the age spectrum but who read an article that didn't emphasize memory problems caused by aging. It was the same in both of the "younger age" spectrum groups, regardless of the article they read.

Research shows again and again that simply hearing about the memory problems associated with aging can lead to consequences with profoundly important implications for people's daily lives. As Sarah Barber, a gerontology professor at the University of Southern California, notes, "Older adults should be careful not to buy into negative stereotypes about aging—attributing every forgetful moment to getting older can actually worsen memory problems."[7]

EVEN UNCONSCIOUS CUES AFFECT MEMORY PERFORMANCE

The research I've described thus far has demonstrated the effects of both clear, explicit negative information about the aging-memory link and subtler methods of framing a test on memory performance. But what is particularly remarkable is that even subliminal cues, meaning cues that are processed at an unconscious level, that remind older adults of this negative stereotype can debilitate memory performance.

To examine the effect of such cues on memory in older adults, researchers can present their participants with subliminal primes. In this type of study, words are flashed very, very briefly on a computer screen so that participants are primed without becoming aware of the specific words or processing them at a conscious level. Researchers can then examine whether such unconscious, or subliminal, primes can influence behaviors.

In one study, older adults, ages sixty and above, were subliminally primed with one of two types of words.[8] Some people were exposed to positive age-related stereotypes, such as *wise, insightful,* and *accomplished,* whereas others were exposed to negative age-related stereotypes, such as *senile, confused,* and *decrepit.* The words were matched on a number of different dimensions, such as word length, frequency with which they appear in the English language, and relative typicality of the aging process, to make sure that other factors did not influence the findings.

After experiencing one of these two distinct types of primes, all participants completed a series of memory tasks to test different types of memory. For example, in one task people were shown a sequence of seven dots arranged on a piece of paper for ten seconds and then had to recreate that arrangement. In another test, a researcher read a list of words and then asked participants to write down as many words as they remembered.

The researchers then examined how people who were exposed to the different types of age-related primes performed on these memory tasks (keep in mind that these primes were briefer than the blink of an eye). They found that people exposed to negative age-related primes performed worse on the memory tasks than those who were exposed to positive age-related primes.

In addition to examining the impact of unconscious primes on memory, the researcher tested whether these primes would also influence people's attitudes and stereotypes about aging. All participants read a story about a seventy-three-year-old woman named Margaret who moves in with her adult daughter and attends a college reunion. Participants were asked to write down as many details from this story as they could recall as part of the memory test. But they were also asked to give their own thoughts and opinions about Margaret, which was the test of their stereotypes about aging.

One person who was exposed to the positive-aging primes wrote, "A rather typical grandmother trying to adjust to a new situation after a traumatic event. Concerned for her children's and grandchildren's welfare. Interested in people who are her own age." In contrast, a person who was exposed to the negative-aging primes wrote, "Getting older and forgetful which is natural for most old people." And another person from the negative-aging prime group wrote only two words: "Alzheimer's disease."

In sum, this study provides really important evidence that stereotypes about aging have an impact on older adults' memory and impressions of aging—and that this process can occur even when negative cues are given without conscious awareness.

HOW OLD DO YOU FEEL?

Reminding people of negative age-related stereotypes, even at an unconscious level, not only has an impact on memory but can also influence how people feel physically. In fact, just the act of taking a memory test can make older adults *feel* even older.

To examine this question, researchers in one study first asked older adults, ages sixty-five to eighty-six, to rate how old they felt by marking an age on a line with endpoints of 0 and 120.[9] Although the adults were on average seventy-five years old, they reported feeling significantly younger, about 58.5 years old. (That's the good news.)

Next, the adults completed brief tests that assessed cognitive functioning and standard memory. This memory task involved spending two minutes reviewing a list of thirty nouns and then writing down as many of those words as they remembered. The researchers then asked participants to rerate how old they felt.

Although the adults had initially reported they felt about 58.5 years old, after completing these tests their subjective age increased by nearly five years, to 63.14 years old. This finding is particularly remarkable in that it shows how simply completing a brief five-minute test seems to have aged people nearly five years! Apparently taking a memory test serves to highlight common stereotypes about aging in our society, which in turn leads older adults to feel even older. In fact, subsequent research revealed that simply reading the instructions for the memory test—and not even actually taking the test—led to similar effects on older adults' perceived age. Researchers believe these actions activate negative stereotypes about aging, which in turn makes older adults feel even older.

In a follow-up to the first study, the researchers tested whether completing such memory tests has similar effects on younger people. After all, maybe simply taking a test makes people feel tired, or mentally challenged, which in turn leads them to feel older. However, the findings on this follow-up study revealed no effect of such a test on subjective age in younger adults. In other words, memory tests don't affect younger adults' perceived age at all.

These findings have immense practical importance since, as you'll learn later in this book, subjective age has an impact on health outcomes.

REAL-WORLD IMPLICATION OF AGEIST STEREOTYPES

One of the major limitations of all the studies I've outlined thus far is that they take place in a controlled laboratory setting. And you may have already questioned whether the findings that I've described about the impact of negative age-related primes have any real-world effects. In other words, even if reminders of such stereotypes affect short-term memory performance in a psychology experiment, do these stereotypes have an impact on older adults' experience in their daily lives?

To examine the real-world effects of negative age-related stereotypes, researchers used data gathered from the Baltimore Longitudinal Study of Aging, which is the longest-running study of memory and aging in the world.[10] This study has examined participants' health and memory over a thirty-eight-year period, thus enabling researchers to examine how changes occur over time.

Overall, the participants in this study are somewhat unusual. They tend to be quite healthy; their self-rating of health is 4.51 on a scale of 1 to 5, with 5 meaning excellent health. They are also highly educated, with 77 percent having finished college.

Researchers examined the participants' initial scores on a scale measuring stereotypes about aging. This scale asked participants to rate their agreement with various statements, such as "Old people are absent-minded" and "Old people cannot concentrate well."

Next, researchers assessed participants' memory in older adulthood, thirty-eight years after they had originally started the study and completed measures of health and aging stereotypes. They conducted a standard memory test in which people are shown a geometric figure for ten seconds and then are asked to draw that picture.

Finally, researchers tested the essential question about whether stereotypes about aging affect memory performance over time by comparing scores on the memory test taken in older adulthood between those with positive versus negative stereotypes about aging when they first began this study. As you can probably guess by now, people with the most negative stereotypes about aging showed significantly worse performance on a memory test than those with more positive stereotypes. In fact, older adults—ages sixty and above—who initially held more negative attitudes about aging showed a 30 percent greater decline in memory performance over time compared to those with more positive initial stereotypes.

These findings are particularly remarkable since researchers took into account many other factors that could explain memory decline over time, including age, depression, education, marital status, number of chronic conditions based on hospital records, race, self-rated health, and sex. In sum, this study provides important evidence that holding negative views about aging not only leads to short-term decreases in memory performance in laboratory settings but also has real and lasting effects on memory over time.

CULTURE MATTERS

It's also important to note that older adults in cultures with a more positive view of aging don't show the same type of declines in memory performance with age. This finding means that changing the negative cultural stereotypes about aging in many Western cultures could go a long way toward improving cognition in older adults.

Although in the United States attitudes about aging are pretty negative, especially regarding the impact of aging on memory, in some other cultures beliefs about aging are much less negative. In China, for example, older people are seen in more positive ways than younger adults, particularly when it comes to wisdom. The Chinese culture has a long history of showing respect for older people and views older people with admiration and reverence.

Researchers thus hypothesized that reminding people of old age should not have the same detrimental impact on memory performance in China and in other cultures with a more positive view about aging. To test this theory, researchers in one study examined memory performance in both younger and older adults in China and the United States.[11] These researchers used distinct types of memory tests to examine whether age and culture impact performance on particular types of tests. One of the tests asked people to reproduce a pattern of dots they had seen for ten seconds; another required people to memorize pairings between particular photos of people and an activity, such as "she swims every day" and "he fell and broke his hip."

As they predicted, younger adults in both China and the United States performed very well on all measures of memory, and there were no differences in performance based on culture. However, older adults in the United States performed substantially worse on such tests compared to older adults in China.

These findings show that biological factors, such as natural memory decay with age, are not accounting for the changes in memory seen in American samples. After all, the aging process at a biological level surely works the same across different cultures. Instead, researchers believe that the negative stereotypes about old age that are so common in the United States are the primary cause of such deficits. As Colin Milner, chief executive officer of the International Council on Active Aging, notes, "In eastern cultures, older adults are revered for their knowledge. It's only in western culture that we say the marketers no longer have an interest in you, jobs are harder to get and that you should want to retire and do nothing."[12]

WHAT'S THE TAKE-HOME POINT?

I hope you now understand the substantial consequences of negative age-related stereotypes about memory and how such stereotypes have a much stronger impact on cognitive abilities than any inherent biological processes. The good news is that people who don't accept the inevitability of aging can counteract the detrimental and self-fulfilling consequences of negative age stereotypes. In fact, simply learning about such stereotypes and their influence may go a long way toward improving memory performance as we age. The poet Henry Wadsworth Longfellow concludes his poem "Morituri Salutamus" thus:

For age is opportunity no less
Than youth itself, though in another dress,
And as the evening twilight fades away
The sky is filled with stars, invisible by day.

For Longfellow, aging is an opportunity full of possibility. If you're starting to feel the same, here are some simple strategies you can use to maintain and even strengthen cognitive skills, no matter your age.

Keep Learning New Skills

We all have a tendency to get stuck in comfortable and familiar routines. But people who take deliberate steps to keep learning new skills stay mentally sharp even as they age. In other words, when it comes to brain function, use it or lose it.

Older adults with early signs of cognitive impairment who are assigned to take country-dancing lessons, which involves pretty complex choreography, show improvements in brain structure six months later.[13] Those who engage in other forms of exercise— brisk walking or gentle stretching—show no such changes.

Here's a vivid example of the importance of learning new skills. In one study, researchers assigned adults, ages sixty to ninety, to engage in some type of activity for fifteen hours a week for three months.[14] Some of them were asked to learn a challenging new skill, such as digital photography or quilting, that required active engagement as well as high-level memory and cognitive processes. Others were asked to engage in more familiar, and passive, activities, such as listening to music or completing word puzzles. Others in a last group were asked to participate in social activities, such as social interactions, field trips, and entertainment.

As you can probably predict, adults who learned new skills showed more improved cognitive functioning than those in the other two groups. This study illustrates the importance of pushing yourself, whatever your age, to experience mental challenges and learn new things. This type of mental stimulation goes a long way toward helping people maintain high levels of cognitive function even in older adulthood. As Denise Park, the author of this study and a researcher at the University of Texas at Dallas, says, "It is not enough just to get out and do something—it is important to get out and do something that is unfamiliar and mentally challenging, and that provides broad stimulation mentally and socially."

So, if you want to stay mentally fit as you age, push yourself to keep learning—take a class, join a book group, travel to new places. It's never too late to develop new skills, and this type of mental stimulation may actually change your brain.

Shift Your Framing

The growing awareness of the hazards of reminding older adults about age-related negative stereotypes has led researchers to examine strategies for overcoming these negative consequences. And encouragingly, some studies show that simple wording changes can help older adults show strong memory performance, even in the face of stereotype threat.

One intriguing study conducted by professors of gerontology at the University of Southern California created a system to reward older adults for good memory performance.[15] In this study, researchers first asked older adults (ages fifty-nine to seventy-nine) to read a fake newspaper article describing age-related memory loss and to complete a standard memory task afterward.

But the researchers then added a creative twist to this standard type of memory study. Specifically, half the participants were told they would receive a reward for each word they remembered correctly, meaning they would get two additional poker chips, which could be redeemed for money at the end of the study. The other participants were given fifteen dollars initially but then were told they would lose three poker chips for each word they forgot, which meant they would owe money to the researchers at the end of the study. So half the participants focused now on *learning* more words, whereas the other half focused on *not forgetting* words.

When researchers then tested how these older adults performed on a memory task, those who had different types of framings of the memory task showed very different scores. Specifically, older adults who were given the chance to earn extra money for learning more words did even less well on this memory test; they scored about 20 percent worse than those who weren't given any information about age-related stereotypes. On the other hand, older adults who were told they would lose money for forgetting words performed even better than those who were not given information about age-related stereotypes.

These findings indicate that an easy approach to improving memory performance in older adults who are taking, say, screening tests for dementia may be for clinicians administering such tests to emphasize the importance of not making mistakes instead of encouraging people to remember as many words as they can. And perhaps older adults can improve memory performance simply by focusing on *not forgetting* instead of on *remembering*.

Change Your Stereotypes

Unfortunately, many of the stereotypes portrayed in the media bolster negative stereotypes about aging. But the good news is that counteracting these images can help create more optimistic—and frankly, realistic—views about growing older. One fascinating study found that countries with older political leaders have more positive views of older adults, suggesting that highly prominent role models have the potential to change people's perceptions about aging.[16] Moreover, simply exposing people to photographs of older adults in high-status positions—think a seventy-two-year-old CEO of a Fortune 500 company—leads to more positive perceptions.

Older adults can change their own negative stereotypes about aging by keeping in mind role models who accomplish great things in their seventies, eighties, and even nineties, like Professor John Goodenough. After all, as astronaut John Glenn says, "Too many people, when they get old, think that they have to live by the calendar."[17] Although Glenn is probably most famous for being the first American to orbit the earth, at age seventy-seven he became the oldest person to fly in space when he joined the crew of the space shuttle *Discovery* as a payload specialist. Moreover, during this nine-day trip—in which the shuttle orbited the earth 134 times—Glenn was also serving as a US senator. Glenn's statement about the importance of not letting the calendar, and our chronological age, define us clearly contributed to his ability to make lasting societal contributions well into his seventies and beyond.

One key step to living longer is therefore to change your stereotypes of what "growing old" really means. How can you do that? Well, as a start, take a look at individuals who continue to be an inspiration and an influence, no matter their age:

- Actor-director Carl Reiner, who published his latest book, *Too Busy to Die*, at age ninety-six
- Sex therapist Ruth Westheimer, who at age ninety released a graphic novel autobiography for children

    entitled *Roller Coaster Grandma: The Amazing Story of
Dr. Ruth

- Clint Eastwood, who was eighty-three when he directed *American Sniper*, which was nominated at the 2015 Academy Awards for Best Picture
- Ruth Bader Ginsburg, who, in her eighties, still serves as an Associate Justice of the US Supreme Court

Changing your mindset about aging goes a long way toward improving the quality—and increasing the longevity—of your life. So, the next time you hear or think of a negative stereotype about aging, think instead of positive older role models who teach, write, act, direct, and practice law in the highest court in the land.

Chapter 4

Secrets of Centenarians: Mindset Affects Longevity

O n September 25, 1942, Dr. Viktor Frankl, an Austrian physician specializing in neurology and psychiatry, his wife, and his parents were sent to the first of several concentration camps, where he would spend the next three years. His wife and parents didn't survive.

Following his release, Frankl returned to Vienna and taught about the importance of finding meaning even in the face of tremendous suffering. In his book *Man's Search for Meaning*, he wrote, "Everything can be taken from a man but one thing: the last of human freedoms—to choose one's attitude in any given set of circumstances, to choose one's own way."[1] Frankl died in 1997 at age ninety-two.

Although most of us fortunately won't ever experience the type of tragedy Frankl experienced, we can all embrace his message. Moreover, considerable scientific evidence now points to the profound importance of adopting this type of positive mindset if you want to live a longer, better life. There are a number of things you can tweak in your life to reap this incredible benefit—but first, the facts.

THE SECRETS OF CENTENARIANS

People who reach a hundred years old tend to take care of themselves physically. They eat a lot of vegetables and beans and not so much meat, drink alcohol in moderation, and don't smoke. They also engage in regular physical activity, such as gardening, walking, and hiking. But there's more to it than that.

Consider the five places in the world where the number of centenarians is truly remarkable:

- Ogliastra, an area of Sardinia, Italy, which has the highest number of male centenarians
- Aegean island Ikaria in Greece, with some of the world's lowest rates of middle-age mortality and dementia
- The Nicoya Peninsula in Costa Rica, with the lowest middle-age mortality in the world
- Loma Linda, California, where Seventh-Day Adventists live on average ten healthy years longer than the average American
- Okinawa, Japan, which has the highest number of female centenarians

People in these cultures spend the majority of their time with others in their extended social network. They live in close-knit communities where inhabitants socialize frequently with family members, friends, and neighbors and where grandparents and grandchildren spend regular time together.

Yes, people in these cultures experience the normal stresses of daily life, just like we all do. But they also use highly effective strategies for reducing their stress. For example, Okinawans take time each day to think about their ancestors, the Ikarians nap regularly, and the Sardinians relax with an alcoholic drink during happy hour each day. These cultures also tend to hold strong religious and spiritual beliefs, which helps to reduce both minor and major stress.

Most important, people in these cultures find meaning and purpose in their lives at every age. The Okinawans use the term *ikigai* and the Nicoyans in Costa Rica say *plan de vida*; these expressions both roughly translate to "why I wake up in the morning." You've probably seen this in yourself, or your relatives, or your friends, with active people in their eighties and nineties who participate in the things they value, whether it's physical exercise, gardening, or passing on traditions to the younger set. We all need a reason to get up in the morning, no matter our age or personal circumstances.

The link between finding meaning and purpose in life and greater life expectancy is also supported by hard facts. Researchers examining data from more than six thousand people between the ages of twenty and seventy-five across the United States over a fourteen-year period found one single consistent difference between those who lived and those who died during this time: those who lived felt a greater sense of meaning and purpose, regardless of age, sex, or whether they were retired or still working.[2]

We can all benefit from this important insight: if you want to live longer, start taking care of yourself physically, but also spend time with loved ones, manage your stress, and find meaning in your life. Dr. Robert Butler, the first director of the National Institute on Aging, says it well: "Being able to define your life meaning adds to your life expectancy."[3]

THE POWER OF EXPECTATIONS

One common feature seen in these cultures where people live to one hundred and beyond is the expectations they have about aging. In fact, people living in Sardinia hold more positive beliefs about aging than do adults living in other parts of Italy.[4] As author Dan Buettner describes in *Blue Zones*, a book about the places in which people live the longest:

> It seems that if you give older people the message that they are needed then they will live much longer. In Sardinia, for example, and Okinawa and to a certain extent in Ikaria, there is no real concept of retirement. As an older person you don't just receive care — you are also expected to cook and help take care of kids or tend the garden.[5]

These cultures adopt a positive mindset about how people in their eighties and beyond are physically active, wise, and still able to make valuable contributions. And holding positive expectations about aging really pays off. In one study, adults ages eighteen to forty-nine completed measures assessing both their negative and positive beliefs about aging.[6] These views included:

- Things keep getting worse as I get older.
- As I get older I am less useful.
- I am as happy now as I was when I was younger.
- I have as much pep as I did last year.

Researchers then examined the participants over the next thirty years to see how these beliefs predicted later health events. Their findings provide striking evidence that expectations matter: thirty years later, 25 percent of those with negative beliefs about aging had experienced some type of cardiovascular development (a heart attack, stroke, angina, etc.) compared to only 13 percent of those who held positive stereotypes about aging.

Other research reveals similar findings about the benefits of holding positive expectations about aging. People with such beliefs are less likely to develop various chronic illnesses and are more likely to recover from disabilities.[7]

Why do beliefs about aging have such a strong influence on health outcomes? Older adults with positive attitudes about aging are more resilient when facing stressful situations. In one study, adults ages sixty to ninety-six were asked about their attitudes toward aging and then about any stress they'd experienced that day.[8] Not surprisingly, people who had experienced more stress overall reported more negative emotions, such as fear, irritability, and distress. But people with positive attitudes about aging easily bounced back from difficult days; they showed no increases in negative emotions.

These findings help explain why having positive stereotypes about aging is good for your health. People with such beliefs probably see aging as less of a big deal, and hence less stressful. This belief, in turn, reduces the negative physiological reactions that lead to poor health outcomes, as described in chapter 2,

"Why Zebras Don't Get Ulcers: Mindset Affects Health." People with such beliefs therefore also have stronger immune systems and are thus less susceptible to minor and major illnesses.[9]

Most important, people's beliefs about getting older actually influence how long they live. Researchers in another study asked adults ages fifty and older to rate their attitudes about aging.[10] Then, over the next twenty-three years, the researchers contacted participants regularly to measure their health. Their findings were remarkable; the people who had registered positive attitudes about aging lived on average 7.5 years longer than those with negative attitudes. Surprisingly, the effect of attitude on longevity mattered even more than loneliness, gender, smoking, and exercise.

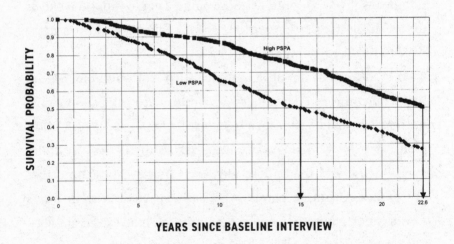

YEARS SINCE BASELINE INTERVIEW

Figure 4.1: The median survival length for those with positive self-perceptions about aging (high PSPA) was 22.6 years past baseline, compared to only 15 years for those with negative self-perceptions (low PSPA).

T. K. Levy, B. R., Slade, M. D., Kunkel, S. R., & Kasl, S. V. (2002). Longevity increased by positive self-perceptions of aging. *Journal of Personality and Social Psychology, 83*(2), 261–270.

So one of the keys to reaching the age of one hundred is developing positive expectations about what aging really means.

WHY FEELING OLD IS BAD FOR YOUR HEALTH

In the last chapter, you learned how simply *feeling* old causes impairments in memory. And, as you might predict, how old you feel, no matter your chronological age, also influences *how* you age.

Researchers in one study asked adults ages 65 to 102 how old they were, measuring their chronological age.[11] Then they asked them how old they *felt*, measuring their subjective age. The researchers then calculated whether people felt older or younger than their chronological age. When the researchers contacted these same people again years later, they asked them whether they had spent a night in the hospital at any point during the last year.

As the researchers predicted, people who felt older than their chronological age were much more likely to have experienced a hospitalization. In fact, people who felt older than they actually were had a 10 to 25 percent increased likelihood of spending a night in the hospital compared to those who felt their age or younger than their age.

These findings point to the powerful impact of our thoughts on physical health. But what's even more remarkable is that people's *perceptions* of their level of physical activity predict how long they live.

To test the impact of people's mindset on longevity, researchers in one study examined data from more than sixty thousand adults living across the United States.[12] These adults provided information on their general health habits, including age, BMI, chronic illness, and level of physical activity. They were also asked one additional question: "Would you say that, compared with others your age, you are physically more active, less active, or equally active?"

Twenty-one years later, the researchers examined death records to track which of the people who completed their survey had died. People who believed they were less physically active than others were 71 percent more likely to die during this follow-up period than those who believed they were more physically active than others. This link between perceptions of physical activity and survival held true even when taking into account other factors linked with longevity, such as BMI and actual level of physical activity.

These findings illustrate the power of mindset—that is, no matter their chronological age, people who feel younger experience better physical health and live longer.

THE POSITIVITY ADVANTAGE

As you learned in earlier chapters, people who look at the world in a positive light are happier and healthier. In fact, people who go through life focusing on what is good, instead of what is bad, even live longer.[13]

Researchers in one study examined autobiographies written by nuns during early adulthood (ages eighteen to thirty-two).[14] They coded the different types of emotional content included in these narratives to assess their degree of positive emotional content. Here are two examples:

- "I was born on September 26, 1909, the eldest of seven children, five girls and two boys . . . My candidate year was spent in the Motherhouse, teaching Chemistry and Second Year Latin at Notre Dame Institute. With God's grace, I intend to do my best for our Order, for the spread of religion and for my personal sanctification."

- "God started my life off well by bestowing upon me a grace of inestimable value . . . The past year which I have spent as a candidate studying at Notre Dame College has been a very happy one. Now I look forward with eager joy to receiving the Holy Habit of Our Lady and to a life of union with Love Divine."

As you can tell, the first passage contains largely objective facts about the person's life. The second, in contrast, contains several positive emotions—"very happy," "eager joy."

Researchers then examined how old the nuns were when they died. Nuns who were in the lowest 25 percent in terms of positive emotions contained in their autobiographies had a mean life expectancy of 86.6 years. Those in the highest quartile of positive emotions had a mean life expectancy of 93.5 years. Even in this unique sample—all women with a strong focus on religion—this gap of nearly seven years shows us that adopting a positive mindset can lengthen our lives.

In another study, researchers asked people ages sixty-five to eighty-five to rate their agreement with various statements assessing optimism.[15] Those who were high on optimism agreed with the following statements:

- I often feel that life is full of promises.

- There are many moments of happiness in my life.

- I still have many goals to strive for.

- Most of the time I am in good spirits.

When researchers then examined the death records of these same people nine years later, the death rate was nearly half that of those who were pessimistic. It also made no difference when other factors that predict longevity were taken into account, including age, sex, body mass index, cholesterol level, level of education, rates of smoking and alcohol use, and a history of chronic disease, cardiovascular disease, or hypertension. Optimistic people tended to live longer.

This link between optimism and life expectancy holds true in study after study, including some with an even longer follow-up period. For example, a thirty-year study by the Mayo Clinic found that pessimists have a 19 percent greater risk of mortality than optimists.[16]

As Lynn Adler, founder of the National Centenarian Awareness Project, notes, "Simply put, centenarians are not quitters. They have a remarkable ability to renegotiate life at every turn, to accept the losses, challenges, and changes that come with aging and not let it stop them."[17]

Even people with terminal diseases survive an average of six months longer when they have an optimistic attitude than those with a pessimistic attitude. In one study, five years after treatment 33 percent of optimistic lung cancer patients were still alive, compared to only 21 percent of pessimistic patients.[18] Once again, the link between optimism and life expectancy holds true even in spite of age, gender, health-related behaviors, stage of cancer, and type of treatment.

SMILE: YOU'LL LIVE LONGER

There's an old Chinese proverb that says, "A smile will gain you ten more years of life." And empirical research now demonstrates there is some truth in that saying.

A clear link between smiling and life expectancy was found in a study analyzing the rookie baseball cards from 230 Major League Baseball players taken from the 1952 register of all players.[19] Some of the photos of these men showed no smile at all, others with a slight smile, and still others with a big smile. The researchers examined how old each player was when he died (as well as other variables that could affect life expectancy, such as year of birth, BMI, career length, marital status, and college attendance). Players with no smiles lived an average 72.9 years; those with partial smiles lived an average of 75 years; and those with big, authentic grins lived an average of 79.9 years.

If you are wondering how holding a big smile could actually increase your life expectancy, here's what some researchers found: The mere act of smiling may actually lead directly to physiological changes in the body that improve health. For example, one clever study asked people to keep chopsticks in their mouths while holding one of three distinct types of facial expressions: a genuine smile, the type that you automatically make when you find something funny; a standard smile, the type that you make when posing for a photo; and a neutral expression.[20]

Then, while holding their assigned facial expression, participants were asked to undergo a pretty painful task: to hold one hand in a bucket of freezing-cold ice water.

Figure 4.2: One of these photographs was shown to participants in the study to help them form the appropriate facial expression. The left photo was shown to those in the neutral group, the center photo was shown to those in the standard-smile group, and the right photo was shown to those in the genuine-smile group.

Kraft, T. L., & Pressman, S. D. (2012). Grin and bear it: The influence of manipulated facial expression on the stress response. *Psychological Science, 23*(11), 1372–1378. Copyright © 2012 by SAGE Publications. Reprinted by Permission of SAGE Publications, Inc.

Their findings revealed the substantial impact of smiling on the ability to tolerate pain. Those who were holding either type of smile had lower heart rates, showing that their bodies were feeling less stress.

What is particularly important about this research finding is that smiling led to benefits even among people who weren't happy. In other words, this study examined only the effects of smiling—meaning the facial expression people held. They weren't examining genuine happiness. And yet they still found that people who held their faces in a genuine smile experienced lower levels of pain.

If adopting a positive mindset doesn't come naturally to you, start smiling more, even when you don't feel like it. Smiling changes how people react to you (always for the better), which will make you feel good. And this good feeling will lead to less stress, lower heart rate, and better health. As Vietnamese Buddhist monk and author Thich Nhat Hanh (ninety-one at the time of writing this book) writes, "Sometimes your joy is the source of your smile, but sometimes your smile can be the source of your joy."[21] So even pretending you feel happy can lead, over time, to happiness—and may also extend your life.

WHAT'S THE TAKE-HOME POINT?

As I've described throughout this book, negative stereotypes about aging are all around us, and have real and substantial consequences—on memory, on walking speed, on health, and even on life expectancy. But actively working to change such stereotypes can result in positive outcomes.

Here's a simple example from Charlotte Yeh, the chief medical officer for AARP Services: After being hit by a car, she used a cane during her rehabilitation and found that strangers regularly interacted with her as if she were totally helpless. These interactions left her feeling terrible, so she decided to decorate her cane with ribbons and flowers. Strangers' reactions changed radically, as they came to associate her with creativity instead of disability. This story illustrates how subtle changes influence how we present ourselves to others, how they respond to us in turn, and, indeed, how we think about ourselves.

Below are some simple strategies you can use to shift your thoughts about aging and thereby improve the quality and quantity of your life.

Challenge Maladaptive Thoughts

Some people naturally have positive thoughts about getting older—and good for them! But if this isn't true for you, working to challenge your maladaptive, and frankly inaccurate, thoughts about aging can result in real and positive changes.

Researchers in one study used a strategy known as *attribution retraining* to change older adults' thinking about what "growing older" really means.[22] These adults, age sixty-five and older, were recruited from three senior citizen centers in the Los Angeles area. None of them were currently engaging in regular physical activity.

These older adults then attended four weekly hour-long group sessions taught by a trained facilitator in which their negative views about aging—such as the belief that growing older inevitably means becoming sedentary—were challenged. They were also taught that older people safely can and do engage in physical activity. Finally, all participants engaged in a one-hour exercise class, which included training in strength, endurance, and flexibility, after each of the group sessions. At the start of this program, all participants were given an electronic pedometer, which was to be worn at all times and measured the number of steps they took each week.

Seven weeks later, the researchers asked all participants to complete surveys assessing their views about the mental and physical changes that occur with aging. They also examined changes in how much activity they were getting compared to before they completed the group sessions and exercise class. Can you guess their findings?

First, participants improved their attitudes about aging, showing increases in positive expectancies about aging, as well as more sleep, lower levels of pain, more energy, and fewer difficulties with daily activities. Second, and more important, older adults who participated in this program became physically active. Specifically, they increased their walking levels about 24 percent, indicating an increase of about 2.5 miles per week. This study demonstrates that merely changing people's beliefs about aging can have a dramatic effect on levels of physical activity.

So, if you've bought into the negative stereotypes about aging that are so prevalent in our culture, start working now to transform these maladaptive thoughts. It's never too late.

Set—and Work Toward—Valued Goals

One of my mentors, Susie Wilson, has achieved considerable success. Susie's professional life included working as a reporter for *LIFE* magazine, assisting Jackie Kennedy in setting up the first White House nursery school (for Caroline Kennedy) and directing the Network for Family Life Education at Rutgers University (now known as Answer—sex ed, honestly) for twenty-three years.

Following her "retirement," Susan has, if anything, increased her overall level of activity. In her eighties, she served on the board of the Fistula Foundation, which provides help to poor women in

Asia and Africa who have experienced childbirth injuries. In May 2016—at age eighty-six—Susie was the top female finisher in the 80-and-over Masters Division of the hundred-meter dash at the Penn Relays. Oh, and she's also written an autobiography, appropriately titled *Still Running*.

What Susan's story demonstrates, in line with considerable scientific research, is that continuing to set and work toward valued goals feels good and is a great way to live longer. In fact, the centenarians I described earlier in this chapter show precisely this type of feeling of purpose in their lives. Similarly, adults ages sixty-five and older who feel they've made progress toward their goals on a given day report feeling happier and experiencing fewer physical symptoms the next day.[23]

The 2016 documentary *Impossible Dreamers* follows senior athletes who are training for national and international competitions in swimming, running, tennis, weight lifting, and other events. Their stories vividly illustrate the immense benefits of setting and working toward valued goals, no matter your age. As Daniela Barnea, age seventy-three, notes about her excitement to move up to the next age group, "I can break new records when I'm the young one in the group."

Now, I'm not suggesting that everyone reading this book start training for a triathlon or international competition. But setting and working toward any type of personal goals—traveling to a country you've never seen, planning a big party to celebrate a milestone birthday or wedding anniversary, learning a new hobby—is a great strategy.

PERSONAL GOALS TO WORK TOWARD
1.
2.
3.
4.
5.

Find Your Meaning

The Holocaust is one of the most devastating events in world history. Therefore, you might assume that people who survived it would have lower life expectancy. Yet researchers find precisely the opposite: men who survived life in a concentration camp during the war lived on average fourteen months longer than men of the same age who escaped.[24] But these findings make sense given what we now know about the value of posttraumatic growth, meaning the benefits experienced after struggling with truly devastating life experiences.

Holocaust survivors show precisely such changes, including a stronger commitment to close relationships, greater resilience, and a deeper appreciation of the small pleasures of daily life. These remarkable findings demonstrate how the power of terrible stress can help bring about positive shifts in mindset, which in turn leads to substantial benefits in the quality and duration of life.

No matter our life circumstances, we can all take steps to find meaning in our own lives by engaging in activities like the following:

- Volunteer with an organization that you find personally meaningful—environmental action, animal rescue, political advocacy.
- Spend time with close family and friends—plan regular activities (see a play or movie, try new restaurants, play golf); take a trip with your children or grandchildren; write down favorite memories, family history, or advice to share with loved ones.
- Donate to causes that speak to you—museums, colleges and universities, political organizations.

The fact is, no matter your age or life circumstances, devoting time and energy to people and causes that you find meaningful is essential. Most important, adopting a positive mindset that focuses on finding such meaning makes for a longer, better life.

PART 2

UNDERSTANDING MINDSET

Chapter 5

Are You Tigger or Eeyore: Personality Matters

D uring the second trimester of my third pregnancy, my husband and I went to our local hospital for a routine ultrasound to check on the health of the baby. As the parents of two sons, we were both ecstatic to learn that this new baby was a girl.

But then the doctor shared some not so good news; the ultrasound revealed spots on a part of the brain that indicated the baby was at increased risk of having a serious genetic disorder, trisomy 18. If she indeed had this disorder, she would have trouble gaining weight and would very likely die before her first birthday.

As soon as we got into the car, I burst into tears. All I could see in my mind was carrying this baby throughout the remainder of my pregnancy while knowing that she was going to die. I couldn't imagine a happy outcome and at this point couldn't talk about my pregnancy without crying.

My husband responded to this potentially devastating news in a completely different way. He dropped me off at home, returned a few hours later with several pink gifts—a blanket, a sleeper, a small bear—and told me, "This baby is going to be fine." His optimistic nature led him to imagine only good outcomes. (For the record, this baby weighed more than eight pounds at birth and is now a very healthy, although somewhat stubborn, fourteen-year-old girl.)

I'm telling you this story to illustrate the tremendous role personality plays in the mindset we adopt. Yes, bad things happen to us all—a failed romantic relationship, a disappointing work outcome, a fight with a friend, scary medical news. But we respond to unhappy events in really different ways.

Some people, like my husband, seem magically able to find the silver lining in any situation. Perhaps you've heard the joke about the very optimistic boy who, upon receiving a room full of horse poop for Christmas, exclaims, "There must be a horse in here somewhere!"

And other people, and I include myself in this group, don't naturally find the silver lining. Instead, we obsess about and ruminate over bad events in our past, replaying them over and over again in our minds, and imagine the worst possible outcomes for events in our future. This approach is certainly not the recipe for feeling better.

In this chapter I'll describe why those who approach life with a more positive mindset are happier regardless of their life circumstances. And if a positive mindset doesn't come naturally to you, the final section of this chapter will provide strategies you can use to adopt a rosier outlook and live a happier life.

THE POWER OF POSITIVE THINKING

Think about a time in which you've been in a really great mood. Perhaps you noticed that when you are feeling happy, you aren't so bothered by the everyday small stresses—traffic jams, long lines, and irritating people just don't get under your skin. Sure, they amount to common annoyances, but your good feelings help you take these types of events in stride. Maybe you cope with the long line at the grocery store by flipping through a magazine, or relish spending an unexpected quiet evening at home watching TV after a friend cancels dinner plans at the last minute. These are all examples of how feeling good helps us adapt and stay positive, no matter what.

Although all of us feel happy at times, some people, like my husband, go through life naturally feeling pretty good. These people go through life expecting things will work out well for them and find it relatively easy to look on the bright side. (This ability to only foresee positive outcomes is vividly illustrated by Sigmund Freud's story about the man who said to his wife, "If one of us should die, I shall move to Paris."[1]) They are also resilient, meaning they bounce back from negative experiences with relative ease.

Not surprisingly, people who adopt this type of positive mindset experience better psychological well-being, including fewer symptoms of anxiety and depression. This ability to consistently see the glass as half full means that they are well poised to respond to life's challenges. In turn, they are able to buffer the effects of really difficult life circumstances, such as a cancer diagnosis or the death of a spouse.[2] For example, people with an optimistic approach to life show lower levels of posttraumatic stress after surviving a school shooting.[3]

But the good news is that, regardless of our natural tendency, with practice we can all get better at responding to life's challenges in more positive ways. In fact, learning and practicing strategies for adopting a more positive mindset changes neural pathways in the brain so that this sort of adaptive response becomes more natural. As Barbara Fredrickson, a psychologist at the University of North Carolina at Chapel Hill, notes, "Taking the time to learn the skills to self-generate positive emotions can help us become healthier, more social, more resilient versions of ourselves."[4]

We often assume that experiencing negative events leads us to feel bad. And although it is true that disappointing and upsetting life experiences can have short- and long-term consequences on our happiness, it is not the mere experience of such events but rather how we react to, or think about, them that really matters. In sum, even when people experience the exact same event, how they respond to and think about it has a major impact on how they feel.

So, let's start by examining what naturally optimistic people do to maintain their positive outlook. And, as I'll describe in this section, there are real differences in how people think about and respond to both common daily stressors and more serious life experiences.

TAKE ACTION

People who approach life with a positive outlook directly face and respond to stressors. When they feel overwhelmed by the sheer number of items on their to-do lists, they sit down and make a plan for tackling each one. When they have an argument with a colleague or friend, they, after calming down, reach out to try to resolve the issue.

This choice to directly confront problems head-on helps eliminate, or at least reduce, the problem. Perhaps the to-do list gets smaller, or the tension caused by the disagreement goes away. Optimists recover from surgery faster, in part because they seek out information about what to expect.[5] This knowledge gives them real and practical strategies for preparing for and recuperating from the procedure, which naturally speeds up their recovery.

Even when circumstances seem dire and hopeless, people with a positive approach to life keep moving forward and persevering. As South African activist and former president Nelson Mandela described,

> I am fundamentally an optimist. Whether that comes from nature or nurture, I cannot say. Part of being optimistic is keeping one's head pointed toward the sun, one's feet moving forward. There were many dark moments when my faith in humanity was sorely tested, but I would not and could not give myself up to despair. That way lays defeat and death.[6]

Those with a more negative outlook, on the other hand, expect bad outcomes, so they give up when facing a difficult situation. They may ignore problems and simply hope they go away—meaning the to-do list simply gets longer and the argument is prolonged. This "stick your head in the sand" approach thereby deprives them of practical information that could potentially help make the situation better. Moreover, their belief that nothing will get better hurts their ability to take action. For example, following the loss of a loved one, they may know objectively that joining a bereavement support group would be a good idea but never actually do so.

People with a positive outlook have an easier time moving forward even during times of stress in part because they have stronger social support networks, including more friends and stronger relationships.[7] And this isn't surprising, since most of us prefer spending time around happy, optimistic people to those who are always gloomy and negative. These good social networks, in turn, help buffer the negative effects of daily life stressors. When bad things happen, people with good support from friends and family know they can rely on loved ones for help. As a result, these events *feel* much less stressful. High levels of support even help people cope when confronting very serious events, such as a cancer diagnosis or natural disaster.[8]

FIND THE SILVER LINING

People who approach life with a positive outlook have a remarkable ability to find some good in any situation. This ability to see the glass as half full enables them to take negative events in stride and always find some magic silver lining.

My oldest child, Andrew, has a clear talent for this type of positive thinking. In ninth grade, he was performing poorly in Spanish class; at the midway point of the fall trimester, his grade was a 50. I was pretty anxious about this until Andrew called at the end of the trimester to tell me he had good news about Spanish. But when Andrew proudly announced his 58 grade, it was not by any stretch of the imagination the good news I had expected to hear.

Nevertheless, Andrew was undaunted and pointed out that this grade was 8 points higher than his midterm average. When I noted that a 58 was still an F, Andrew in his optimism responded that it was really an F+. I then reminded him, perhaps less calmly by this point, that I was a professor, and there was no such thing as an F+ grade. But again, he pointed out that his trajectory—meaning the 8 point improvement—suggested he would have a 66 at the end of the second trimester.

Obviously, Andrew is a master at seeing all things in an optimistic light, and while his Spanish grade is clearly disappointing, his interpretation of his (F+) grade is actually quite encouraging. After all, anyone who can call home with the good news about a 58 clearly has a remarkable ability to find the silver lining.

Empirical research bears out the immense benefits of this type of optimistic framing. In one study, researchers brought in dating couples and told them they would be completing the exact same questionnaire to see if people in a dating relationship saw each other in the same way.[9] The couple was seated across from each other at a small table and handed what appeared to be identical questionnaires. Initially, the questionnaires were in fact identical; the first page of each asked where the couple had met and how long they had been dating.

On the second page, however, the researchers threw in a distinct twist. One person was asked on this page to write down all the things they hated about their dating partner. The other person was asked to write down every single item in their dorm room, bedroom, or apartment; they were also told to make sure to list at least twenty-five items.

Now, think for a minute about the experience of the first person, who was asked to write down things they hate about their dating partner and believed that their partner has been given the same instructions. They had to watch their partner frantically scribble to fill the lines, assuming that he or she in fact hates many—at least twenty-five—things about them.

Finally, each person was asked to rate their feelings about their partner and their satisfaction with their dating relationship.

The researchers' findings were not entirely what we'd expect. For people who didn't feel very good about themselves, believing that their partner had a pretty negative view of them led to lower levels of satisfaction and closeness. This finding makes sense; after all, most of us would feel pretty offended if we believed that our romantic partner had so many critiques about us.

But for those who felt good about themselves, meaning those who go through life with this positive outlook, their findings were the opposite. In fact, for these people, believing that their partner had a long list of complaints about them led to *greater* feelings of closeness. Why? Well, their partner is still dating them, so surely they must love them so intensely to stay with them, given all their faults? Perhaps this person is really their soul mate? In other words, those who have high self-esteem can take what really should be a relationship-damning experience and find some good. And this ability to see the positive—in all situations—creates greater relationship satisfaction.

LET IT GO

Randy Pausch, a professor of computer science at Carnegie Mellon University, was forty-five years old when he was diagnosed with pancreatic cancer. After undergoing a year of unsuccessful treatments, doctors told him the disease was terminal and that he should expect only three to six months of "good health."

Less than a month after receiving this dire prognosis, Pausch delivered an upbeat and inspirational speech, titled "The Last Lecture," in which he shared his considerable wisdom about how to live life to its fullest. One of his main points was to recognize the value of simply having fun. As he noted, "Never underestimate the importance of having fun. I'm dying and I'm having fun. And I'm going to keep having fun every day because there's no other way to play it."[10]

Pausch's message illustrates precisely how optimists cope, even when facing truly dire circumstances. They focus on what they can control—having fun, in his case—and they don't ruminate or wallow in sadness and regret.

This ability to let things go helps people maintain a positive outlook, especially when they have absolutely no control over the situation, and thus can't simply take action to fix or solve it. Those without this natural inclination to look on the bright side, in contrast, often become mired in negative thoughts in the face of serious, yet uncontrollable, events.

Researchers in one study examined people's reactions to a local major natural disaster—the 1989 Loma Prieta earthquake near San Francisco, which killed fifty-seven people and caused tremendous property damage.[11] Some people reported they tended to distract themselves from negative feelings about this disaster, such as by doing something fun with friends or going to a favorite place to take their mind off the event. Other people reported they tended to ruminate about the disaster, such as by repeatedly thinking about the moment the earthquake hit, the people who died, and what might happen in the next earthquake.

Two months later, researchers surveyed those in both groups to examine how they were faring. As you can probably predict, ruminating about this disaster led people to feel worse. Those who dwelled on negative aspects about the earthquake had more symptoms of depression and posttraumatic stress disorder than people who didn't have such thoughts.

Repeatedly focusing on negative thoughts can, over time, even lead to clinical depression. For example, people who ruminated following the death of a partner to a terminal illness were more likely to be depressed six months later, even when taking into account level of social support, pessimism, gender, and other life stressors.[12] In fact, people who ruminate over traumatic events are four times as likely to develop clinical depression as those who do not (20 percent versus 5 percent).[13]

This type of cycling in negative thoughts can also lead to physical symptoms.[14] Women with breast cancer who report persistent negative thoughts show not only higher levels of depression but also more pain, more severe physical symptoms, and lower quality of life.

These findings illustrate that one of the key predictors of depression is simply a failure to let the bad things go. In other words, people who are depressed get fixated on bad thoughts, and just can't seem to pull themselves out of this negative cycle. As psychologist Jutta Joormann notes, "They basically get stuck in a mindset where they relive what happened to them over and over again."[15] And, not surprisingly, going over and over the negative in life brings us down.

THE POWER OF GENETICS

Here's one reason why people see themselves and the world in such different ways: personality is at least partially rooted in your genes, so some people have an easier time adopting a positive mindset. In fact, research suggests that our genes may determine approximately 50 percent of our happiness. For example, genes may help explain why some people are more optimistic, or more extroverted, or even more resilient.

How exactly do genes predict happiness? Although this is an ongoing and obviously important question, researchers are just beginning to understand the mechanisms that explain this link.

Researchers in one study examined more than 830 pairs of adult twins, identical and fraternal, to test the role of both genetic makeup and environment in predicting people's well-being.[16] Participants first completed measures of different factors predicting happiness, including self-acceptance, feelings of autonomy, personal growth, positive relationships, pursuit of goals, and sense of control over their lives.

Their findings suggest that genetics predicts all six components of happiness. However, different genetic factors are linked with different components. In other words, a single gene doesn't predict happiness, and different genes predict different components of happiness.

Genes also help explain why some people seem to skate through life, even when confronted with difficult circumstances, whereas others get bogged down in negative thoughts. One longitudinal study examined people from birth to age twenty-six to examine how stressful life events—such as unemployment, abuse, and disabling injuries—predicted depression.[17] For people with one type of genetic makeup, no matter how many stressful life events they experienced, they were no more likely to become depressed than those who had experienced no stressful events at all. But for people with another version of a particular gene, nearly half of those who experienced four or more stressful life events became depressed. They were also more likely to have thoughts of committing suicide.

Now, some people find the information about the power of genetics in predicting happiness pretty depressing. After all, this means that some people have a much easier time finding happiness than others. And while that is true, I think of the genetic link to happiness much like I think about metabolism—that is, how quickly our bodies burn off the calories we consume. Some people have a higher metabolism than other people, meaning they can largely eat whatever they want and still not gain weight. (I don't like these people, but they do exist.) Other people don't have the benefits of a speedy metabolism, so they need to more carefully watch what they eat and engage in regular exercise in order to stay thin. But even people without a fast metabolism can stay thin, as long as they focus on achieving this goal through a healthy diet and regular exercise.

So, yes, some people do have a genetic head start on finding happiness—they may not need to exert much effort at all in order to find happiness (my son, the Spanish scholar, probably fits into this category). But all people can do things in their daily lives that make them happier, regardless of their DNA.

WHAT'S THE TAKE-HOME POINT?

Everyone experiences challenges—a lingering health issue, difficult financial circumstances, the loss of a friendship, and so on. It is simply impossible to go through life avoiding all such challenges.

But what we do have control over is how we think about and respond to such events. As Randy Pausch described in his last lecture, "You just have to decide if you're a Tigger or an Eeyore." Tigger, as you probably know, is energetic, enthusiastic, and positive about all things. Eeyore, on the other hand, is pessimistic, gloomy, and depressed.

But no matter what your natural inclination, you can learn, with practice, to shift your thoughts, and improve the quality, and potentially increase the longevity, of your life. And this is a really important step to take, given the considerable scientific evidence that consistently thinking about, and ruminating over, the negative things in our lives can actually hurt our ability to think clearly and even, over time, lead to major depression. All you need are some relatively easy tweaks of your mindset.

Frame Challenges in a Positive Light

One relatively easy strategy for changing mindset to increase happiness is to reframe daily life challenges by focusing on what's good about them instead of what's bad. One of my friends has a great strategy for finding the positive during frustrating traffic jams caused by a car accident: he reminds himself that he's in a much better situation than the person who just had the accident.

People with a positive outlook are also able to find some humor, even when coping with difficult circumstances. As *New York Times* columnist Arthur Brooks described his wife's reaction to a difficult parent-teacher conference about one of their teenage children, "At least we know he's not cheating."[18]

Finding humor helps people cope with the small irritations of daily life, but it is particularly important in coping with serious life circumstances. For example, people with fibromyalgia, a debilitating and chronic condition marked by widespread bodily pain, who relied on smiling and laughter to cope with small daily life stressors—such as a waiter spilling water on you—report lower levels of psychological distress and fewer physical symptoms.[19] This ability to take things in stride reduces stress and its negative physiological effects on the body, as you saw in chapter 2, "Why Zebras Don't Get Ulcers: Mindset Affects Health." In other words, laughter may be—at least in some cases—the best medicine.

The next time you are faced with an unpleasant situation, search out any benefit, no matter how small, and focus on it with all your might. Here are some examples of ways you can start to reframe negatives experiences:

- Stuck in an airport? We all complain that we never have free time for ourselves, so take this opportunity to call a friend or read a good book.
- Passed over for a promotion? Now's the perfect time to polish your resume or explore other—perhaps even more fulfilling—career options.
- No plans on New Year's Eve? Don't get depressed— it's not even a safe night on the road. You're not the only one at home. Cozy up in front of the TV and watch the festivities in comfort, or start early on that

New Year's resolution to get organized and clean out that overflowing closet.

Although these are simple solutions to minor stresses that are a fact of life, the mindset you use to deal with them is up to you, and framing them in a positive light will make a real difference in how you feel.

Accept Negative Feelings—Then Move On

One of the major differences between the positive-thinking Tiggers and the negative-thinking Eeyores is whether they can let the bad go. Tiggers can; Eeyores generally don't. And then, to make matters worse, people who beat themselves up for feeling bad tend to feel—not surprisingly—even worse.

Researchers in one study asked more than 1,300 people whether they tended to criticize themselves for having negative thoughts and feelings.[20] People who felt bad about having such negative emotions had higher levels of depression and anxiety, and lower levels of psychological well-being and life satisfaction. They basically get into a negative cycle, in which they feel bad about having negative thoughts and feelings, and then ruminate about these bad feelings. As you can imagine, this quickly becomes a vicious cycle.

Want to test your own tendencies toward this type of negativity? Researchers from the University of Kentucky have created a mindfulness questionnaire[21] that we can adapt to measure one's inclination to self-criticize. Rate your agreement with each of the statements in the table on the following page.

	STRONGLY DISAGREE	DISAGREE	MIXED	AGREE	STRONGLY AGREE
1. I tell myself I shouldn't be feeling the way I'm feeling.	1	2	3	4	5
2. I make judgments about whether my thoughts are good or bad.	1	2	3	4	5
3. I tell myself that I shouldn't be thinking the way I'm thinking.	1	2	3	4	5
4. I think some of my emotions are bad or inappropriate and I shouldn't feel them.	1	2	3	4	5
5. I disapprove of myself when I have illogical ideas.	1	2	3	4	5

TOTAL SCORE:

Add up your scores on these five items to see how much you tend to self-criticize. Higher numbers mean more self-criticism. If you find that you do tend to engage in this type of self-criticism, an important first step is working on accepting these thoughts and feelings, and not beating yourself up about having them. As Brett Ford, a professor of psychology at the University of Toronto, says, "It turns out that how we approach our own negative emotional reactions is really important for our overall well-being. People who accept these emotions without judging or trying to change them are able to cope with their stress more successfully."[22]

So, if you find yourself ruminating about a fight with a friend, a difficult situation at work, or the current state of American politics, try a new approach: identify and accept these negative thoughts and feelings. For example, you might think, "I'm feeling lonely," or "My job isn't going well." Acknowledge how you feel, accept it, and then move on.

Find Happy Friends

You probably already know that happiness, like the flu, is contagious. Many of us have friends and loved ones who always seem to be in a good mood, and spending time with them lifts how we feel.

One of the clearest studies to demonstrate this effect of other people's happiness on our own happiness examined data from a large social network study. Researchers in this study had gathered data from more than 5,000 people living in Framingham, Massachusetts, over a thirty-year period (1971 to 2003).[23] Although the study was designed specifically to measure risk factors related to heart disease (obesity, smoking, and alcohol use), the researchers had also asked participants about their "social ties." These social ties included relatives (parents, spouses, siblings), friends, coworkers, and neighbors. People in this study listed the names of these people in their lives so researchers could examine their broader social networks as well as the proximity of their contacts, meaning how close they lived to the person in the study. (Remember, this study was started in 1971, before people could rely on cell phones, email, and texting to stay in good touch with those who lived far away.)

The findings from this social network analysis clearly indicate that happiness is contagious. Specifically, people who are surrounded by many happy people show increases in happiness over time. For example, a happy friend living within a mile of a person's home increases that person's happiness by 25 percent. Having a happy spouse, happy next-door neighbor, and happy sibling (who lives within a mile) also leads to increases in happiness.

What is perhaps even more surprising is that happiness can also be increased indirectly, meaning through broader connections within a social network. For example, having a happy friend increases your own happiness about 15 percent. But having a friend who has a happy friend (even if your actual friend isn't happy) increases your own happiness nearly 10 percent. And even more distant connections can make us happy: having a friend who has a friend with a happy friend still yields us a 5.6 percent increase in our own happiness.

PEOPLE WHO MAKE ME FEEL BETTER	PEOPLE WHO MAKE ME FEEL WORSE
1.	1.
2.	2.
3.	3.
4.	4.
5.	5.

Although this social network analysis has focused on the advantages of having happy people in our social networks, these relationships can of course also work in the opposite way. You probably already know from life experience that being around people who are negative can make you feel worse. In the box on the previous page, take a minute to make two kinds of lists: people who make you feel better and people who make you feel worse. Then, try to spend more time with those in the first group, whenever you can.

In a creative test of the power of negative experiences to spread within a social network, researchers in one study examined how unhappiness can spread through social media. In this study, researchers first evaluated both positive and negative emotions conveyed in people's Facebook posts.[24] Then they compared the frequency of these emotional expressions to the amount of rainfall in each poster's city. As you might expect, people tend to post more negative emotions, and fewer positive emotions, on rainy days. In fact, in a large city, such as New York City, a rainy day leads to an additional 1,500 negative posts by those living in that city compared to on a nonrainy day.

But what is even more interesting about this study is that the researchers then examined how one person's Facebook post could influence the expressions posted by friends in other cities. These findings again provide strong evidence for the power of emotional contagion within a network. In other words, having a friend post something negative on Facebook increases the likelihood of a negative post and decreases the likelihood of a positive post, by one's own friends. To return to the New York City example, a rainy day in New York City not only yields another 1,500 negative posts by those living in the city (and experiencing the rain) but an additional 700 negative posts by friends living elsewhere (and not necessarily experiencing rain).

Although you can't always eliminate negative people from your life—a close family member, a neighbor, a coworker—you can make a deliberate attempt to spend more time with those who make you feel good, and less time with those who don't. This strategy is particularly good advice for those of us who don't naturally adopt a positive mindset. I started this chapter by describing my husband's optimistic outlook about our daughter's health, even as I was mired in worry and sadness. Perhaps you can see now why I chose to marry him!

Chapter 6

"Comparison Is the Thief of Joy": Environment Matters

I t's hard to imagine a more idyllic setting in which to grow up than Palo Alto, California, a quiet town in the heart of Silicon Valley just across from Stanford University. Children grow up in million-plus-dollar homes, attend top-notch public schools, and seemingly have every advantage money can bring.

Yet in the last decade a number of teenagers in this highly educated and wealthy town have committed suicide—many by jumping in front of a train. In fact, the teen suicide rate in Palo Alto is four or five times the national average.

Although many factors contribute to suicide, virtually everyone agrees that the intensively stressful high school experience in Palo Alto plays some role. The competition for admission to top colleges is fierce; 64 percent of the 2015 graduating class at one of the two local high schools had a GPA of 3.51 or higher. Most students take multiple AP classes, spend a ton of time on homework and extracurricular activities, and feel tremendous pressure from their parents, teachers, and peers to excel.

But take a minute to think about what "stress" really means in this elite environment. These kids aren't worried about having enough food to eat or a safe place to sleep at night, or the physical threat of living in a crime-ridden or war-torn community. Stress—at least as these students are experiencing it—is almost entirely driven by their own thoughts and probably the thoughts of their parents, peers, and teachers. And these high school students are experiencing stress precisely because they've bought into the mindset that attending a prestigious college is the secret to happiness.

In this chapter, you'll learn how environmental factors—including our neighborhoods, countries, and social media feeds—lead us to think about ourselves in particular ways, and how these mindsets can, at least in some cases, make us feel worse. You'll also learn valuable strategies for reducing the influence of these external factors that can bring us down and for focusing instead on finding true happiness within yourself.

THE DOWNSIDE OF COMPARISON

Social comparison is a fundamental and automatic human impulse. It helps us understand how we stand next to other people, including what we're good at and what we're not so good at. We use these comparisons to evaluate ourselves on virtually any aspect—appearance, income, success, and so on.

Such comparisons serve an important purpose since many factors in life have no clear objective standard. For example, let's say someone has a salary of $100,000 a year. How is that salary? To a teacher in rural Arkansas this could be considered a really impressive salary, but to a Manhattan lawyer it could be considered pitiful. The comparisons we make to other people in our environment therefore provide a simple way of assessing our own circumstances.

Although social comparisons can provide a useful way to measure how we are doing, they can also create feelings of envy. One of my favorite cartoons shows two men talking, with one person saying to the other, "I do count my blessings, but then I count those of others who have more and better blessings, and that pisses me off." That message demonstrates precisely how comparisons can make us feel worse about our own lives.

In one study, researchers informed state workers in California about the existence of a website that contained precise salary information of every person working for the state, listed by name.[1] As you might expect, many people chose to visit this website to learn what their coworkers made; this email sent to thousands of employees produced a clear spike in traffic.

A few days later, the researchers sent these same employees a follow-up email. This email asked them how satisfied they were with their jobs and in particular with their salaries. As the researchers predicted, people who had just learned they were earning less than their peers with the same job were annoyed. Compared to those who didn't get the email, they were less happy with their current job and more interested in finding a new one. After all, they now realized their own salary didn't measure up to what their peers were getting, and this comparison certainly didn't make them happy.

Here's a thought experiment on the hazards of comparison: Have you ever received a particularly braggy holiday letter? You know what I mean—a letter in which all members of the family seem to be thriving, from award-winning sports seasons, to impressive academic achievements, to fabulous family bonding during trips to exotic and expensive destinations?

How do you feel after reading such a letter? For most of us, these letters force a particular type of social comparison that leaves us feeling worse about our own mediocre lives. Hearing about other people's great lives—a fabulous vacation, impressive professional accomplishments, packed social calendar—makes us feel worse about our own lives. As Teddy Roosevelt supposedly said, "Comparison is the thief of joy."[2]

EXPLAINING THE WEALTHY NEIGHBORHOOD PARADOX

These findings about the hazards of comparison help explain a consistent, yet perplexing, phenomenon: why making more money does not necessarily lead to greater happiness. We often *expect* that having more money will lead to greater happiness. After all, money buys us things that should make us happy.

Although *absolute income*, meaning the total amount of money that we have, is associated with greater happiness, *relative income*, meaning whether we have more or less income than those around us, is at least as important, and potentially more important, in predicting satisfaction. Why? Because our feelings about how much money we make aren't driven simply by our objective wealth but rather by how our wealth compares to that of those in our comparison group.

In one clever study to evaluate the importance of relative income, researchers forced people to choose between two options:[3]

- Option A: Your current yearly income is $50,000; others earn $25,000.
- Option B: Your current yearly income is $100,000; others earn $200,000.

This experimental design sets up a clear choice—would you rather make more money objectively (option B), or would you rather make more money than those around you (option A)? This answer seems pretty obvious—I mean, surely we would all prefer to make more money, right?

Perhaps surprisingly, more than half of the study participants chose option A, indicating they preferred to make less overall money, as long as they would make more money than other people. This example illustrates how well we know that the comparisons we make have a major impact on how we feel.

This finding about the role of comparisons in influencing our own happiness also helps explain why people who live in wealthier neighborhoods are actually less happy.

Researchers in another study asked nearly three thousand people across the country to rate their overall desire for material possessions, using statements like the following:

- I admire people who own expensive homes, cars, and clothes.
- I like a lot of luxury in my life.

- I like to own things that impress people.
- My life would be better if I owned certain things that I don't have.[4]

These items were rated on a scale of 1 (strongly disagree) to 5 (strongly agree), and then summed together so that higher scores indicated more interest in owning material possessions. They also assessed these people's overall household income and the general socioeconomic status in their neighborhoods by examining both overall income and rate of poverty in their zip code.

Consistent with prior research, the researchers found that people who made more money were less interested in buying material possessions. This finding makes sense because people with a comfortable standard of living should be less focused on the need for acquiring more possessions.

However, people who lived in wealthier neighborhoods were more interested in buying material possessions. They also showed greater impulsive buying and less savings behavior. The researchers believe that constant exposure to wealth in one's environment creates a feeling of *relative deprivation*. In turn, people respond to such feelings by increasing their own desire to acquire material possessions, presumably in an attempt to maintain social status.

But the pursuit of material possessions does not lead to happiness. In fact, people who are intently focused on purchasing products—which are often intended to convey status and prestige to others—have greater unhappiness in their relationships and more psychological problems.

And feelings of relative deprivation hurt happiness even at a national level. One large-scale study examined overall feelings of life satisfaction and daily mood in more than eight hundred thousand people living in 158 different countries.[5] Although making more money was consistently associated with greater happiness, people living in wealthier countries report higher levels of worry and anger. Wealthier countries may have a faster pace of life and greater industrialization—and less opportunity to spend time in nature—which may all contribute to higher levels of negative affect.

In addition, people living in wealthier countries are more likely to engage in social comparisons that hurt well-being. When people are living in wealthier countries, they experience a so-called *aspiration gap*, meaning a discrepancy between what they have and what they want. And, as you might predict, the bigger this gap, the worse we feel.

THEY AREN'T AS HAPPY AS YOU THINK THEY ARE

I was invited once to give a talk to a small group of alumni from a particular school. I arrived at the host's home, and it was lovely inside and out—professionally chosen furniture, rugs, and window treatments; beautifully manicured landscaping; a staff of caterers passing out drinks and food on silver trays. The family was equally impressive: a stunning husband and wife and two well-dressed and well-behaved young children. The evening was delightful, and as I got in my car at the end of the event, I thought, *What a perfect life this family must have.*

In all honesty, I compared this perfect life I witnessed to my own much less perfect life: my messy house, my overgrown lawn, my sullen children. So, really, I was thinking, *This family has a perfect life, and my own can never measure up.*

The next day, I mentioned attending this event to a friend, who asked me if I knew this family's history; of course, I did not. I then learned that this marriage was the husband's first but the wife's second. She had married her college boyfriend a few years after graduation; less than a month after their wedding, he died instantly when a plane crashed into his office in the North Tower of the World Trade Center. He never saw their wedding photos.

I learned an important lesson about the faulty logic inherent in making comparisons: we never know the true story about other people's lives. Our comparisons are based on the external reality they present, or in some cases choose to present. As economist Seth Stephens-Davidowitz points out, people spend six times as much time washing dishes as they do golfing, yet there are roughly twice as many tweets about golfing as there are about doing the dishes.[6] Similarly, although the budget Las Vegas hotel Circus Circus and the luxury hotel Bellagio have an approximately equal number of rooms, people report checking into the Bellagio hotel on Facebook about three times as often.

And even when these images are impressive, we never know what other people are really experiencing. As Chekhov's Ivan Ivanovitch says, "We see those who go to the market to buy food, who eat in the daytime and sleep at night, who prattle away, merry . . . But we neither hear nor see those who suffer, and the terrible things in life are played out behind the scenes."[7]

There's strong support for Chekhov's intuition. In one series of studies, researchers asked college students how frequently they had experienced a variety of negative events (such as receiving a low grade or being rejected by a potential romantic partner) and positive events (such as attending a fun party and going out with friends) in the past two weeks.[8] They were also asked to estimate how often other students had experienced these same events.

Can you predict their findings? For every single negative event, students believed they were experiencing these events more often than were their peers. For example, although 60 percent of students had received a bad grade in the past two weeks, they believed that only 44 percent of their peers had had this experience. On the other hand, students also believed that their peers were experiencing the positive events more frequently than they themselves were. For example, although only 41 percent of students reported attending a fun party in the last two weeks, they believed that 62 percent of their peers had had this experience.

Sadly, perceiving such discrepancies—even when they are wrong—is associated with negative consequences. Students who underestimated how often their peers were experiencing negative events and overestimated how often their peers were experiencing positive events reported feeling lonelier and less satisfied with life.

Many colleges and universities are now trying to counteract the negative consequences of such misperceptions by encouraging people to share their own failures. For example, Smith College in Northampton, Massachusetts, has started a program called "Failing Well," in which students and professors share their experiences of personal and professional failure in an attempt to create awareness of the negative events we all face. Similar programs have been adopted at other schools, including Stanford's

Resilience Project, Harvard's Success-Failure Project, and the University of Pennsylvania's Penn Faces.

Johannes Haushofer, a professor of psychology and public affairs at Princeton University, created a "CV of Failures" that recounts all the rejections of his academic career.[9] This list includes graduate programs that rejected him, academic positions that turned him down, and scholarships that he did not receive. His motivation for creating this document was his awareness that people's successes are often obvious, but their failures are not. As Haushofer notes, "Most of what I try fails, but these failures are often invisible, while the successes are visible. I have noticed that this sometimes gives others the impression that most things work out for me . . . This CV of Failures is an attempt to balance the record and give some perspective."

Here's a list of some of my own professional failures, which doesn't even include the long list of journal editors and book publishers that have rejected my work:

Doctoral Programs I Did Not Get Into

1991	Department of Psychology Yale University
1991	Department of Psychology, University of Michigan
1991	Department of Psychology, University of California – Los Angeles

Academic Positions I Did Not Receive

1996	Department of Psychology, Rutgers University
1996	Department of Psychology, Georgia State University
1996	Department of Psychology, Stanford University
1996	Department of Psychology, University of Missouri–Columbia
1997	Department of Psychology, University of Minnesota

We can all find greater happiness by keeping in mind that what people present to others almost never tells the true story of what they are experiencing. As writer Anne Lamott says, "Try not to compare your insides to other people's outsides."[10]

THE HAZARDS OF TECHNOLOGY

Advances in technology—from the internet to cell phones to Facebook and Twitter and Instagram—have in some ways made our lives happier. After all, this sort of technology lets us connect with loved ones even when we are far apart.

Unfortunately, there is clear and consistent evidence that technology can also decrease happiness. One of the earliest studies on the consequences of the internet on individuals' well-being was conducted by Robert Kraut, a researcher at Carnegie Mellon University, in 1998. His research found that the more people used the internet, the higher their rates of loneliness and depression, the less they communicated with family members living in their own home, and the smaller their social circle.[11] Most recently, a 2010 review of forty studies found that internet use had a small but significant, detrimental effect on happiness.[12]

To examine the impact of social media on loneliness, Hayeon Song, a professor at the University of Wisconsin, and her team analyzed data from relevant existing studies on the link between Facebook use and loneliness.[13] The researchers chose to focus on Facebook because it is by far the most popular social media site, with Facebook use accounting for 54 percent of users' time online globally and 62 percent of users' time in the United States.

These findings, which combined the results of many different studies on the impact of Facebook use on loneliness, found that as loneliness increases so does the time spent on Facebook. In other words, people who feel lonely feel more attracted to Facebook, perhaps in part because this type of social connection is more comfortable for those who are shy or feel lacking in social skills. But unfortunately the greater time these people spend on Facebook does not make them feel more connected to others—it doesn't reduce loneliness.

Researchers in another study examined the impact of Facebook use on happiness by sending text messages to residents of Ann Arbor, Michigan, five times each day.[14] Each time they asked the residents how much they had used Facebook, how worried and lonely they were, and how much direct interaction they had had with other people in the time since the last text.

Once again, these findings showed a real downside of Facebook use: the more people used Facebook in the time between the two texts, they less happy they felt. Moreover, the more people used Facebook over the course of the study, the greater was the decline in overall life satisfaction compared to at the beginning of the study. The conclusion seems unavoidable—Facebook clearly seems to be making people less happy.

But what is it about Facebook use that impairs our happiness?

One possibility is that increased Facebook use leads to higher levels of envy. Envy is especially likely to occur through repeated Facebook use since we are typically connected with people who are similar to ourselves in some ways. It's not surprising that hearing about the successes of others who are similar to ourselves may be particularly difficult.

Facebook may also make it particularly hard to avoid comparisons, which in turn may have a negative impact on happiness. Just think about the constant images many people see of their friends on Facebook and Instagram having what appears to be a great time. Surely our own lives can't really measure up. (I'm certainly thankful that I didn't have to see photos of parties I wasn't invited to on the internet when I was in high school, as my three kids have to endure now.) This type of constant comparison helps explain why adolescents who spend more time on social media and electronic devices, such as smartphones, have higher rates of depression and more suicide attempts.[15]

One recent study provides compelling evidence that Facebook use in particular is truly bad for our health.[16] In this study, researchers first examined how much time people spent on Facebook each day, as well as the types of activities they engaged in, such as "liking" other people's posts, posting their own updates, and clicking links. They then examined whether the frequency of such interactions was associated with overall well-being one year later. Researchers found that people who spent more time on Facebook had lower levels of physical health, mental health, and life satisfaction one year later.

So for those of us in search of greater happiness, a relatively simple strategy is to quit the social media habit. This choice reduces opportunities for depressive social comparisons and frees up time to spend in better ways, as I'll describe in chapter 8, "Change Your Behavior and Your Mindset Will Follow." And when you do spend time on social media, try to present your real life, not just the good bits. When I'm on Facebook, I make a deliberate effort to post things like "All my kids have lice." Which, for the record, has been true far too often.

WHAT'S THE TAKE-HOME POINT?

The desire to "keep up with the Joneses" is perhaps human nature. But the constant pressure to reach standards set by others makes us feel worse about our own lives. People who engage in more social comparisons are less happy, less satisfied with their lives, and more depressed.[17]

If you find yourself constantly making such comparisons, here are some simple strategies you can use to shift your mindset away from others and focus on finding happiness within yourself.

Avoid Comparisons

There's a great poem by Kurt Vonnegut in which he writes about talking to author Joseph Heller while attending a party hosted by a billionaire. When Vonnegut asks Heller how he feels knowing that this billionaire makes more money in a single day than Heller will ever earn from sales of his novel *Catch-22*, Heller responds that he has something that the billionaire will never have. "And what's that?" asks Vonnegut.

"The knowledge that I've got enough," says Heller.

This poem vividly illustrates how disregarding comparisons is the only route to finding true happiness. As a famous quote from the Torah says, "Who is rich? He who is happy with his lot" (Pirkei Avot 4:1). People vary considerably in how much they tend to compare themselves with others. Want to test your own tendencies? The Iowa-Netherlands Comparison Orientation Measure (INCOM) lets people measure how much they tend to compare themselves to others.[18] Try rating your agreement with each of these statements.

	STRONGLY DISAGREE	DISAGREE	MIXED	AGREE	STRONGLY AGREE
1. I often compare myself with others with respect to what I have accomplished in life.	1	2	3	4	5
2. I always pay a lot of attention to how I do things compared with how others do things.	1	2	3	4	5
3. I often compare how my loved ones (boy- or girlfriend, family members, etc.) are doing with how others are doing.	1	2	3	4	5
4. If I want to find out how well I have done something, I compare what I have done with how others have done.	1	2	3	4	5
5. I often compare how I am doing socially (e.g., social skills, popularity) with other people.	1	2	3	4	5

TOTAL SCORE:

Add up your scores on these items to see how much you tend to make comparisons. If your score is high, which indicates a stronger inclination toward making comparisons, try to stop yourself whenever possible.

We can also learn, with practice, to focus on comparisons that make us feel better, not worse. One of the reasons why people who volunteer report better health and happiness—as you'll read more about in chapter 11, "Give a Gift—to Anyone"—is that this experience changes the nature of comparisons they make.[19]

If shifting these comparisons doesn't come naturally to you, I can tell you that I've improved my own ability to adopt such framing with happier results. When my son, the Spanish scholar, was really struggling, and I was pretty depressed about his academic future, I reminded myself (sometimes hourly) that "at least he doesn't have leukemia." Pretty bleak, I know, but the reality is there are parents all over the world who would far prefer their child to be struggling with Spanish than struggling with chemotherapy.

Express Gratitude

It is perhaps human nature—at least for many of us—to focus on what's bad in our lives, instead of what's good. But as the philosopher Epictetus says, "He is a man of sense who does not grieve for what he has not, but rejoices in what he has."[20]

Research points to a very simple strategy for increasing our happiness: focus on what we are grateful for. In one study, researchers assigned people to one of three groups:

- Those in the first group were asked to write down five things they were grateful for in their lives over the last week (the "gratitude condition"); their lists included such things as God, kindness from friends, and the Rolling Stones.

- Those in the second group were asked to write down five daily hassles from the last week (the "hassles condition"); their lists included such things as too many bills to pay, trouble finding parking, and a messy kitchen.

- Those in the third group simply listed five events that had occurred in the last week (the "control condition"); their lists included attending a music festival, learning CPR, and cleaning out a closet.[21]

Before the experiment started, all participants had kept daily journals recording their moods, physical health, and general attitudes. The researchers could then compare how people in these different conditions changed over time.

What do you think they found? People who were in the gratitude condition felt fully 25 percent happier—they were more optimistic about the future and they felt better about their lives. What was particularly remarkable was that people in this group also did almost 1.5 hours more exercise a week than those in the hassles or events condition, and had fewer symptoms of illness.

Does this type of simplistic approach work only on relatively young, healthy people—who, after all, have many things in their lives to feel grateful about and relatively few major stressors? To test this question, in a subsequent study these researchers recruited adults who had neuromuscular disorders, which cause joint and muscle pain as well as muscle atrophy and thus are seriously debilitating.

Researchers asked these people to write each day for three weeks about one of two topics: Some people were asked to simply write about their daily life experiences (these people were in the control condition), while other people were asked to write about what they were grateful for in their daily lives (these people were in the gratitude condition).

Once again, this research revealed that writing about gratitude led to substantial benefits. People in the gratitude condition were more satisfied with their lives overall and more optimistic about the upcoming week. Interestingly, they were also sleeping better, which is a really important finding since good sleep tends to predict happiness as well as better health.

Similarly, women with breast cancer who complete a six-week online gratitude intervention, in which they spend ten minutes writing a letter expressing gratitude to someone in their life each week, show better psychological well-being and adaptation to cancer.[22] These findings suggest that simply writing about things you are grateful for has physical benefits, not just psychological ones, even among people who are struggling with serious and even life-threatening health conditions.

So, take a minute now and make a plan for increasing gratitude in your own life. First, make a list in the box below of things you are grateful for right now in your own life—not things that you will be grateful for once you retire, or once you win the lottery, or once you buy a new house.

THINGS I AM GRATEFUL FOR IN MY LIFE—RIGHT NOW
1.
2.
3.
4.
5.

Next, make a plan for regularly finding ways to focus on gratitude. Write in a gratitude journal before you go to sleep each night or when you first wake up, start a family tradition of going around the dinner table each night and saying one thing you are grateful for that day, or make a point of sending a thank-you email or letter once a month to someone in your life.

Find Your Meaning

I started this chapter by describing the relentless pressure that Palo Alto teenagers experience in their pursuit of an Ivy League acceptance. But these students, and their parents and peers, are looking for happiness in all the wrong places. There's no evidence that people who attend prestigious colleges or pursue financially lucrative careers experience greater happiness.

So, what *does* predict happiness? Doing things—in your job, your community, your family—that you find personally meaningful. Depending on your life stage, this could mean choosing a college major that you feel passionate about, or picking up a volunteer activity in your community, or selecting a particular career or industry. As Emily Esfahani Smith, the author of *The Power of Meaning: Finding Fulfillment in a World Obsessed with Happiness*, writes about the challenges young adults face in a world of comparisons, "They won't become the next Mark Zuckerberg. They won't have obituaries that run in newspapers like this one. But that doesn't mean their lives lack significance and worth. We all have a circle of people whose lives we can touch and improve—and we can find our meaning in that."

I have a friend whose husband worked for years in a top
financial firm on Wall Street. One day he returned home and
confessed to his wife that he hated his job and needed to quit.
Although they still had college loans to pay off, she supported
his decision; he is now working as a firefighter. When I asked her
how life had changed following his major career shift, she vividly
described his passion for his job. Apparently, he now "skips to
work," precisely because he has finally found his meaning. And
this brings him—and her—much more happiness than his former high salary ever did.

Empirical data supports the importance of engaging in meaningful activities as a key component of happiness. For example, a
recent study revealed that public service lawyers—public defend-
ers, in-house counsel lawyers for nonprofits, and criminal pros-
ecutors—reported higher levels of daily mood and well-being
than lawyers in traditional (and more prestigious) firms.[23] What
accounts for such differences? Well, it probably isn't about hours
worked, since lawyers in both groups work long hours (although
those working in firms who have requirements to bill a certain
number of hours report lower happiness). And it certainly isn't
about the money, since lawyers in public service make much less
than those in firms.

What really accounts for the big difference in happiness
between these two groups of lawyers is most likely a direct result of
the greater personal meaning and interest those in public service
careers derive from their jobs. As these researchers note, "A happy
life as a lawyer is much less about grades, affluence, and prestige
than about finding work that is interesting, engaging, personally
meaningful, and focused on providing needed help to others."

The constant comparisons in our society create a false impression that happiness lies in the pursuit of extrinsic goals, including material possessions, status, and prestige. But these findings demonstrate that true happiness actually lies in the pursuit of intrinsic goals, which focus on personal growth and connecting with others in meaningful ways.

Chapter 7

Embrace Adversity: Trauma Matters

O n November 27, 1990, BJ Miller, a sophomore at Princeton University, was walking back to his dorm late at night when he made a life-changing decision. At 3 AM, after a night of drinking, he decided to climb on top of an electrified shuttle train parked on campus. BJ was exposed to eleven thousand volts of electricity, which left him near death. He was taken by helicopter to a nearby hospital, where doctors had to remove his legs below the knees and amputate his left arm below the elbow.

After several months of surgeries and physical therapy, BJ returned to Princeton and graduated with his class in 1993. Although he continued to experience considerable pain, BJ regained much of his physical strength and even competed on the

US volleyball team at the 1992 Summer Paralympics in Barcelona. BJ is now a doctor in San Francisco.

This story is truly inspirational on a number of levels, and certainly BJ's ability to cope with such a tragic event speaks to his tremendous personal mental strength. And yet, despite all the good that he has made from this experience, and the impressive life that he has built, one must imagine how much easier his life would have been without having to deal with this type of pain and loss.

However, BJ's response to the question on everybody's mind— "If you could, would you go back in time and undo the night of that accident?"—might surprise you. His answer was "No." As he told a reporter for the *Princeton Alumni Magazine,* "Too much good stuff has come out of it. I was not headed toward a career in medicine before the accident, and I don't think I'd be as good a palliative-care physician if I hadn't had that experience."[1]

BJ speaks powerfully about the instant rapport and empathy he has with his patients. He works with veterans who have lost limbs and people who have been paralyzed by accidents and notes that his physical appearance actually helps his patients. After all, when he walks into their hospital rooms, they know from simply looking at his body that on some level he gets what they have experienced.

This ability to see the positive in truly dire circumstances illustrates how our mindset shapes consequences. Although we can't go through life avoiding all loss, we do have considerable control over how we think about even terrible trauma. Learning how to adopt a positive mindset is therefore an essential part of maintaining happiness, no matter what.

UNDERSTANDING POSTTRAUMATIC GROWTH

Experiencing life-threatening illness, physical abuse, the death of loved ones, and other difficult circumstances forces us to think about ourselves and the world in new ways. It helps to be aware of this phenomenon and to be able to use it to transform sad experiences into opportunities to reevaluate and find greater meaning in life.

Although it may seem really difficult to see any positives when facing devastating personal circumstances, it is possible to find some beneficial aspects of virtually any adverse situation. For example, many people who are diagnosed with cancer report experiencing a change in life priorities, a richer spiritual life, and closer relationships with loved ones. As Elizabeth Alexander, a poet and professor of humanities at Columbia University who lost her fifty-year-old husband to a heart attack, says, "Somehow, we have to let the ravages shape us and make our souls stronger and more beautiful."[2]

Psychologists describe this type of perspective-taking as *posttraumatic growth*, meaning experiencing significant positive shifts after struggling with a major life crisis. This growth occurs as people struggle to make sense of and cope with a trauma, and can result in meaningful and lasting change.

If you've experienced a major trauma, you can test your level of posttraumatic growth from this event with the Posttraumatic Growth Inventory (PTGI). To take a short form of the test,[3] respond to the following ten statements and sum up your answers to get your total score.

	STRONGLY DISAGREE	DISAGREE	MIXED	AGREE	STRONGLY AGREE
1. I changed my priorities about what is important in life.	1	2	3	4	5
2. I have a greater appreciation for the value of my own life.	1	2	3	4	5
3. I am able to do better things with my life.	1	2	3	4	5
4. I have a better understanding of spiritual matters.	1	2	3	4	5
5. I have a greater sense of closeness with others.	1	2	3	4	5
6. I established a new path for my life.	1	2	3	4	5
7. I know better that I can handle difficulties.	1	2	3	4	5
8. I have a stronger religious faith.	1	2	3	4	5
9. I discovered that I'm stronger than I thought I was.	1	2	3	4	5
10. I learned a great deal about how wonderful people are.	1	2	3	4	5

TOTAL SCORE:

Higher scores indicate a greater amount of overall posttraumatic growth. This scale assesses five distinct components of such growth: appreciation of life, relationships with others, new possibilities in life, personal strength, and spirituality. Each of these types of growth helps people cope with traumatic events in a positive way.

As you might expect, people who are able to find some positive aspects in difficult situations experience better outcomes. For example, people who are able to see benefit in a cancer diagnosis report lower levels of distress and depression, higher levels of positive affect, and an overall increased quality of life.[4] Moreover, as you learned in chapter 2, "Why Zebras Don't Get Ulcers: Mindset Affects Health," adopting a positive mindset in the midst of adversity leads to better physical well-being over time. For example, adolescents who are diagnosed with diabetes but can find some benefit in this experience more closely follow their recommended treatment regiment, which in turn predicts better health.[5]

Being able to recognize that experiencing major hardship brings value and meaning helps promote calm and staying on an even keel, even when the circumstances are so terrible that there seems no way to be truly happy. For example, after her twenty-two-year-old sister was killed in the 2010 earthquake in Haiti, Jordan Hightower shifted her mindset about how to live her own life. She said, "I realized that waiting to experience life was stupid because hers had been taken so suddenly and I could be next. I began living."[6] Jordan has now traveled to more than twenty-three countries, seen dozens of plays and concerts and sporting events, and spends quality time with friends and family. And she no longer worries about her relatively low salary as a teacher or living in a small apartment.

Most of us will at some point experience great loss, be it the death of a loved one, a serious illness or injury, or a divorce. We can't go through life avoiding all bad experiences, but we can choose to see these tremendously difficult experiences in a positive light by focusing on what is gained, instead of what is lost. As Anna Berardi, director of the Trauma Response Institute at George Fox University, says, "Most people emerge from a trauma wiser, with a deeper appreciation of life."[7]

ADVERSITY ENHANCES SMALL PLEASURES

How exactly do stressful life events help us experience better well-being? Having experienced and survived negative events increases our ability to recognize and take pleasure from simple things—a gorgeous sunset, a gripping novel, a delicious glass of wine. Experiencing some adversity may also help remind us to appreciate the small joys of daily life, to stop and smell the roses.

Researchers in one study asked fifteen thousand adults to complete a measure of savoring, a type of emotion regulation in which people prolong and enhance positive emotional experiences.[8] (You might savor the taste of a really great chocolate bar by imagining how good it is going to taste before you start eating it, taking very small bites to help the taste last longer, and really concentrating on how fabulous the chocolate tastes in your mouth.) They then asked people which types of adverse events they had experienced, such as the death of a loved one, divorce, or a severe illness or injury. Although people who were still struggling with an event reported a lower ability to savor positive events, those who had experienced more adverse events in the past reported higher levels of savoring. In other words, having experienced—and coped with—negative life experiences in the past seems to increase people's capacity for enjoying pleasurable experiences.

These findings help explain a puzzling phenomenon— happiness tends to increase with age. By age sixty, we will all have experienced difficult life events, such as the loss of loved ones, career setbacks, or health problems. And although we might think that experiencing these types of events would cast a pall over the later years, and thus lead people to feel gloomier, helpless, and pessimistic as they age, fear no more. People experience fewer negative emotions, and more positive emotions, with age, meaning those in their seventies and eighties report greater happiness than teenagers![9]

Researchers in another study asked fifteen hundred adults ages twenty-one to ninety-nine about their overall life functioning, including physical, cognitive, and psychological functioning.[10] Although older people predictably reported lower levels of physical and cognitive functioning, they reported higher levels of psychological well-being. Specifically, the older the person, the greater their satisfaction with life, and the lower their perceived stress, anxiety, and depression. As Dr. Dilip Jeste, director of the Center for Healthy Aging at the University of California, San Diego, notes, "Participants reported that they felt better about themselves and their lives year upon year, decade after decade."[11]

Many different factors contribute to the increase in happiness as we age. But one explanation is that experiencing difficult life events changes our mindset, and this shift makes us feel happier.

According to the *age-related positivity effect*, older adults generally prefer and pay more sustained attention to positive versus negative information.[12] For example, when researchers show people a crowd of faces with different expressions, younger people look most at the threatening faces, whereas older people's attention naturally gravitates to the happier ones.[13] They also remember more positive than negative events. In other words, older adults tend to deliberately focus their attention and memory on the good, whereas younger people tend to focus on the bad. And guess which type of focus leads to greater happiness?

This shift in mindset is evident in how our brain processes different types of events. For example, researchers in one study showed two groups of people, ages nineteen to thirty-one and ages sixty-one to eighty, photographs while they were in an MRI machine.[14] Some of the photographs conveyed positive experiences, such as a skier winning a race, while others portrayed negative experiences, such as a wounded soldier. The researchers measured brain activity to see if age made a difference in how these photos were perceived.

Contrary to what they expected, there was no difference between the groups when viewing negative images—at least neurologically. However, when the older group viewed photos depicting positive experiences, the areas of the brain that process emotion (the amygdala) and memory (the hippocampus) were both activated. This demonstrates that the older adults registered positive events very strongly; the brain regions that process good things were basically saying "remember this." This type of activation was not witnessed in the younger group.

So, with age we get better at focusing on the good and ignoring the bad, and this change in mindset, not surprisingly, makes us feel happier. As Alvin Mann, age ninety-four, described his strategy for aging well to the *New York Times*, "Of course, one part of it is medical science, but the bigger part is that we live worry-free lives; we do not let anything we cannot control bother us in the least."[15]

ADVERSITY BUILDS COMPASSION

On April 15, 2013, Carlos Arredondo was watching the Boston Marathon when he heard a loud explosion. Although he had no idea whether additional explosions would occur, he rushed immediately to a young man whose legs were badly bleeding. A photo of Carlos, the man with the cowboy hat, pushing Jeff Bauman in a wheelchair became one of the iconic images of the heroism seen that day.

What prompted Carlos to immediately jump into action, potentially imperiling his own life? His personal experience with adversity almost certainly played a role. Carlos's older son, a marine, died in 2004 in Iraq. His younger son, who developed severe depression following this loss, died by suicide in 2011. These tragedies likely increased his ability to empathize with others and to engage in life-saving altruism.

This type of compassion among those who have experienced significant loss is not unusual. Longitudinal research shows that many people who experience the death of a spouse to lung cancer show substantial changes in personality.[16] These changes include increases in sociability and dependability as well as in prosocial beliefs. In fact, nearly 40 percent of bereaved spouses show substantial increases in their orientation toward altruism.

Lab-based research reveals similar findings about how adversity increases prosocial behavior. For example, researchers in one study measured people's experience of adverse events as well as their levels of compassion and empathy.[17] They then allowed study participants to either keep all the money they were paid for being in the study or to donate some of their earnings to the Red Cross. As predicted, people who had experienced more negative life events—and hence could empathize with others in need of such help—were more likely to donate.

Keep in mind, however, that recovering from trauma takes time. Immediately after Carlos Arredondo learned his older son had been killed, he was severely distressed, and even sought inpatient psychiatric treatment for his grief. His ability to show tremendous courage and compassion during the Boston Marathon attacks came only after time had passed, and he had come to terms with his loss.

ADVERSITY BUILDS RESILIENCE

Perhaps most important, a growing amount of research points to the benefits of adversity in increasing resilience, meaning the ability to react to negative experiences in an adaptive and productive way. Adverse events seem to provide people with opportunities to practice coping with trauma, and therefore to develop valuable strategies for functionally managing future loss.

Here's a simple example of the benefits of experiencing even a relatively low-level adverse event. Researchers in one study examined the effects of a ten-day sailing trip in New Zealand on resilience in teenagers.[18] The teenagers experienced tough conditions, including hard physical work, seasickness, bad weather, crowded living conditions, and extensive daily chores. The researchers measured levels of resilience in students during the trip and again five months later, and then compared those levels of resilience to those of college students who did not participate in such a trip.

The differences in resilience between these two groups of students were long lasting. The experience of tough conditions, coupled with the knowledge that one has the ability to cope with these challenges, led to significantly higher levels of resilience compared to college students who didn't experience such a trip. In this way, stressful experiences seem to "immunize" us against future stressors. We learn from experience that we have the strength to navigate tough challenges and that belief is tremendously helpful when we later encounter other stressors in daily life.

Now, the stress of adventure travel is obviously not entirely comparable to the serious stressors we face in daily life. But real-world stressors, and even tragedies, provide similar advantages in terms of teaching resilience.

For example, researchers in another large-scale study surveyed nearly two thousand adults ages 18 to 101 for several years to assess how their well-being changed over time.[19] Participants listed any stressful life events they had experienced before the start of the study, and then any new ones that occurred. These events included divorce, death of loved ones, serious illnesses, and natural disasters. The researchers then measured the link between the number of stressful life experiences and overall psychological well-being.

You might expect that people who had avoided major stresses would have greater life satisfaction. But in fact, those with relatively stress-free lives were no happier than those who had experienced as many as a dozen major life events. Who was happiest? Those who had experienced some, but not too many, stressful events (two to six).

These findings suggest that resilience doesn't happen—at least for most of us—by accident. Instead, we get better at recovering from difficult events with practice. People who've managed to avoid major stressors haven't had a chance to develop these skills; thus, when difficult things do happen, they have trouble coping. These findings help account for the counterintuitive finding that among those coping with a serious neurological illness, widowed people experience higher levels of happiness than married people.[20] In sum, having already faced a tremendous loss helps people develop adaptive strategies for coping with subsequent life stressors, such as diagnosis with a life-threatening illness.

This research provides compelling evidence that what doesn't kill us does indeed make us stronger. As Roxane Cohen Silver, a psychologist at the University of California, Irvine, notes, "Each negative event a person faces leads to an attempt to cope, which forces people to learn about their own capabilities, about their support networks—to learn who their real friends are. That kind of learning, we think, is extremely valuable for subsequent coping."[21]

But keep in mind that there are, of course, limits to the value of adversity. After all, people who experienced a high number of such events were worse off than those who experienced only a moderate number of events. Elizabeth Smart, who was kidnapped from her Utah home at age fourteen and spent nine months experiencing physical and psychological abuse before being rescued, writes, "I'm a stronger person than I would have been. I wouldn't wish it on anybody, though. I don't think anybody needs to become strong that way."[22] But even in the face of too many adverse experiences, the human spirit still displays a remarkable capacity to adapt, as you'll read about in the next section.

THE POWER OF ADAPTATION

On July 23, 2007, two men who had recently been released from jail broke into a home in Cheshire, Connecticut. They tied up the father, Dr. William Petit, in the basement. They then tied his wife, Jennifer, and the couple's two daughters, Hayley and Michaela, to their beds and proceeded to sexually assault all three of them. The girls were ages eleven and seventeen. Then, to hide evidence of their crimes, the men set the house on fire. William was able to escape from the basement, but his wife and both girls died of smoke inhalation.

The horrific details of this story are impossible for most of us to imagine, as is the depth of loss that William experienced. The loss of his wife and two daughters seems unbearable, particularly given the heinous circumstances of their last hours alive. Most of us probably wonder how he could ever experience happiness again.

And yet in 2012 William remarried. He met his second wife, Christine, when she volunteered as a photographer with the Petit Family Foundation, a charitable foundation he started to honor his family's memory. His first wife's family attended their wedding and expressed how happy they were that he had found love again. And on November 23, 2013, William and Christine Petit welcomed a new baby, William Arthur Petit III.

What does this tragic story tell us about achieving happiness? The loss of his first wife and daughters clearly changed and shaped William Petit in fundamental ways and will deeply affect him for the rest of his life. Yet his story also vividly illustrates the power of the human spirit to adapt, even to circumstances that may at first seem impossible to bear. After experiencing horrifically difficult circumstances, we can—over time—find happiness again. As the poet and novelist Rainer Maria Rilke writes, "Let everything happen to you. Beauty and terror. Just keep going. No feeling is final."[23]

Aside from anecdotal evidence, scientific research also demonstrates the power of the human spirit to adapt to negative events, even when we can't imagine this is possible. Studies with people who have experienced a job loss, spinal cord injury, or blindness reveal that after an initial period of adaptation, many do report positive well-being.[24] Time after time, humans have shown that no matter how bad things may seem in the moment we can all, eventually, find happiness again.

WHAT'S THE TAKE-HOME POINT?

One of my favorite quotes about the value of adversity is from an excellent book—*My Losing Season* by Pat Conroy. This book chronicles a very unsuccessful high school basketball season, and what this season taught players on that team. Here's the quote:

> Sports books are always about winning because winning is far more pleasurable and exhilarating to read about than losing.

Winning is wonderful in every aspect, but the darker music of loss resonates on deeper, richer planes. Loss is a fiercer, more uncompromising teacher, coldhearted but clear-eyed in its understanding that life is more dilemma than game, and more trial than free pass. My acquaintance with loss has sustained me during the stormy passages of my life when the pink slips came through the door, when the checks bounced at the bank, when I told my small children I was leaving their mother, when the despair caught up with me, when the dreams of suicide began feeling like love songs of release . . . Though I learned some things from the games we won that year, I learned much, much more from loss.

This quote speaks to the true benefit we all can experience from loss, as long as we are able to frame that loss with a positive mindset. And since it is impossible to go through life without experiencing loss, at least we can all try to hold onto such experiences and recognize what they have added to our lives and not just what they have taken away.

In July 2004 my fifty-seven-year-old mother died of ovarian cancer, only four months after her diagnosis. It was, as you can imagine, devastating, and I spent months grieving this loss and wondering if I would find happiness again. But over time, and with practice, I have learned to recognize and appreciate what I gained after her death, such as a closer relationship with my brother and a much-needed shift in career goals.

It can be really hard to find the silver lining in the midst of difficult life circumstances, especially for those of us who don't find it easy to naturally focus on the bright side. But for those who may need help in adopting this type of positive mindset, there are specific strategies empirical research shows can help, even when facing tremendous tragedy and loss.

Focus on the Small Joys of Daily Life

If you are struggling to cope with major loss, it's going to be really hard to find much happiness in this situation. But if you just focus on even the small joys of daily life, it can make a world of difference in getting through a devastating event. Instead of being preoccupied with the event, divert your attention with one of the following activities:

- Take a walk outside and focus on the beauty of nature—the smell of freshly cut grass, the colors of flowers, the sound of birds singing.
- Connect with a dear friend—write a letter, make a call, meet for coffee and really catch up.
- Distract yourself in some way—read a novel, watch television or a movie, clean out a closet.
- Exercise (in whatever way feels good to you)—attend a yoga class, go for a jog, take deep breaths and stretch your muscles.

No matter your circumstances, try to find a few good moments every day. As Sheryl Sandberg notes, "It is the greatest irony of my life that losing my husband helped me find deeper gratitude—gratitude for the kindness of my friends, the love of my family, the laughter of my children."[25] And this shift in mindset increases happiness.

Make Connections

One of the challenges of finding happiness following a great loss is that people feel isolated and alone in their grief. Social support may be in abundance immediately following a loss but then disappear within a few days or weeks—much faster than grief dissipates. Even when support is available, people may lack the ability to really empathize with the loss.

People who make connections with others, especially those who understand the nature of the loss, find it easier to cope and find happiness again. Both formal and informal grief support groups can provide valuable support for those who have experienced the loss of a loved one. Survivors can share their experiences, obtain guidance on coping, and discuss big questions (e.g., Why did this happen? Is life fair? Is there a God?). Many people find participating in a support group with others who understand what they are going through helps them feel less alone. Moreover, some evidence suggests that group-based interventions for bereaved people may lead to greater reductions in grief severity than individual therapy.[26]

Researchers in one study assessed how survivors responded to the 2007 mass shooting at Virginia Tech, in which thirty-three people died.[27] Although some students, as expected, showed higher levels of depression and anxiety over the next year, others didn't show a big change in their overall mood state, for better or for worse. But the most remarkable finding was that some students actually felt *better* in the year after experiencing this tragedy. In fact, students who sought out social support from and developed stronger connections with other students showed decreases in anxiety and depression. Thus, even in the case of truly devastating events, people who make connections with others experience substantial benefits.

Create Some Good, No Matter the Circumstances

Even when facing terrible tragedy, in many cases we can create some good—for others, if not for ourselves. Life is full of the inspirational stories of those who survived and even thrived in the face of immense tragedy by creating good from their loss. Here are three powerful examples:

- When Amy Anderson's son Bryson was stillborn at just twenty weeks, she was devastated. But when her doctors suggested she bind her breasts to stop breast milk production, Amy instead chose to start pumping milk to donate to help premature babies. (The use of human milk for premature babies can substantially reduce the risk of very serious health problems.) Amy pumped for eight months, donating a total of ninety-two gallons of breast milk, and found great meaning in her choice. She said, "This was Bryson's life purpose and I'm going to embrace that."[28]

- On October 25, 2012, Marina and Kevin Krim faced an unspeakable nightmare: their nanny had stabbed their six-year-old daughter, Lulu, and their nearly two-year-old son, Leo, to death. The following month, the Krims established the Lulu

& Leo Fund to bring arts and science programs to disadvantaged children. As Kevin Krim said at their first (sold-out) fund-raiser, "It's that inspiration of their lives that motivates us."[29]

- You undoubtedly remember the horrific Columbine shooting in April 1999, in which two students shot and killed thirteen people before committing suicide themselves. In February of 2016, Sue Klebold, the mother of one of the shooters, published a book called *A Mother's Reckoning: Living in the Aftermath of Tragedy*, which tells her family's story. Her goal in writing this very personal story was to help other families recognize the signs she missed in her own son, with the hope that such knowledge could help prevent future tragedies. All her profits from this book will be used to fund charitable organizations that focus on mental illness and suicide prevention.

These real-world examples prove the power a positive mindset has in helping to find meaning in life and strength in coping with truly dire circumstances. If you are struggling after an immense loss, find a way to create some good out of the experience—perhaps by working to create awareness of a disease, establishing a scholarship or award in honor of a loved one, or volunteering with an organization that helps others who have experienced such a loss. By adopting a positive mindset with a focus on creating good, you can cope with unthinkable loss, and, over time, find contentment, happiness, and peace.

PART 3

CHANGING MINDSET

Chapter 8

Change Your Behavior and Your Mindset Will Follow

On July 19, 1989, United Airlines Flight 232 experienced engine failure leading to the loss of all flight controls about an hour after takeoff in Denver, Colorado. For approximately thirty minutes, the pilots worked unsuccessfully to regain some power, dump fuel, and navigate to a runway in Sioux City, Iowa. Passengers were aware of the emergency situation and were told to expect a rough landing. Of the 296 people on board, 111 died and 185 survived the crash.

How did people cope with their fear as they prepared for the crash landing? Interviews with survivors showed many relied on their religious faith.[1] Here are some of their words:

- "I closed my eyes and thought, *'Dear Lord, I pray that you'll guide the pilot's hands.'* I also thought that if God wanted to take my life, that it was OK with me. I was full of peace. Here I was sitting on the edge of eternity. I wasn't facing the end of my life."

- "I did what I needed to do to prepare to die. My thought at the time was that I wanted to be reborn into a family where I would be able to hear the teachings of Buddha. I'd done a lot of Buddhist meditation in my life, and this trained me to become one-pointed in my awareness. I was totally focused on the brace position."

Adopting religious and spiritual beliefs improves psychological well-being and physical health, at least in part because such beliefs help us cope with small daily life stressors as well as major traumatic events.

In this chapter, I'll describe how simple tweaks in behavior—getting enough sleep, reading a novel, practicing meditation—can change how you think about yourself and the world. Most important, adopting such behaviors can increase happiness, improve physical health, and extend our lives.

GO TO BED

Perhaps the easiest way to increase happiness is to get enough sleep. A 2015 Gallup poll surveying more than seven thousand American adults found that people who reported getting enough sleep had higher overall well-being than those who got less sleep.[2]

For example, the average well-being score for people who reported getting eight hours of sleep a night was 65.7 (out of 100), compared to 64.2 for those who got seven hours of sleep, and 59.4 for those who got six hours of sleep. This survey confirmed the results of multiple scientific studies showing that getting enough sleep helps improve psychological well-being, including reducing rates of anxiety, depression, and loneliness.[3]

Why is adequate sleep so important? One reason is that people who are well rested are better able to cope with daily life stressors.[4] People who are sleep deprived are more irritable and make more errors in thinking and memory. Maybe you can think of a time in which you were too short with a family member, friend, or colleague after getting too little sleep one night?

People who don't get enough sleep get stuck on negative thoughts and lose the ability to instead focus on positive things.[5] In fact, people who don't get enough sleep engage in more repetitive negative thinking, including worrying obsessively about the future, replaying events from the past, and experiencing intrusive thoughts. As described in chapter 5, "Are You Tigger or Eeyore: Personality Matters," this type of thought pattern increases the risk of depression and anxiety.

Sleep deprivation is also bad for our physical health. Poor sleep weakens the immune system, which increases the risk of developing various illnesses, including cancer, stroke, heart disease, and diabetes.[6] Better sleep even leads to better recovery from surgery.

To examine the impact of sleep deprivation on the body's ability to fight off disease, researchers in one study recruited healthy volunteers.[7] They measured these people's overall health habits, such as alcohol use and smoking, as well as their sleep patterns during the prior week. Then, with permission, the researchers inserted cold virus into the participants' bodies using nasal drops.

The researchers then monitored these people over the next week to see who developed a cold.

Their findings provide powerful evidence that getting enough sleep is an essential part of staying healthy. People who had slept on average less than six hours a night the prior week were more than four times as likely to develop a cold compared to those who had slept more than seven hours a night.

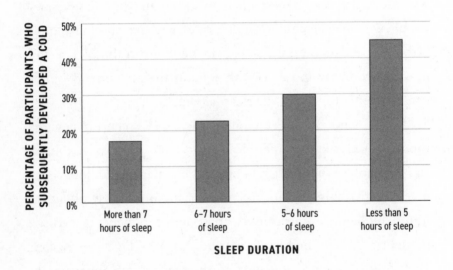

Figure 8.1: People who slept more than seven hours a night were significantly less likely to develop a cold than those who slept fewer than five hours a night.

Prather, A. A., Janicki-Deverts, D., Hall, M. H., and Cohen, S. "Behaviorally Assessed Sleep and Susceptibility to the Common Cold." *SLEEP* 2015; 38 (9): 1353–1359.

"Short sleep was more important than any other factor in predicting subjects' likelihood of catching cold," said Aric Prather, a professor of psychiatry at the University of California San

Francisco. "It didn't matter how old people were, their stress levels, their race, education or income. It didn't matter if they were a smoker. With all those things taken into account, statistically sleep still carried the day."[8]

I hope you now understand the importance of getting a good night's sleep—which is one of the easiest ways you can feel happier and be healthier. So make a goal to get in bed early enough to allow for a full night of sleep and avoid eating and drinking, especially caffeine, late at night. Also, make sure not to use electronics, like a computer, iPad, or e-reader, right before trying to sleep; the "blue light" that most of these devices emit actually makes it more difficult to fall asleep.

PICK UP A BOOK

Here's another small change you can make in your daily life that increases happiness: Read a book you love! Many people can remember times in childhood in which they were fully caught up in reading a beloved book, such as the Harry Potter series. I remember removing my oldest child's light bulbs at night because he literally couldn't stop reading.

As adults, however, we often believe we "don't have time to read." (Interestingly, we somehow find time to watch TV, search the internet, and update our Facebook posts.) Unfortunately, this means we miss out on some of the many benefits of reading.

Scientific research suggests reading helps us feel connected to other people—even feeling a connection to characters in a book creates a sense of belonging, an important component of happiness.[9] Reading can increase positive feelings, especially if the book inspires you to think about your own life in a new way or to take action toward reaching your own goals.

Reading, especially fiction, can also improve our ability to empathize with someone else and thus improve our social skills. When we become absorbed in a novel, we imagine the world through the characters' eyes, which increases our ability to take on someone else's perspective in the real world.[10] This skill, in turn, may increase our ability to empathize with others and work through conflict. For example, fifth graders who read the Harry Potter series, which examines prejudice between wizards and nonwizards, become more empathic and less prejudiced toward people in stigmatized groups.[11] As Keith Oatley, a psychologist at the University of Toronto, notes, "Fiction might be the mind's flight simulator."[12]

Moreover, some recent evidence suggests that reading books may extend our lives. One study compared three groups of people (all fifty and older): those who read no books, those who read books up to three and a half hours a week, and those who read books for more than three and a half hours a week.[13] Compared with people who didn't read, those who read for up to three and a half hours a week were 17 percent less likely to die over the twelve-year follow-up period, and those who read more than three and half hours a week were 23 percent less likely to die during this period. In fact, people who read books lived an average of almost two years longer than those who did not read at all. What accounts for these astonishing findings? People who regularly read books, not newspapers or magazines, show higher levels of cognitive skills, including memory, critical thinking, and concentration. These abilities, in turn, likely provide a survival advantage.

So, an easy way of increasing happiness is to pick up a book you find personally enjoyable (not a book you "should read") and make a point of reading every day—a few minutes before bed, or on a lunch break, or during your daily commute on public transportation. It may even lengthen your life!

TAKE A WALK

We already know exercise is good for us physically. It helps us maintain a healthy weight, strengthens muscles and bones, and leads to lower heart rate and blood pressure. Most important, exercise reduces the negative physiological effects of stress on the body, which is why people who engage in regular exercise experience fewer illnesses.[14]

But exercise isn't just good for our physical health—it also helps improve thinking and memory skills, and may even reduce the risk of dementia.[15] Even pretty low amounts of exercise, such as walking a few times a week, leads to changes in brain function that predict better cognitive functioning.

The benefits of exercise on mental sharpness are also seen among those showing early signs of dementia. One study of older adults who had been diagnosed with mild cognitive impairment randomly assigned people to one of two groups.[16] One group of people walked for one hour three times a week; the other group received education in nutrition and healthy living each week. Before the study, none of these people were currently engaging in regular exercise. Six months later, people who had started the walking program had lower blood pressure, and, intriguingly, now had better scores on cognitive tests.

Engaging in regular physical activity is also good for our mental health.[17] Have you ever been in a bad mood but then exercised and felt better? Exercising helps us feel better in part because it can get our minds off any problems we may be facing. It lets us manage stressful life events without becoming irritable and upset.[18]

But exercise also leads to physiological changes in our bodies that make us feel better. When we engage in physical activity, the brain releases chemicals, called endorphins, that reduce pain and make us feel better.

Exercise may even help treat depression, and, at least in some cases, may be as helpful as psychotherapy or antidepressants.[19] In one study, researchers examined whether exercising could help people who are depressed feel better.[20] To test this hypothesis, they assigned 156 adults with clinical depression—a severe level of depression that disrupts daily life—to one of three groups:

- People in one group engaged in aerobic exercise (three forty-five-minute sessions a week for four months). They did not receive any drugs to combat depression.

- People in another group received drugs to relieve the symptoms of depression (also given for four months) but did not engage in aerobic exercise.

- People in the third group engaged in both aerobic exercise and received drugs (again for four months).

The researchers then examined people in all three groups over time to see if levels of depression changed. They found that people who engaged in aerobic exercise, even when they received no drugs to help with their symptoms of depression, showed improvements in mood for as long as four months. In fact, people in all three groups improved at the same rate. This study provides important evidence that moderately strenuous exercise can be as effective as pharmaceuticals in treating depression.

Although the benefits of exercise are clear, it can be hard to make time to exercise. But changing your exercise mindset can help you start and stick with an exercise routine. Specifically, don't focus on the long-term benefits of exercise for improving cardio-vascular fitness or maintaining a healthy weight or preventing depression. Instead, focus on the short-term and immediate plea-sures of exercise. Maybe taking a yoga class is a time to clear your head and relax after a busy day. Maybe going for a walk with a friend is a chance to catch up. Maybe you'll get better sleep—and feel more refreshed the next day—after working out. Adopting this type of focus on immediate gratification makes it easier to stay motivated because you don't have to wait so long for the payoff.

Also, try not to stress about finding more hours, or even min-utes, in your day to add in an exercise program. Make small shifts in your behavior, such as taking the stairs instead of the elevator and parking farther away from store entrances. One recent study even found that simply getting up and moving every thirty min-utes or so, instead of just sitting for long periods, reduced the risk of early death.[21] In sum, when it comes to exercise, almost any-thing counts—just start moving.

SEX

So, let's turn now to a different type of exercise . . . having sex. Does sex make you happy? The answer, which is perhaps the least surprising thing you will learn in this book, is yes!

To test the strength of the relationship between frequency of sex and happiness, researchers examined data on the self-reported levels of sexual activity and happiness of sixteen thousand people.[22] Their findings revealed that sex is a strong (and positive) predictor of happiness. After controlling for many other factors, including income, education, marital status, health, age, race, and other characteristics, respondents who reported having sex at least two to three times a month were 33 percent happier than those who reported having no sex during the previous twelve months. In fact, having sex even just once a month generates the same increase in happiness as having an additional $50,000 in annual income!

So, how often should you have sex in order to feel happiest? Tim Wadsworth, a professor of sociology at the University of Colorado, Boulder, examined national survey data gathered from over fifteen thousand Americans on both levels of happiness and sexual frequency. The happiness effect appears to rise with frequency. Compared to those who had no sex in the previous year, those reporting having sex once a week were 44 percent more likely to report a higher level of happiness. Those reporting having sex two to three times a week are 55 percent more likely to report a higher level of happiness.

Interestingly, people's satisfaction with their frequency of sex also depends on how often they think their friends are having sex. Although overall people who had more frequent sex reported higher levels of happiness, even after controlling for their own sexual frequency people who believed they were having less sex than their peers were unhappier than those who believed they were having as much or more than their peers. As a result of this knowledge, if members of a peer group are having sex two to three times a month but believe their peers are on a once-weekly schedule, their probability of reporting a higher level of happiness falls by about 14 percent. (This finding is further proof of the hazards of comparison, as described in chapter 6, "'Comparison Is the Thief of Joy': Environment Matters.")

Let me just note that this effect does not mean that having more sex is a great way to find more happiness. In fact, when couples are asked—as part of an admittedly odd research study—to double their frequency of sex for three months, they don't feel happier.[23] Instead, they feel exhausted and decidedly less happy; they also report less enjoyment of sex.

So what's the point of this study? The frequency of sex in and of itself is probably not the essential part of behavior that makes us happy. After all, this study shows a correlation between frequency of sex and happiness, but it doesn't show whether this connection is due to happy people having sex more frequently, more frequent sex creating more happiness, or whether some other factor predicts both happiness and frequency of sex (such as not having small children). Instead, sex is a pretty good indicator of whether people have a close relationship with a spouse or romantic partner and having this type of intimacy is clearly conducive to happiness. I'll describe more about the power of relationships in creating happiness in chapter 12, "Build Relationships: All You Need Is Love."

EXPLORE RELIGIOUS OR SPIRITUAL BELIEFS

Regardless of their specific creeds, people with religious or spiritual beliefs have higher levels of happiness and life satisfaction.[24] National surveys of Americans find that 47 percent of those who attend religious services more than weekly report being "very happy," compared to only 26 percent of those who never attend religious services. Those who attend religious services also have lower levels of depression and rates of suicide.

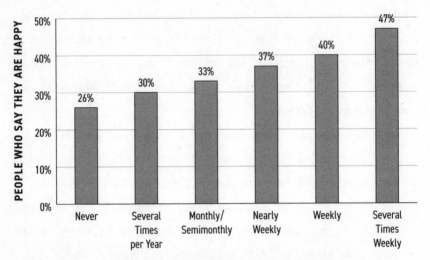

Figure 8.2: People who frequently attend religious services are more likely to report feeling happy than those who rarely or never attend services.

Myers, D. G., & Diener, E. (2018). The scientific pursuit of happiness. *Perspectives on Psychological Science, 13*(2), 218–225. Copyright © 2018 by SAGE Publications. Reprinted by Permission of SAGE Publications, Inc.

Moreover, religious involvement is associated with better health, including lower levels of cancer, heart disease, and stroke.[25] People with stronger religious beliefs also have fewer complications and shorter hospital stays following heart surgery.[26]

In fact, these beliefs help people live longer. In one study, researchers examined data from more than seventy-four thousand women, who answered questionnaires about their diets, lifestyles, and health every two years, and about their religious-service attendance every four years.[27] Compared with people who never attend religious services, those who attended more than once per week had 33 percent lower mortality risk during the sixteen-year study period and lived an average of five months longer, even when researchers took into account a variety of other factors, such as diet, physical activity, alcohol consumption, smoking status, body mass index, social integration, depression, race, and ethnicity. Those who attended weekly had a 26 percent lower risk and those who attended less than once a week had a 13 percent lower risk, and this behavior lowered their risk of both cardiovascular mortality (27 percent) and cancer mortality (21 percent). These lower rates of mortality mean that people who attend religious services more than weekly live to about age eighty-three, compared to only about age seventy-five for those who never attend religious services.

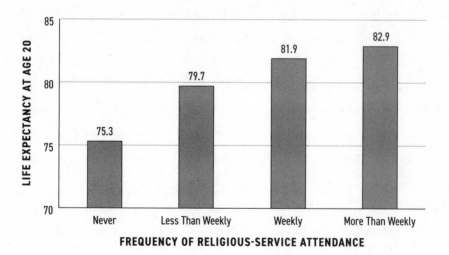

Figure 8.3: People who attend religious services more frequently live longer than those who never attend services.

Myers, D. G., & Diener, E. (2018). The scientific pursuit of happiness. *Perspectives on Psychological Science, 13*(2), 218–225. Copyright © 2018 by SAGE Publications. Reprinted by Permission of SAGE Publications, Inc.

How does adopting religious or spiritual beliefs lead to such beneficial outcomes?

One possibility is that substantial social support is provided within many religious communities. People who are religious may belong to a church, temple, or Bible study that creates a network of support, which provides valuable social support. For example, people with religious beliefs recovering from cardiac surgery not only felt more hopeful but also *believed* they had more social support.[28] These beliefs, in turn, led to lower levels of anxiety and depression.

Another explanation is that religious beliefs make people feel better precisely because these beliefs help people face major life stressors using a positive mindset, which in turn reduces the harmful physiological effects of stress on the body. When cancer patients who have a sense of meaning and peace undergo stem cell transplants, they experience fewer physical symptoms, such as nausea, and show lower levels of depression, anxiety, and fatigue in the year following the transplant.[29] Patients with congestive heart failure who report having strong spiritual beliefs are 20 percent less likely to die in the five years following their heart episode than those without such beliefs.[30] This link between spirituality and mortality holds true even when researchers take into account other variables that predict life expectancy, such as age, sex, and health behaviors. Even in the face of serious, life-threatening illnesses, religious and spiritual beliefs help reduce stress and thereby improve health.

Finally, religious beliefs also give people ways to understand traumatic events and provide some type of meaning to even seemingly senseless tragedies. Seeing the benefits of a negative experience gives people a chance to confront and cope with thoughts and feel-ings about the trauma but with a focus on its positive aspects, which in turn can lead to greater psychological and physical well-being. For example, believing that God won't give you more than you can handle, or that your deceased loved ones are now in a better place, or even that bad things do happen for a reason, makes peo-ple feel less anxious and depressed. As I described at the start of this chapter, many people facing the trauma of a plane crash and their potential imminent death relied on religious beliefs to man-age their anxiety.

These findings about the link between religious views and finding meaning help explain why people living in poor countries have a greater sense of meaning than those in wealthier ones.[31] Although we might predict that it is harder to find meaning while living in the midst of high levels of poverty, people living in poor countries do consistently report having a greater sense of mean-ing; this relationship is at least partially due to their stronger reli-gious beliefs. Religion may therefore play a particularly important role in helping people find meaning in dire circumstances.

One strategy for finding greater happiness—and better health—is to participate in whatever type of religious or spiritual activities fit your own preferences. For some people, this could be attending religious services weekly. For others, this could mean set-ting aside time each day to pray. Or it could mean participating in a Bible study group. So, if you believe adopting religious and spiritual beliefs would help you manage the small, and even large, stressors of daily life, find a way to integrate this practice into your routine (and you'll learn more about how exactly to do that in the final section of this chapter).

PRACTICE MEDITATION

As I've described throughout this book, our thoughts have a substantial impact on psychological and physical well-being. In many cases, how we *think* about an event plays a major role in how we feel and respond.

One way to gain control over our thoughts and focus entirely on the present is to practice meditation. Meditation involves focusing all our attention on a single feeling, such as breath coming in and out of the body, or a single thought or phrase—a *mantra*. Practitioners of meditation are intensely concentrating on being in the moment and not letting their minds drift to various thoughts and concerns.

Meditation can have powerful effects on psychological well-being.[32] For example, people who participate in a loving-kindness meditation group for six weeks report increases in positive emotions, social connections, and purpose in life. They also experience increases in life satisfaction and decreases in feelings of depression.[33] The benefits of meditation are so well known that large corporations—such as Target, Google, General Mills—and school boards are encouraging the practice of meditation. Celebrities such as Goldie Hawn, Howard Stern, and Richard Gere also tout its benefits.

Meditation also leads to better physical health. People who practice meditation report fewer symptoms of illness and lower levels of pain.[34] These benefits are seen even for people who have serious, life-threatening illnesses. For example, people with cancer who receive training in meditation show not only less fear about recurrence but also less fatigue, improved physical functioning, and better immune response.[35]

How exactly does meditation lead to such powerful effects? One explanation is that meditation helps people manage stress and thereby minimize the wear and tear on the body caused by our physiological stress response. As you learned in chapter 2, "Why Zebras Don't Get Ulcers: Mindset Affects Health," managing stress can go a long way toward making us feel better— psychologically and physically. Teenagers with high blood pressure who are trained to meditate twice a day—for just fifteen minutes each time—are less likely to develop cardiovascular disease than those who simply received education about how to lower blood pressure and the risk for cardiovascular disease.[36] Patients with heart disease who received training in meditation may even show decreases in their degree of arteriosclerosis.[37]

Meditation can also help interrupt destructive thought patterns that bring us down. The intense and deliberate focus on the here and now helps people break out of cycles of negative thought that can create depression, as described in chapter 5, "Are You Tigger or Eeyore: Personality Matters." And even if their thoughts occasionally drift away from the present, people who meditate report less mind-wandering to unpleasant topics.[38] This strategy for maintaining a focus on the present day during the act of meditating lets people cope more effectively even while anticipating upcoming stressful events, such as waiting to hear bar exam results.[39]

Meditation may also lead to changes in the brain that encourage physical and psychological health. For example, researchers from Massachusetts General Hospital examined the brain scans of sixteen people before and after they participated in an eight-week course in mindfulness meditation.[40] They found that parts of the brain linked with compassion and self-awareness grew, whereas parts of the brain linked with stress shrank. People who meditate show fewer age-related changes in the brain, suggesting that meditation may help slow down the naturally occurring developments that come with age.[41]

Meditation may even work to reverse the aging process.[42] One remarkable study found that practicing meditation may lead to cognitive improvements in older adults who show early signs of dementia. Researchers at UCLA examined the effectiveness of a training program that combined yoga and meditation in reducing cognitive and emotional problems in people fifty-five and older who had early signs of cognitive impairment, such as misplacing things, missing appointments, and forgetting faces.[43] People with this type of cognitive impairment are more than twice as likely to develop Alzheimer's disease and other forms of dementia.

People who underwent three months of yoga and meditation, which included a one-hour yoga class each week and twenty minutes of meditation at home daily, showed improved memory and lower levels of anxiety and depression. In fact, this type of training was even more effective than traditional memory training, such as doing crossword puzzles and learning computer programs, which is often used for patients with signs of cognitive impairment. These findings indicate that training in meditation can not only help improve memory but also give people coping skills for managing their emotional reactions to difficult diagnoses.

So if you are looking for a relatively simple—and cheap—way to reduce your stress and feel better, start meditating. You can find information on how to go about adopting the practice in books, on the internet, and even through apps on your phone. It takes relatively little time and can have substantial benefits for happiness, aging, and health. As Sara Lazar, a professor of psychology at Harvard Medical School, notes, "Mindfulness is just like exercise. It's a form of mental exercise, really. And just as exercise increases health, helps us handle stress better and promotes longevity, meditation purports to confer some of those same benefits."[44]

WHAT'S THE TAKE-HOME POINT?

Throughout this chapter I've described various types of behaviors that empirical research shows help us feel better and live longer. Start thinking about which of these speak to you, and find ways to start adopting some new behaviors as part of your daily routine (more on how to do that in the next section).

But keep in mind that making any type of long-term behavior change is easier to do if you have support. So, try to find a friend—or two or more—who can help support this transformation. Want to start reading more? Form a book club with friends in your neighborhood. Want to start exercising more? Get a Fitbit that measures your steps and set up weekly competitions with your spouse or a coworker.

Here are some other strategies you can use to adopt a new behavior—and really stick with it over time.

Shift Your Framing

It can be really hard to adopt a new habit, especially if that means dropping an old one. But modifying how we frame our new behavior can go a long way toward helping us make such a change.[45]

Here's an example about how shifting our mindset about a behavior can actually help us adopt a new habit: Imagine you are finishing a lovely dinner at a fancy restaurant, when the waiter asks if you'd like to try their famous chocolate cake for dessert. Now, your new intended behavior is to lose weight, which would mean trying not to eat the chocolate cake. How do you respond to his request? Some people might say, "No, thank you. I can't eat chocolate cake." And this approach is technically true, of course; you certainly can't eat chocolate cake if you are trying to lose weight. But this type of framing sets up not eating the dessert as something that is imposed on you, practically against your will; it implies you are not *allowed* to eat this cake. Here's an alternative wording you could use: "No, thank you. I don't eat chocolate cake." This framing is barely different from the earlier option—a single word has changed. But the meaning behind this phrasing is dramatically different. This sentence establishes that you have made a choice, which is empowering and self-affirming, about your decision to lose weight, and thus you *choose* not to eat this cake.

In other words, the language you use to think about, and talk about, your behavior has a powerful influence on your ability to successfully make a long-term change. Words do matter. In a simple demonstration of the difference between "I can't" and "I don't," researchers instructed people with a goal to eat healthy foods to use one of these two phrases when faced with a tempting food. Then, as they left the study, the researcher told the study participants to pick one of two snacks—a candy bar or a granola bar—as a "thank-you" for coming in.

Which group chose the healthier option? Of those who learned to say "I don't," 64 percent chose the granola bar, compared to only 39 percent of those who learned to say "I can't."

Both of these examples illustrate the power of wording in changing how we think about a behavior, which in turn helps us maintain a new behavior over time.

Make a Plan

One of the hardest parts of shifting your behavior is just getting started with a new routine, whether it's some type of physical activity every day, or learning to meditate, or putting down the phone in favor of a book at night. So, figure out the change you want to make, and then set a specific plan for how you'll implement this behavior in the next week. This type of short-term approach helps you start a new routine, which, over time, can become a regular part of your life.

Make sure to think through how this change in habit can fit within your daily schedule. It is much easier to stick with a new behavior when it easily fits into our daily lives. Let's say you want to start meditating or walking for twenty or thirty minutes a day. Think through your day and where you can realistically find this time. Is it first thing in the morning? Is it at lunch? Is it in the evening right after dinner? In some cases, finding brief periods of time may be more realistic than longer blocks. For example, people who commit to engaging in several short exercise breaks—say, four ten-minute bouts of climbing the stairs or walking briskly outside—are more successful at maintaining this behavior than those who attempt to find a single longer period of exercise such as a one hour-long exercise class.

Last, write down your plan. The very act of recording your plan—what it is and when you will do it—helps create more specific intentions and increases your odds of actually following through. And once you've recorded this plan, post it somewhere to remind yourself of your new intentions.

Take a Technology Break

Technology is supposed to make our lives easier. But the reality is that technology actually creates considerable stress. As described in chapter 6, "'Comparison Is the Thief of Joy': Environment Matters," technology increases our ability to engage in destructive social comparisons. Technology also takes away time from other things that we know bring us happiness—reading a book, spending time with friends, getting enough sleep.

But perhaps most important, the mere presence of technology creates an expectation that we are always available—to friends, colleagues, family members, and so on. This means that we never really get a break away from the ongoing demands of daily life, which leads to considerable stress.

In one study, researchers recruited a sample of adults to participate in a study on their use of technology.[46] They randomly put all study participants, which included undergraduate and graduate students as well as community members, with a mean age of thirty, in one of two groups for one week. One group of people were told to check their email as often as they wanted to each day, to keep their email inboxes open so they could see when new emails arrived, and to keep notifications of new emails turned on. People in the other group were told to check email only three times a day, to close their inboxes, and to turn off all email notifications.

At the end of each day, participants in both groups completed measures of how they felt, particularly their level of stress.

The researchers found that people who were told to check email less frequently reported significantly less stress. In fact, the benefits of reducing email checking were as large as those gained from learning other relaxation techniques!

Here's a simple way to increase your happiness: turn off your phone. Set clear and specific rules about the use of technology—no phone use after 9 PM, or during meals, or for large blocks of time on the weekend, when you really should be spending time interacting with people and relaxing, not checking email and texts. Limiting your use of technology will decrease your stress and increase the quality of your relationships, as you'll learn in chapter 12, "Build Relationships: All You Need Is Love."

Chapter 9

Nature Does the Mind and Body Good

More than forty thousand employees work in the Amazon headquarters in downtown Seattle. But even in this urban environment, employees can walk through trees, watch water flow in an indoor creek, and have meetings in rooms with vine-covered walls. This building includes plants from four hundred different species, ranging from small plants like moss and ferns to trees as tall as fifty feet.

Amazon is one of many companies to deliberately bring nature into the workplace. Airbnb has a wall of plants at its headquarters in San Francisco; Apple features a forest of more than eight thousand trees at its campus in Cupertino, California; and Google's new headquarters in Mountain View, California, will include trees, extensive landscaping, and bike paths.

Why are companies spending so much money on creating such environments? These choices are clearly based on the

177

considerable scientific research demonstrating the impact of nature on inspiring creativity, reducing stress, and, yes, increasing work productivity.

HOW DOES NATURE MAKE YOU FEEL?

Think about a time you've walked on a beach, strolled through a flowering garden, heard the sound of birds chirping, or merely looked through a window at grass and plants. How did you feel? For many people, seeing, hearing, or even thinking about nature makes us feel more energetic, peaceful, and alive. This is why we pay more for a hotel room with a view of the ocean or a home with a great yard.

To quantify the benefits of nature researchers asked participants in one study to simply imagine how they would feel in different situations.[1] Here are two such situations:

- "You and a friend are walking briskly together along a long hallway in a modern building."
- "You and a couple of friends are at a local park, exercising together on the grass."

Both these situations are very similar: they involve spending time with a friend and engaging in a physical activity. Yet people report feeling different depending on which of these situations they imagine. Specifically, those who imagine spending time outside report feeling higher levels of vitality, including feeling more energetic, alert, and alive.

In a second study, researchers asked people to look at photographs of either nature or non-nature scenes. The photographs depicting nature included, for example, a desert with surrounding cliff edges and a scene of a lake at night. The non-nature photographs depicted scenes of a city street with buildings on either side and a road at night. Once again, people who saw the nature scenes reported higher levels of vitality than those who saw the non-nature scenes.

The benefits of nature on feelings of well-being are even stronger when people *actually* spend time outside instead of just imagining spending time outside or looking at photographs. Simply walking for fifteen minutes on a tree-lined footpath beside a river leads to higher levels of energy and alertness than walking in an interior space without any views of the outside.

THE BENEFITS OF LIVING NEAR NATURE

How does nature produce feelings of happiness in real-world settings? In one study, researchers examined data from a very large sample—more than ten thousand people living in Britain.[2] All these people provided ratings for their overall mood as well as life satisfaction. This data also included information on where the people lived, so that the "amount" of nature—including gardens, parks, and water—they are exposed to daily could be measured. But perhaps most important, this data was collected annually for eighteen years, so the researchers could also see how moving to a new location (which could contain a different amount of green space) was associated with mood and life satisfaction.

These findings revealed substantial benefits of living in environments near nature. Specifically, people who live near nature showed significantly lower rates of anxiety and depression, and significantly higher rates of overall life satisfaction. These were not small or subtle effects. In fact, living near nature was about 33 percent as beneficial for people's mental health as being married.

Results from a study conducted in various neighborhoods in Wisconsin revealed similar findings about the beneficial effects of nature.[3] Across all income levels, people who lived in a neighborhood with less than 10 percent tree canopy were much more likely to report depression and anxiety. In other words, a poor person living in a forest area was more likely to be happy than a wealthy person living on a treeless block in a fancy neighborhood.

And there's more good news. Just brief exposure to nature— even if you don't live near nature—leads to momentary happiness. People who simply walk past clusters of greenery in a city show spikes in happiness, suggesting that even flower beds, trees, and small strips of green in an urban environment make us feel good. Similarly, people in New York City who are in or near a public park feel happier, at least when assessed by the positivity of their tweets (in words and emoticons).[4]

In contrast, can you guess where the least happy tweets occur? Near transportation hubs, such as Penn Station, Port Authority, and the entrance to the Midtown Tunnel, presumably indicating frustration with commutes and travel delays.

OK, so perhaps none of this is particularly surprising. As the researchers themselves note, "Who wouldn't be happy amidst the greenery of a public park, or borderline-suicidal while stuck in traffic or waiting for a late train?" But later in this chapter, I'll describe the benefits of nature on our physical well-being.

INDOOR PLANTS COUNT, TOO!

So, nature clearly matters in terms of our psychological well-being. But we aren't all lucky enough to live or work in environments surrounded by nature, especially for those who live and work in cities. (Ironically, as I'm writing this chapter, a new five-story dormitory is being built just outside my office window, effectively blocking the entire lovely view of a mountain range). Encouragingly, however, evidence suggests that even indoor plants can count as "nature" and lead to positive effects.

In one of the first studies to examine the effect of indoor plants on well-being, researchers asked office workers in several states to rate their overall job satisfaction and to provide information on their office environment.[5] Specifically, workers were asked whether their office windows looked out on to green spaces and whether they had live indoor plants in their offices.

Overall, workers who had live indoor plants in their offices reported being happier and more content than those without plants. Below is the proportion of those in each group who reported feeling "content" or "very happy":

- 82 percent of the "plants and windows" group
- 69 percent of the "plants but no windows" group
- 60 percent of the "windows but no plants" group
- 58 percent of the "no plants and no windows" group

Interestingly, although workers with both indoor plants and a view of nature reported the highest life quality, having indoor plants was even more beneficial than having a view of nature. Workers with offices containing both plants and views of nature also reported feeling better about their jobs and the work they performed.

Now, a key question about this data is whether other factors explain this relationship between office and life satisfaction. After all, workers who are older, have more prestigious positions, and make more money are probably more likely to work in offices with window views. But these other factors didn't explain the relationship: there were no differences in reported happiness even when the data was controlled for age, salary, education level, and position.

There's another concern about the data from the study I just described. This study collected data from people working in particular environments, and therefore other factors might have contributed to the differences in contentment and happiness. For example, perhaps people who are happier overall and more content in their lives choose to buy indoor plants—meaning it isn't so much that the plants create positive well-being but that the presence of plants is a deliberate choice by people who have good well-being.

To examine this possibility, researchers tested how changes in an office environment could lead to changes in workplace satisfaction.[6] First, all workers completed measures of workplace satisfaction, concentration, and productivity. Then, eight weeks later, half the workers experienced a modified environment: an interior designer brought in a number of green large-leafed plants, which were distributed around the work floor. On average, three plants were placed for every five desks, with at least two plants in

direct sight of each desk. The other workers experienced no differences in the office environment.

Three weeks after the plants were installed, the workers again
completed measures of workplace satisfaction, concentration, and
productivity. Although there were no differences in workplace satisfaction between those in the two groups, workers who now saw
plants in their office environment reported increases in their ability
to concentrate and in their productivity. Moreover, workers' own
reports of their feelings of greater productivity were supported
by objective data showing those in office settings with plants completed tasks more quickly (and just as accurately) as those in office
settings without plants.

What do these findings suggest for those of us not fortunate
enough to have a great view of nature from our office (or home)
windows? Go buy some plants!

GIVE YOUR BRAIN A
BREAK—TAKE A WALK OUTSIDE

So, what is it about spending time in nature that leads to such
dramatic benefits? Our daily life is filled with constant stimulation from phones, traffic, television, and so on. All these events
grab our attention. But our brain's ability to stay focused over
time is limited. Eventually, we can become overwhelmed and feel
mentally drained; scientists informally call this "brain fatigue." In
other words, our brains need a break.

According to *attention restoration theory*, spending time in nature
provides a cognitive break from all the external distractions we
face in our daily lives. Nature settings allow the brain to relax,

and thereby serve a really important function in helping restore our cognitive capacities. In fact, people show improvements in memory and attention after walking for an hour in a quiet nature setting, but not after walking down a noisy urban street.[7] Remarkably, such benefits are seen even among those with clinical depression.[8]

Even brief nature breaks can help improve memory, attention, and concentration. For example, high school students perform better on tests if they are in a classroom with a view of a green landscape, rather than a windowless room or a room with a view of man-made space, such as a building or parking lot.[9] Similarly, people who glance at a grassy green roof for only forty seconds show better concentration and commit fewer errors on cognitive tasks than those who look out on a bare concrete roof.[10]

So, here's an easy way to give your brain a break: spend some time in nature.

FEELING STRESSED? GO OUTSIDE!

Spending time in nature helps both our brains and our bodies to relax. Exposure to nature basically switches the body from a state of high arousal to one of rest and relaxation. Spending time in nature is therefore a great strategy for reducing stress and the harmful effects of constant physiological arousal on our bodies.

One recent study, in which participants wore caps containing electrodes so that researchers could assess brain activity, directly compared how the brain responded to different types of environments.[11] People walking in a parklike setting show calmer brain waves, including lower levels of arousal and frustration, than people walking in urban areas.

People who walk through a park for an hour later feel less anxious than those who walk along a busy street.[12] They also show lower levels of rumination, which, as you learned about in chapter 5, "Are You Tigger or Eeyore: Personality Matters," leads to depression.[13] They also show reduced neural activity in an area of the brain linked to risk for mental illness.

This type of short-term exposure to nature even helps reduce the physiological toll of stress. For example, research from Japan on *shinrin-yoku* ("forest bathing," meaning spending time in a forest area) shows simply walking in a forest for twenty or so minutes leads to lower levels of blood pressure, heart rate, and the stress hormone cortisol compared to walking in an urban area.[14]

These findings explain why people who regularly spend time in nature—including city parks and private gardens—report lower rates of stress and stress-related illnesses.[15] As Kristen Malecki, a professor at the University of Wisconsin School of Medicine and Public Health, notes, "If you want to feel better, go outside."[16]

Moreover, even seeing pictures of nature scenes reduces the body's natural stress response. Researchers in one study attached sensors measuring electrical activity in the heart to college student participants.[17] They then showed them a series of pictures on a computer screen. Some of the screens displayed pictures of urban spaces, such as buildings and parked cars, whereas others displayed nature spaces in urban settings, such as trees along a city sidewalk.

After viewing the photos, researchers deliberately induced feelings of stress in the study participants. First, they were given a series of difficult math problems. Then, they were given fake feedback showing their scores on this test weren't as good compared to other students'. This procedure, not surprisingly, did indeed cause feelings of stress. Students were then shown the same pictures again to examine whether viewing signs of nature would help reduce their physiological stress reaction.

As the researchers predicted, viewing scenes of nature helped students recover from stress. Students who saw photos of green spaces had lower heart rates than those who viewed concrete spaces. This study suggests that even pictures of greenery may help people recover from low-level stress.

More recent research from neuroscience helps explain why looking at nature reduces feelings of stress. In this study, researchers showed people pictures of both urban scenes and nature scenes while they were in an fMRI machine, which measures brain activation.[18] The photographs were carefully matched so that each was visually appealing and showed a range of colors; the urban scenes showed attractive city skylines, not traffic or smog. Each type of photograph was presented for two minutes, with a new photo appearing every one and a half seconds to keep people engaged in the task.

Despite the similarities between the two types of photos, the data measuring brain activation indicated remarkable differences. The parts of the brain that are in charge of empathy, altruism, emotional stability, and positive mental outlook were much more active when the nature scenes were shown. In contrast, the parts of the brain in charge of assessing threat and experiencing stress and anxiety were much more active when the urban photographs were shown. These findings indicate that people looking at nature show calmer brain wave activity, indicating greater relaxation and lower anxiety.

THE POWER OF A ROOM WITH A VIEW

In one of the earliest tests of the link between nature and physical health, researchers reviewed the medical records of patients who underwent gallbladder surgery at a suburban hospital in Pennsylvania over a ten-year period.[19] This hospital had a unique setting on the second and third floors, in that patients with rooms on one side of the hall overlooked a pretty group of trees, whereas those on the other side overlooked a brown brick wall.

The researchers then compared rates of recovery for those who had been assigned to a room with a view of nature versus the brick wall. Now, they also wanted to make sure that other factors weren't contributing to the speed of recovery, so patients with each type of view were carefully matched based on their sex, age (within five years), whether they were smokers, and whether they were obese.

Their findings were particularly remarkable. First, nurses' reports revealed that patients with a view of the brick wall were more negative in their recovery, recording observations like "needs much encouragement" and "upset and crying," than those with a view of nature. Patients who overlooked a wall also required more—and stronger—pain relief. Finally, and most important, patients with a view of nature were discharged nearly a day earlier on average: 7.96 days compared to 8.70 days.

Although this study provides powerful evidence that views of nature help patients heal from surgery, the practical limitations are clear. After all, many hospitals are in urban settings, and providing every patient with a window overlooking nature may just not be feasible.

Fortunately, other forms of nature can also lead to positive effects. For example, the pain, anxiety, and fatigue ratings of surgical patients who have a live plant placed in their hospital rooms during recovery are lower than those put in rooms without plants.[20] They also show lower levels of physiological arousal, including lower blood pressure and heart rate, and require fewer painkillers.[21]

Moreover, looking at pictures of nature can have very similar effects. In another study, patients who were recovering from heart surgery were given rooms that were identical in every regard except for one important difference: the art present in that room.[22] Some patients had no art in their rooms at all, others had an abstract painting, and still others had a large nature photograph (either of a tree-lined stream or a shadowy forest). It turns out that patients in the room with the photograph of the tree-lined scene were less anxious and needed less pain medicine than those in rooms without art, with abstract art, or even those with the photograph of the dark forest.

NATURE'S GOOD FOR YOUR HEALTH

Given the role nature plays in reducing stress and arousal, it's not surprising that people who spend time in nature experience better overall physical well-being and fewer health-related complaints.[23] For example, people who live in neighborhoods with more green space, such as trees and parks, have lower levels of chronic illness, including diabetes (14 percent lower risk), hypertension (13 percent lower risk), and lipid disorders (10 percent lower risk).[24]

People who spend time in nature also have lower rates of high blood pressure. In fact, some evidence suggests that visits to outdoor green spaces of thirty minutes or more each week could reduce the prevalence of hypertension, which is a major contributor to other chronic disorders, by as much as 9 percent.[25]

Most important, longitudinal research provides strong evidence that spending time in nature can actually lengthen our lives. Researchers in one study monitored more than one hundred thousand women who completed health questionnaires over a period of eight years.[26] With the aid of satellite imagery, they also examined the amount of green vegetation in a person's neighborhood. Even after adjusting for other factors that increase the risk of death, such as age, smoking, BMI, and socioeconomic status, women living in areas with the most greenness had a 12 percent lower rate of mortality than those living in areas with the least greenness.

Now, this is not to say that spending time in nature can prevent or cure all diseases. As Clare Cooper Marcus, a landscape architecture professor at the University of California, Berkeley, notes, "Spending time interacting with nature in a well-designed garden won't cure your cancer or heal a badly burned leg. But there is good evidence it can reduce your levels of pain and stress—and, by doing that, boost your immune system in ways that allow your own body and other treatments to help you heal."[27]

WHAT'S THE TAKE-HOME POINT?

Spending time in nature is tremendously beneficial for physical as well as psychological well-being, as you've read about throughout this chapter. Yet we consistently underestimate the value spending time in nature has for our happiness. People who take even a relatively brief walk outdoors—approximately seventeen minutes long—underestimate the effects of such a walk on their mood and feelings of relaxation.[28]

Now that you know the benefits of nature, take steps to spend more time in nature. Here are some easy ways to start.

Integrate Nature into Your Life

Spending time in nature has a ton of benefits, from improving attention and concentration to reducing depression and anxiety to lowering heart rate and blood pressure. All these effects are strongest when people actually spend time in nature, and there are many easy ways to integrate some form of nature into your everyday life. Here are some easy examples:

- Go for a walk outside.
- Buy plants for your home and office.
- Listen to sounds of nature on a CD while driving in the car or cleaning the house.

And remember that almost any type of nature counts. People who report more exposure to any type of nature in their work environment—from seeing nature outside their window to having a live plant in their office to spending breaks outside—report lower levels of stress and fewer health complaints.[29] Similarly, people who simply stop and photograph signs of nature—such as a tree, plant, or sunset—show higher levels of happiness and joy than those who photograph man-made objects.[30] So, don't worry if you can't imagine finding the time for a thirty-minute stroll outside each day; just start by finding small and simple ways of integrating nature into your life in some way.

Plant a Garden

Now, this is a hard one for me, since I decidedly do not have a green thumb. But empirical research tells us that the act of planting and caring for a garden is a great way to reduce stress and give our brains a much-needed break.

Researchers in one study gave people a stressful activity to complete, and then asked them to perform one of two activities.[31] Half the people were asked to read indoors for thirty minutes. The others were asked to garden outside for thirty minutes. Although both these activities led to lower levels of stress, gardening actually reduced stress better than reading.

Gardening also leads to health benefits, including reductions in depression and anxiety and increases in life satisfaction.[32]

Go to the Beach

Many of us have fond memories of spending time on a beach, from building sand castles to swimming in the surf to watching the waves crash on the sand. And there's a reason why spending time at the beach feels so good: looking at water helps calm the body and reduce arousal. It decreases our heart rate and blood pressure and increases hormones, such as serotonin and endorphins, in the body that make us feel good.

Now, one of the benefits of spending time at the beach is the break it gives our brains from the constant stimulation of daily life. But it's not just the leisure that makes us feel good when we look at water. Surprisingly, pictures of nature that feature water can lead viewers to more positive states, even more so than nature pictures featuring only green landscaping.[33]

Want to learn more about the benefits of spending time by the water? Check out *Blue Mind*, a book by marine biologist Wallace Nichols that describes how water is good for both mental and physical health.

Chapter 10

Spend Money Wisely: Take a Trip, See a Play, Go to a Game

There's a wonderful short story by the German author Heinrich Böll about a wealthy tourist who comes across a fisherman taking a nap in his boat.[1] The tourist approaches the fisherman and urges him to continue fishing, pointing out that working harder could, over time, allow him to earn enough money to own multiple boats and have other people do the fishing for him. The fisherman asks why that should be his goal. The tourist responds, "Then, without a care in the world, you could sit here in the harbor, doze in the sun, and look at the glorious sea."

Of course, that's exactly what the fisherman is already doing.

This story illustrates what considerable empirical research now demonstrates: We find more happiness by spending our days in ways that bring us joy than in the relentless pursuit of money. While the wealthy tourist encourages the fisherman to spend his time pursuing more and more money, the wise fisherman already understands that his true happiness comes from spending time sleeping in the sun. In this chapter, I'll explain why money doesn't bring us happiness, why a materialistic mindset can be hazardous, and why spending the money we have on experiences is the clearest route to happiness.

WHY MORE MONEY DOESN'T BRING HAPPINESS

The tendency to think that having more money will bring more happiness is hard to resist. After all, most of us covet various big-ticket items, from fancy cars to bigger homes to more lavish vacations. So surely people who are able to experience this type of luxurious lifestyle are happier, right?

But it turns out money really can't buy happiness. As shown in figure 10.1, income per person has increased substantially over the last sixty years, but the percentage of people who report feeling "very happy" during this time is quite stable.

One of the first studies to demonstrate this perhaps counterintuitive finding compared happiness in major lottery winners to those who had not experienced this type of financial windfall.[2] Although there was no difference between these two groups in ratings of how happy they were, lottery winners actually rated the pleasure of various ordinary activities—watching television, hearing a funny joke, talking with a friend—as lower than those who had not won.

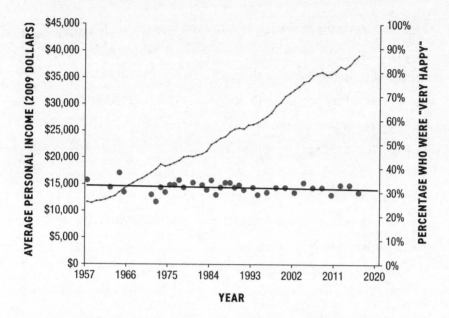

Figure 10.1: Personal income—as shown by the line with the small dots—has increased substantially over the last sixty years. But the percentage of people who report feeling "very happy"—as shown by the line with the bigger dots—hasn't changed.

Myers, D. G., & Diener, E. (2018). The scientific pursuit of happiness. *Perspectives on Psychological Science, 13*(2), 218–225. Copyright © 2018 by SAGE Publications. Reprinted by Permission of SAGE Publications, Inc.

These findings on the relative lack of a link between money and happiness also help explain why people living in wealthier countries don't feel happier. As Carol Graham, a professor of public policy at the University of Maryland, notes in her book *Happiness Around the World: The Paradox of Happy Peasants and Miserable Millionaires*, "Higher per capita income levels do not translate directly into higher average happiness levels."[3] For example, the percentage of people living in Bangladesh who report they are happy is twice as high as the percentage of Russians, even though Russians are more than four times as wealthy. Similarly, happiness rates are twice as high in Nigeria compared to Japan, even though the Japanese have nearly twenty-five times more income than Nigerians.[4]

Subsequent research with large samples provides even stronger evidence that higher income doesn't increase our happiness. One large-scale survey of nearly half a million Americans measured household income, life satisfaction, and emotional well-being.[5] Life satisfaction assessed people's overall contentment with the current state of their lives, whereas emotional well-being assessed whether people regularly experience positive emotions, such as happiness and enjoyment.

These findings revealed that more income is linked with more life satisfaction; people with higher levels of income are indeed more satisfied overall with their lives. However, more income is linked with more emotional well-being only up to a point. For those with incomes of about $75,000 and up, there is no happiness gain from more income. Though people who make more than $90,000 a year are nearly twice as likely to report feeling "very happy" as those who make less than $20,000, there's basically no difference in happiness between those who make $50,000 and $89,999.[6]

But there is an exception to the general rule that more money doesn't bring more happiness. For people living below the poverty line, lack of money can exacerbate daily life stressors, such as health issues and car troubles. Such people may worry about having enough money to satisfy basic needs—food, shelter, heat, and so on. For them, more money does increase happiness. After all, it is impossible to feel happy when concerned about whether your children will have enough food to eat or your family will have heat this winter. In turn, programs that give money to alleviate poverty directly lead to increases in happiness, in part because additional income reduces stress for people living in such conditions.[7]

In other words, after our basic needs are met, what matters in terms of happiness is how we choose to spend our time. And spending more time in ways that make us happy—reading a book, watching television, socializing with friends—is a much better way to increase our happiness than spending more time working to make even more money.

THE HAZARDS OF MATERIALISM

The temptation to think that happiness lies in acquiring more and better possessions lurks around us everywhere. Advertising images clearly send the message that having a better car, nicer jewelry, or a bigger house is the route to greater life satisfaction.

But not only does empirical research refute this idea, it actually indicates that the mere pursuit of material possessions can undermine happiness. In fact, people who are high in materialism overwhelmingly experience lower levels of life satisfaction. They experience fewer positive emotions each day, are more likely to be depressed, and report more health complaints, including headaches, backaches, and sore throats.[8]

Materialism is even linked with lower marital satisfaction. Marriages in which both spouses are low in materialism have less conflict, better communication, and more satisfaction than those in which one or both spouses are high in materialism.[9] They are also more likely to last over time.

The incessant need to buy things is often rooted in feelings of low self-esteem. People who don't feel so good about themselves feel—falsely—that purchasing material objects will make themselves feel better. And although they may experience a temporary boost from such acquisitions, this positive feeling soon fades. More-over, and as described in chapter 6, "'Comparison Is the Thief of Joy': Environment Matters," purchasing things to demonstrate wealth is a losing battle, since someone else will always have more and better things. This is why people who live in wealthier neigh-borhoods are more focused on buying things, but are not happier.

But even for those who aren't generally focused on purchasing material possessions, a temporary mindset focused on consumer-ism can hurt our happiness.[10] In one study, researchers showed some people images of luxury goods, such as cars, electronics, and jewelry, while others saw neutral images. Those who saw material-istic images later reported higher levels of depression and anxiety, indicating that even a transient materialistic mindset can impair psychological well-being. They were also less interested in engag-ing in social activities.

So, what can we do to reduce our emphasis on materialism, given its negative effects on happiness? Keep in mind that trying to find happiness by buying material possessions is a losing proposition. In fact, Buddhists feel that material objects actually serve as imped-iments to true happiness. As Roger Corless, a professor of religion at Duke University and the author of *The Vision of Buddhism*, once said, "Trying to be happy by accumulating possessions is like trying to satisfy hunger by taping sandwiches all over your body."[11]

WHY MONEY IS NOT
THE ROUTE TO HAPPINESS

One reason why more money doesn't bring us the lasting happi-ness we expect is that we adapt to our newfound wealth. Initially, it is great to have some extra money, but over time we simply adapt to this higher level of income or unexpected windfall, and thus it no longer leads to greater happiness. Psychology researchers call this adaptation the *hedonic treadmill*.

Here's an example of the power of adaptation. Think back to getting your very first cell phone: how excited did you feel? Probably very excited, because all of a sudden you could call people from the car! This new device was initially thrilling.

But imagine right now how you'd feel if your current cell phone were replaced with that same cell phone that so excited you fifteen or twenty years ago. I bet you wouldn't feel so excited, because we now have adapted to the ever-increasing technology available in a cell phone. We therefore now expect our cell phones not only to allow us to call people from the car but also to take photos, read the newspaper, or buy books. This is a clear example of how we adapt over time and find that the things that initially increased our happiness—a raise, a cell phone—no longer do so over time.

Moreover, increases in wealth can also change the comparisons we make, as described in chapter 6, "'Comparison Is the Thief of Joy': Environment Matters." Perhaps an increase in income leads us to move to a fancier neighborhood or send our children to private school, which we anticipate will make us happier. But in reality, these new environments just change the nature of the comparisons we make, and these comparisons make us feel worse. For example, maybe everyone in our new neighborhood drives a pricey car or pays for an expensive lawn service, and our children's friends at their new school take more lavish vacations and have second homes. All of a sudden, our newfound wealth doesn't feel so good. As Benjamin Franklin said, "Money has never made man happy, nor will it, there is nothing in its nature to produce happiness. The more of it one has, the more one wants."[12]

A third explanation for the overall absence of a money-happiness link is that money may change how we spend our time. And, ironically, people with more money may inadvertently spend their time in ways that don't lead to happiness. People with above-average income spend less time pursuing activities that increase happiness, such as exercising or relaxing, and more time on activities that don't necessarily, such as working or commuting. For example, people making more than $100,000 a year spend about 20 percent of their time on leisure activities, whereas those making less than $20,000 spend about 34 percent of their time on such activities.[13] People with higher incomes also spend fewer evenings socializing, and a smaller portion of their days interacting with others.[14]

This overall tendency for people who make more money to spend more time alone may even influence how they experience happiness. One recent study found that people with higher incomes report experiencing more self-focused emotions, such as pride and contentment.[15] In contrast, people who make less money report experiencing more other-focused emotions, such as compassion and love. As Paul Piff, a professor of psychology at the University of California, Irvine, notes, "Wealth doesn't guarantee you happiness, but it may predispose you to experiencing different forms of it—for example, whether you delight in yourself versus in your friends and relationships."[16]

As I'll describe in chapter 12, "Build Relationships: All You Need Is Love," social relationships are the best predictor of happiness, so people with more income may miss out by spending less time with others. In this case, greater wealth could actually lead to less happiness.

WHY BUYING EXPERIENCES IS THE BIGGEST BANG FOR YOUR BUCK

This chapter has focused thus far on explaining why more money does not lead to more happiness. But the good news is that we can spend our money in ways that does bring happiness. One way of spending money that increases happiness is spending money on other people, including friends and family members and even strangers, as I'll describe in chapter 11, "Give a Gift—to Anyone."

What other types of spending are good for our psychological well-being?

People who spend money on life experiences—*doing things*— show greater enduring happiness than those who spend money buying material possessions—*having things*.[17] So, spending money on tickets to the big game, a Broadway show, or a fabulous trip is a great way to increase happiness. Spending money on an expensive car, watch, or shoes, on the other hand, only has a fleeting impact on happiness. As Martin Seligman, director of the Positive Psychology Center at the University of Pennsylvania, describes, "Material objects are all like French vanilla ice cream. The first taste is great, but by the seventh taste, it is cardboard."[18] In other words, choose to make memories over remodeling a bathroom.

Unfortunately, people's estimates of what types of spending would bring them the most happiness are pretty consistently wrong. People expect that buying material goods will make them happier; after all, we keep material possessions and thus get repeated use and enjoyment out of them. Experiences, in contrast, are fleeting, so surely can provide only temporary happiness.

Researchers in one study asked people to think about how much happiness a particular purchase would bring them.[19]

Overwhelmingly, people thought buying a material good would bring them more happiness than buying an experience. But when researchers asked these same people two to four weeks later how happy they felt about their purchase, people were much happier with their experience purchase.

Why is spending money on experiences better than spending money on material objects? We get to anticipate them, we get to share them with others, and we get to relive them.

THE PLEASURE OF ANTICIPATION

Have you ever taken a fabulous trip that you thought about and planned for weeks and months ahead? Thinking about where you were going to go, what you were going to see, and so on? If so, congratulations—that type of anticipation is a great way to milk more happiness out of a single event! This is the type of anticipation children experience leading up to Christmas morning—they savor that day in part because they've anticipated the joy of opening fabulous gifts for days and weeks ahead. (The Germans even have an expression for it—*Vorfreude ist die schönste Freude*, which means, "Anticipation is the greatest joy.")

There's a great quote in one of the Winnie-the-Pooh books by author A. A. Milne that precisely illustrates the joy of anticipation:

"Well," said Pooh, "what I like best," and then he had to stop and think. Because although Eating Honey was a very good thing to do, there was a moment just before you began to eat it which was better than when you were, but he didn't know what it was called.

And, of course, that word is *anticipation*.

But you don't have to just take my word for it. Scientific research demonstrates that people who anticipate something experience greater enjoyment than those who do not. For example, researchers in one study asked college students to participate in a "chocolate rating" study.[20] Half the students were asked to immediately eat Hershey's Kisses or Hugs, and then to rate their enjoyment of this chocolate. The other students were also asked to eat and then rate the chocolate but only after waiting for thirty minutes. Can you predict their findings? Students who had to wait thirty minutes reported liking the chocolate much more than those who were able to eat it immediately.

Thus, one reason why we get more happiness out of spending money on experiences is that it is more enjoyable to anticipate experiences than a new material good.[21] Think about the pleasure you might get from anticipating a long-awaited European vacation—the things you will see, what will you eat. Now think about the pleasure you might get from anticipating the upcoming arrival of a material possession, such as a car, large-screen television, or new computer. For most people, the anticipation of the arrival of the material object ("I can't wait to have my new purse!") evokes much less happiness than the anticipation of the trip ("I can't wait to see Machu Picchu!").

The findings from this research led me and my husband to fundamentally change the types of gifts we give our children at Christmas each year. Instead of purchasing a pricey possession, we spend money on some type of experience. For my daughter one year, this was tickets to *Hamilton*, and another year it was tickets to the Dancing with the Stars tour. (As it turns out, the Dancing with the Stars tour is not the most appropriate choice for an eleven-year-old girl.) For my sons, these experiences always revolve around sports—tickets to see the Boston Celtics or the Boston Bruins.

So, when you are shopping for loved ones, consider opting out of buying yet another material possession and instead buying an experience—a day at a spa, tickets to a concert, or a gift certificate to a favorite restaurant.

THE POWER OF SHARED EXPERIENCES

Another explanation for the benefits of buying experiences is that people are more likely to share experiences with others, whereas they are more likely to acquire material possessions for solo use. After all, you are probably more likely to go on a trip or to the theater with a friend than alone, but are likely buying that new purse, watch, or laptop for your own use, not to share. And perhaps this tendency to share experiences with those we care about accounts for their greater impact on happiness. As noted hiker and wanderer Chris McCandless wrote, "Happiness is only real when shared."[22]

Researchers in one study directly tested this question by comparing the relative benefits on happiness of spending money on experiences versus possessions, as well as spending money for solitary versus social purposes.[23] What did this research tell us about the best way to spend money?

First, social spending led to greater happiness than solitary spending, meaning we find more happiness from buying a new large-screen television the whole family can enjoy than a new purse or watch we plan to use ourselves. This finding held true for buying both material possessions and experiences; people who spent money on socially shared experiences—going to a concert with a friend or taking a vacation with a spouse—reported higher levels of satisfaction than those who spent money acquiring solo experiences—attending a sporting event on their own or taking a solo trip.

But the very best predictor of happiness was spending money on socially shared experiences—such as planning a trip with a spouse or taking the whole family to a Broadway play. In fact, socially shared experiences had a greater impact on happiness than spending money on solitary experiences or material possessions (solitary or shared). These results point to the profound benefits of spending money on experiences, especially if those experiences can be shared with people we care about, on happiness.

THE POWER OF RELIVING

Imagine you've taken a great trip—a relaxing week at an all-inclusive Caribbean resort, an exciting week touring museums and historic sites in Rome, a hiking trip to Yosemite National Park. Now imagine you've just spent a bunch of money on belongings—a fancy new car, a luxury watch, a fur coat. Which of these purchases would you be more likely to share with others? As you can probably predict, we are much more much likely to talk about our experiences with other people than our purchases of material objects.

Moreover, talking about experiences increases our enjoyment of the original event.[24] We love describing our trips to others in part because in the telling we are reliving the experience in our minds. This ability to reflect back on experiences is part of what makes these events so worthwhile.

We find it much less enjoyable to talk about similarly expensive material purchases with people. Initially, we may mention in passing that we've bought a new car, but we're pretty unlikely to keep describing its purchase or our experience driving it to others.

As Amit Kumar, the author of these studies, notes, "Experiences live on in our memories and in the stories we tell, while our material goods 'disappear' as we inevitably get used to them. A once-cherished Walkman is now obsolete, but, as Humphrey Bogart once told Ingrid Bergman in *Casablanca*, 'We'll always have Paris.'"

THE CUBS WORLD SERIES TICKET DILEMMA

My brother Matt has been a long-time season ticket holder for the Chicago Cubs baseball team. In October 2016 he faced a very unusual dilemma: what to do with the four tickets he had for a World Series game. One option was to take his wife and two kids to the game—clearly a really special opportunity. Another option was to sell the tickets and make $10,000.

After reading this chapter, you can probably imagine my advice to Matt. Based on research on the science of happiness, there are two best answers. One, of course, is to take his family to the game and enjoy that shared experiences (and savor and remember those memories for a long time). Another good option is to sell the tickets and then take the proceeds and go on a great family trip—

Disneyland, or the Grand Canyon, or Hawaii. Either of these choices should lead to greater happiness than buying a new car or living room furniture. They went to the game and miraculously saw the only Cubs World Series game win in Wrigley Field.

For my brother and his family, spending money going to the game was a much better choice than making a quick $10,000. They anticipated going to the game, attended the game together as a family, and continue to relive this night as they share the story with others about this unique experience. That's the type of happiness that money truly can buy!

WHAT'S THE TAKE-HOME POINT?

We all want to find more happiness, but so often we are pursuing happiness in all the wrong ways. There's a great *New Yorker* cartoon depicting a person on his deathbed saying, "I should have bought more crap." Try to stop being swayed by the constant messages we get about the value of material objects. Instead, prioritize things that really matter—spending money on experiences, especially shared ones we can anticipate, is the true route to happiness.

Here are some simple strategies you can use in your own life to find greater happiness.

Prioritize Time over Money

As I've described earlier in this chapter, how we spend our day has a major impact on our happiness. So, whenever possible, eliminating tasks that drag down happiness is a great way to increase overall well-being. This could mean just not doing certain things as often. For example, if you hate changing your sheets, or vacuuming, perhaps those tasks could be done every other week instead of once a week. In other cases, making a decision to hire someone else to perform particular tasks, such as cleaning your house or mowing the lawn, could substantially increase your happiness.

In studies involving both college students and older adults, people who report prioritizing their time over their money report greater psychological well-being and life satisfaction.[25] The benefits of spending money to save time are seen across cultures and in people from various socioeconomic backgrounds.

Here's an example of how spending money that saves us time feels really good. In one study, people were given forty dollars on two consecutive weekends but were given strict instructions on how to spend the money.[26] One weekend people were told to spend the money on material purchases, such as books or clothes. On the other weekend, people were told to spend the money on something that saved them time, such as taking a cab instead of walking or eating in a restaurant instead of cooking.

The researchers then asked people after each weekend to rate their overall level of stress and well-being. Can you predict what they found? Compared with the days in which they bought stuff, people reported lower levels of stress and negative mood, and higher levels of positive mood, on days in which they were told to spend the money on time-saving ways. Spending money to save ourselves time seems to reduce the stresses of daily life, and therefore creates greater happiness.

There are many time-saving choices we could make in our daily lives:

- Hire a service to clean the house, rake the leaves, mow the lawn, or shovel the driveway.
- Get takeout dinner instead of cooking.
- Take a more expensive nonstop flight as opposed to a cheaper flight that requires a layover.

In many instances, you'll find that prioritizing time over money is the best route to increasing happiness.

Take Photos

Imagine visiting a city for the first time and taking a bus tour to see the major sights—museums, statues, famous buildings. Would your enjoyment of this experience differ if you took photos?

Researchers in one study set out to test precisely this question.[27] Visitors in one condition were told to take at least ten photos during the one-hour tour, whereas those in the other condition were told to leave their cameras and cell phones behind, and thus could not take pictures. People who took pictures reported greater enjoyment of the tour. Why? Taking photos leads people to report more engagement in the experience.

Although this study only examined the impact of taking photos on people's enjoyment of the actual experience, taking photos may well have an additional benefit; having photos of an experience allows people to reflect back on the experience later, which may also lead to increased happiness. Just imagine the happiness you might feel in looking over photos from a vacation, a milestone birthday celebration, or documenting a monumental moment in your child's life.

Plan a Trip

Planning a trip is actually a wonderful way to create happiness because it allows us to anticipate. And, as you learned earlier in this chapter, anticipation increases enjoyment. It is interesting to note that while, predictably, people who are planning a vacation are happier than those who are not planning a vacation, the increase in happiness doesn't persist after the vacation is over.[28] Although we can find moments of happiness following a vacation, by talking about our experience with friends and reliving it through photos, once we return to the routine of daily life, we don't get a lasting boost in happiness.

Anticipating a trip creates even more happiness than reminiscing about a trip we actually took.[29] After all, we typically anticipate only the positive—the great meal we are going to have, the wonderful museum we will tour, the thrill of seeing a new city, and so on. When we reminisce, some of the less-than-positive realities of the trip seep into our memories—the lost luggage, the long lines, the noisy hotel room.

So, an easy way to increase happiness is to plan some trips. When I'm having trouble sleeping, or feeling anxious, here's my go-to strategy: I pull out a travel book and start planning a trip. Sometimes this planning actually results in a trip, but more often than not the planning never gets off the ground—although I still hope to see the beaches of Normandy, visit the ruins of Pompeii, and take a Mediterranean cruise someday.

Chapter 11

Give a Gift—
to Anyone

On the morning of December 26, 2004, Petra Němcová, a model from the Czech Republic, and her boyfriend, Simon Atlee, a British photographer, were vacationing at a resort on the coast of Thailand when an earthquake triggered a tsunami in the Indian Ocean. Petra and Simon were in their bungalow when the first wave hit, sweeping them both outside in seconds. Petra broke her pelvis and suffered severe internal injuries, but was rescued after clinging to a palm tree for eight hours; Simon did not survive.

After recovering from her injuries, Petra decided to return to Thailand to help others whose lives had been shattered by this natural disaster. She started the Happy Hearts Fund, which focuses on rebuilding schools and helping young victims. Her motivation was in part, she reports, selfish: "When we make someone happy, we become even happier. If you decide yourself that you will help in some way, you will benefit the most because it will create amazing joy."[1]

In this chapter, I'll describe why giving to other people is one of the best ways to find happiness. In fact, giving to others increases our own happiness, improves our health, and may even extend our lives. And what's perhaps most important, any type of giving counts, from giving money to charitable organizations to volunteering in your community to donating blood.

LOOKING FOR HAPPINESS IN ALL THE WRONG PLACES

Imagine you find a crumpled twenty-dollar bill in your car one morning and decide to spend this "found money" to bring some extra joy to your day. What's the best way for you to accomplish this goal? Most of us probably imagine treating ourselves to something we'd like—getting lunch at a favorite restaurant, buying a book we've been wanting to read, or having a manicure.

But our intuition about the best way to spend this money turns out to be quite incorrect. To examine how spending money in different ways leads to happiness, researchers asked random people on the street if they were willing to participate in a quick psychology study.[2] People who agreed were asked to rate their happiness and provide their phone numbers. They were then handed an envelope that contained either five or twenty dollars. They were told to spend the money in the envelope by 5 PM that day and were also given specific instructions about how to spend this money. One group of people were told to spend the money on themselves, such as to pay a bill, cover an expense, or a buy gift for themselves. Another group of people were told to spend the money on someone else, such as a gift for someone else or a charitable donation. Participants were then called that evening, after they had spent the money, and were asked to report their happiness.

Perhaps not surprisingly, there was no difference in happiness between those who got five versus twenty dollars. However, people who spent money on someone else reported greater levels of happiness than people who spent the money on themselves, even though there was no difference in happiness between people in these two groups at the start of the day. Rather, it is how we spend the money that influences how we feel, and spending as little as five dollars on someone else—even someone we don't know—increases our own happiness.

Results from another study on how giving something to others feels even better than keeping it for ourselves reveal similar findings. In this study, researchers gave participants the option to purchase a goody bag with the money they earned for helping with their study.[3] Half the participants were told that the goody bag was theirs to keep, whereas the other half were told their goody bag would be donated to a sick child at a local hospital. People who were told their bag was going to a sick child reported higher levels of happiness than those who got to keep their goody bag.

What's particularly interesting about this research is that people are consistently wrong in their estimates about how best to spend money to increase their own happiness. In fact, most people think that spending money on something for themselves will make them happier than spending money on someone else. Unfortunately, this error in intuition means that we aren't spending our money in the right way.

THE PERK OF PROSOCIAL SPENDING

The research described thus far illustrates how spending small amounts of money on others increases our own happiness. And although these findings may not fit with our intuition about how to get the biggest happiness boost, perhaps they only apply when we are talking about relatively small sums.

To examine the link between giving more substantial amounts of money and happiness, researchers asked Americans across the country how they generally spent their annual income, and to rate their general level of happiness.[4] The major monthly expenses people reported included bills and expenses (mortgage/rent, car, electricity), gifts for themselves (clothes, jewelry, electronics), gifts for others, and donations to charity. The researchers then combined the first two categories—as a measure of "personal spending"—and the second two categories—as a measure of "prosocial spending." Next, they examined the link between happiness and each type of spending.

Their findings were very clear: there was no association between happiness and personal spending, meaning that things people bought for themselves did not predict happiness. In contrast, the more people spent on other people—either people they knew and bought gifts for or people they didn't know but donated to through charitable organizations—the happier they were. This association between giving to others and happiness remained even when researchers took into account annual income.

Now, one problem with this study is that the researchers couldn't determine whether generosity reflected people's happiness or caused it; in other words, maybe happy people give more to others instead of giving leading to happiness. To better answer this question, these researchers later conducted another study in which they examined how a certain type of giving was associated with happiness.

This research, which examined how people spend bonus money (worth about $5,000) they receive from their company, reveals identical findings. People who spend it on other people experience more happiness later on than those who spend this money on themselves. This finding held true even when researchers took into account overall income as well as size of the bonus. In sum, employees who devoted more of their bonus to prosocial spending experienced greater happiness after receiving the bonus, and the manner in which they spent that bonus was a more important predictor of their happiness than the size of the bonus itself.

These findings about the link between giving and happiness emerge in study after study. For example, a worldwide survey conducted by Gallup found that in 120 out of 136 countries people who donated to charity in the past month reported greater satisfaction with life.[5] Thus, even in poor countries, spending money on other people is a stronger predictor of happiness than spending money on ourselves.

Now, clearly meeting our basic needs requires spending a fair amount of money on personal spending. After all, personal spending includes many necessities such as mortgage payments and groceries and gas. But even making small shifts to allocate more money to prosocial spending can bring us more happiness.

GIVING TIME COUNTS, TOO

Although giving in general increases happiness, we get a particular boost from giving in ways that let us form connections with other people. For example, researchers in one study handed out ten-dollar Starbucks gift cards to random people on the street.[6] However, the lucky recipients were given specific instructions on how to use these cards:

- Some people were told to use the gift card to take another person out for coffee.
- Some people were told to give the gift card away to someone else, and that they could not accompany that person to Starbucks.
- Some people were told to spend the gift card entirely on themselves by going to Starbucks alone.
- Some people were told to go to Starbucks with a friend, but to use the gift card only on themselves.

This study design allowed researchers to examine the relative benefits of spending time with a friend, giving a gift to someone, and receiving a gift for oneself.

The researchers found that people who used the gift card to benefit someone else *and* spent time with that person at Starbucks reported the highest levels of happiness. So, giving is good, but giving in ways that involve interacting with others is especially good.

This finding explains why volunteering, which connects people to other volunteers as well as with those in need in a given community, increases happiness.[7] Compared with people who never volunteer, those who volunteer monthly are 7 percent more likely to be "very happy," and those who volunteer weekly are 16 percent more likely to be "very happy."[8] One inspirational quote often attributed to Mahatma Gandhi is, "The best way to find yourself is to lose yourself in service to others."

National surveys on the link between neuroticism—measuring respondents' level of depression, anxiety, and tension—and volunteerism provide an even clearer demonstration that giving makes us happy. States with the highest rates of volunteerism— Utah, South Dakota, and Minnesota—are all in the top ten least neurotic states. On the other hand, states in which residents are more neurotic have lower rates of volunteerism.[9] And although states with wealthier people do report more volunteerism, presumably because more income allows for more free time, these findings take into account overall state income levels. So, even when researchers stratified the data according to state wealth, states with higher rates of volunteerism also report higher levels of overall well-being.

WHAT'S SO GOOD ABOUT GIVING?

A number of years ago, I was driving my kids to our local McDonald's when a car ran a red light and nearly hit us as I was making a turn into the parking lot. That car swerved and braked in one direction as I swerved and braked in the other direction, and somewhat miraculously, we didn't experience a high-speed collision. After catching my breath, I drove into the drive-through lane . . . at which point I realized that the car that had nearly hit us was right in front of us.

The other driver placed his order and then drove to pick up his food at the window. As I waited in line, I noticed that driver having a really long conversation through the drive-through window—like the cashier was the man's long-lost cousin or something. I became more and more irate, as my McDonald's drive-through experience had started with a narrow miss of a serious car accident and now was taking twenty minutes.

Finally, the other car pulled away from the window, and as it did, the driver rolled down the window and put his hand out and did a little wave at me.

At the point, I was pretty mad, so I also rolled down my window. And I made a different type of a gesture.

Then, I pulled up to get my food and handed the cashier my credit card, which she promptly returned, saying, "Oh, that other driver just paid for your whole order."

Now I felt really embarrassed—after all, this was that driver's apology for the near accident. ("I almost killed you, but your Egg McMuffin is free, so we are good, right?") And unfortunately, I couldn't take back that gesture I had made or that my kids had seen.

So, why did that driver pay for my food? Almost certainly to feel better about what had happened—in effect, to apologize for aggressive driving and nearly crashing into me. This gesture made me feel better, but it also made *him* feel better.

And this story illustrates one of the major reasons why helping makes us feeling better—it can help bring us out of not-so-good moods. Giving to others can even help people recover from grief, as described at the start of this chapter. As Mark Twain wrote, "The best way to cheer yourself is to try to cheer somebody else up."[10]

Empirical scientific research provides strong support for Twain's intuition. Helping people can even assuage our guilt and make up for something bad we did, which in turn increases our own happiness.

In one study, a researcher asked a woman on the street to take his picture with a very expensive-looking camera.[11] He mentioned that the camera was sensitive but that all she needed to do was aim and push one button. However, when she pushed the button, the camera did not work. In some cases, he dismissed the problem by saying, "The camera acts up a lot," whereas in other cases, he made the woman feel guilty by saying she had jammed the camera by pushing too hard. Then, as the woman walked down the street, another woman dropped a file folder full of papers that scattered on the street.

Who stopped to help her pick up the papers? Only 40 percent of those who did not feel guilty helped her, compared to 80 percent of those who felt guilty. This study provides a simple illustration of how giving can be used to help bring us out of a bad mood.

GIVING FEELS GOOD

In 2007 my cousin's son, Parker Brown, died at age seven of leukemia. The loss of a child at such a young age, of course, is tragic and life-changing, but Parker's mom, Sarah, was determined that some good come from his death. So she asked all her friends and family members to honor Parker's memory by signing up for the bone marrow registry.

I dutifully signed up. My own son Robert was exactly the same age as Parker, and I couldn't even imagine what Sarah was going through. So, the request to sign up for the bone marrow registry was a very easy way for me to show my support for Sarah. After all, signing up only involved a small cheek swab with a Q-tip, which I did in my kitchen and then mailed back.

I then gave the registry very little thought, until I received a call in the fall of 2015. "It appears you may be a match," I learned.

And a month later, I spent a day in the hospital undergoing the procedure.

As I left the hospital that evening, I felt tremendously happy. After all, I was given the opportunity to possibly save someone's life. And even though I don't know this person, and will probably never meet her, this experience was one of the most meaningful experiences I've ever had.

This story illustrates how giving to others doesn't just help someone else—it also makes us feel good. Think about a time you've written a check to a charity, given money to a homeless person, or helped a stranger who was lost and needed directions. Your motivation for giving in all those cases was probably to be kind or generous—to help someone else. But all these types of giving also make us happier.

GIVING FEELS GOOD IN THE BRAIN

After every natural disaster—from wildfires burning in California to hurricanes flooding Texas—strangers step up to help in some way. Some people donate money and supplies, others help search for survivors and rebuild communities. These acts of generosity occur spontaneously, and with no obvious benefit for the do-gooder.

Why do so many people voluntarily give time, money, and supplies to people they've never met, and may live across the country—or even across the world? Giving may literally help our species survive, and thus has been evolutionarily selected for. Specifically, people who give to others often receive help in return, which therefore increases the likelihood of their (and their genes') survival.

In line with this view, the link between giving and feeling good even exists among small children, who couldn't really have come to understand that society values giving. For example, children as young as two years of age are happier when they give treats—such as Goldfish crackers—to other children than when they keep the treats for themselves.[12]

Other support for the view that giving may be in our genes comes from recent research in neuroscience. For example, researchers in one study put people in an fMRI machine to measure brain activation, and then asked them to think about receiving money themselves or donating money to a charitable organization.[13] Merely thinking about giving to others activated a part of the brain that processes rewarding experiences; in fact, this is the same part of the brain that is activated when eating chocolate! (And also when using cocaine, but that seems like a less appropriate example.) In contrast, receiving money for ourselves results in lower levels of brain activation, suggesting giving to others does in fact feel better than getting something for ourselves.

Such activation is greater when people freely choose to donate than when they are required to do so. But even mandatory giving to charitable organizations elicits some brain activation, suggesting that the mere act of giving does feel rewarding.[14]

GIVING IS GOOD FOR OUR HEALTH

Here's another reason why giving to others is a really good idea: Giving is literally good for our health. In fact, giving to others is linked to health benefits even among people with serious chronic illnesses, such as cardiovascular disease and AIDS.[15]

In one study, people with high blood pressure were given $120 and told to either spend that money on themselves or on other people over a six-week period.[16] Those who were told to spend money on others had lower rates of blood pressure at the follow-up, suggesting that giving to others may directly benefit one's own health. A longer-term study over two years revealed similar findings; in fact, the more money people spent on others, the lower their blood pressure. So, telling people to be generous to other people may be as effective as starting an exercise routine or even taking medication.

Why does giving to other people lead to such positive health outcomes? Giving help to others seems to buffer us from the negative effects of stress.[17] Here's a simple example of the power of even small types of prosocial giving: People who experience stress on a given day generally report feeling worse.[18] But those who engage in some type of prosocial behavior—from holding a door open for someone to asking if someone needs help—don't experience the negative effects of stress on mood.

As described in chapter 2, "Why Zebras Don't Get Ulcers: Mindset Affects Health," high stress is bad for our health, so people who find ways to manage this stress reduce its negative physiological effects on health. People who give social support to others have lower blood pressure and higher levels of oxytocin, a hormone that increases feelings of closeness to others, suggesting that giving to others may have physiological benefits that directly link to health.[19]

Most important, giving to others can lengthen our lives. Although we often assume—correctly—that receiving social support helps buffer the negative effects of stress, giving help to others also provides important health benefits. In fact, a study of older married couples found that those who provided help to friends, relatives, or neighbors had a lower risk of dying over the next five years than those who did not.[20] Receiving help, on the other hand, was not linked with a lower risk.

Researchers in one study examined rates of volunteerism in a sample of elderly people living in California.[21] They then examined survival among these people five years later. Those who volunteered for two or more organizations were 44 percent less likely to have died during this follow-up period than those who did not volunteer. This life expectancy gap between volunteers and nonvolunteers persisted even when researchers took into account other factors predicting longevity, such as age, general health, smoking, and exercise.

Researchers in one intriguing study directly examined whether providing help to others is especially beneficial for those experiencing major stressors.[22] First, their findings revealed that older adults who experienced at least one stressful event—such as a serious illness, job loss, or death of a loved one—in the past year had an increased risk of dying in the subsequent five years.

However, the impact of this stressful event differed substantially for different people. Those who did not report engaging in helpful behaviors toward others had about a 30 percent lower rate of survival over the next five years. But for people who reported helping others, there was no increased risk of dying. These findings are a powerful demonstration that helping other people can actually increase our own life expectancy.

This data is particularly important since we so often hear about the benefits of seeking out social support during times of stress, but not so much about the benefits of helping others. As the researchers who conducted this study point out, "At-risk populations are frequently advised to seek support from their social networks. A less common message, but one that perhaps deserves more prominence, is for them to support others as well."

BUT MOTIVES MATTER

But let me end with a note of caution: motives matter. We reap most of the benefits of giving to others when our giving is freely chosen; people who are required to give to others—think mandatory school volunteerism programs—won't get nearly the same mood boost from helping.

Researchers in one study asked college students to keep a daily diary for two weeks and to write down how they felt each day and whether they had either helped someone else or done something for a worthy cause.[23] As they expected, students felt better on days in which they had engaged in some type of prosocial behavior.

However, the benefits of helping were only seen when the students helped because they wanted to do so; students who were required to help or felt they had to or others would be mad at them did not experience such benefits.

Similarly, volunteering helps buffer the negative effects of stress on health, and leads to longer life expectancy, but only for those who care about others and truly want to provide help.[24] People who are motivated to volunteer out of true compassion for others do live longer than those who don't volunteer.[25] But people motivated for self-focused reasons, such as feeling better about themselves or escaping from their own troubles, don't live longer than people who don't volunteer.

WHAT'S THE TAKE-HOME MESSAGE?

If you want happiness for an hour, take a nap.
If you want happiness for a day, go fishing.
If you want happiness for a year, inherit a fortune.
If you want happiness for a lifetime, help someone else.

As this Chinese proverb teaches, giving is one of the best ways to find happiness. Moreover, helping in all sorts of different ways makes us feel good: donating to charity, volunteering, giving a gift to a friend, buying coffee for a stranger, and so on. All the diverse ways of giving bring about a more positive, empathic mindset, which, in turn, makes you feel good.

So, figure out what type of giving makes you feel best, and create a plan. Set aside twenty dollars a week and resolve to spend it on someone else sometime during the week—give it to a homeless person, buy lunch for a friend, buy coffee for the office. Write one letter a month to someone who's meant something to you. Spend a few hours each month volunteering.

Here are some specific, and relatively simple, strategies we can all use to increase happiness in our own lives by giving to others.

Perform Random Acts of Kindness

We've all heard about strangers performing random acts of kindness, from long chains of people in Starbucks drive-throughs paying for the car behind them to strangers paying off layaway purchases at Toys "R" Us during the holidays. These random acts of kindness are touching demonstrations of the power of giving—with no expectation of receiving something in return.

But scientific research now tells us that selfless giving does lead to concrete benefits—for the giver, not just the receiver. In fact, people who perform a random act of kindness every day for ten days report a significant boost in happiness.[26]

So, find ways in your daily life to perform small acts of kindness to others. Here are some easy examples:

- Bring coffee to a coworker, neighbor, or friend.
- Give a compliment to a stranger.
- Tip well.
- Let a car merge in front of you.
- Donate blood.
- Sign up to be a bone marrow donor (you just might save someone's life).
- Carry around care kits with small food items and give them to homeless people.

Random acts of kindness are especially meaningful for people who are going through a hard time. After my mother died, I realized how hard Mother's Day and Father's Day are for people who've lost a parent, so I send an email to all my friends who've experienced this loss telling them I'm thinking of them on that day. My family buys holiday gifts each year for kids who are living in foster care to help make this day a little better than it might otherwise be. Find ways that fit into your own life to perform random acts of kindness; many of these are small gestures that can have big effects.

Donate in Concrete Ways

Giving can take many forms: we can donate money to large charitable organizations such as the ASPCA or the Sierra Club, volunteer our time at a local soup kitchen or as a Big Brother or Big Sister, or donate blood through the American Red Cross. And although all these ways of giving can have a positive impact, different ways of giving can bring us more or less happiness.

The best forms of giving are those that feel personally meaningful. For some, that may be donating to environmental causes, whereas for others, that could be donating to an animal rescue organization, a political action committee, or a local soup kitchen.

We also show a larger boost in happiness when our donation has a concrete impact. For example, people who give to Spread the Net (an organization that provides malaria nets to sub-Saharan Africa) experience greater boosts in happiness than those who contribute to the United Nations Children's Fund (UNICEF).[27] Why? UNICEF donations help children in various ways throughout the world. This is obviously a valuable organization that does tremendous good for kids, but it is hard for donors to see exactly how their contributions really matter. In contrast, Spread the Net tells donors that each ten-dollar contribution sends one malaria net to a family, and that a single bed net can protect up to five children for five years. Thus, a small donation has a clear, powerful, and concrete impact.

So, prosocial giving overall feels good, but it feels best when we can understand and appreciate the value of our giving in the real world.

Write a Gratitude Letter

This chapter has focused on various types of giving—money, time, blood, and so on. But giving thanks to others is also a powerful way of increasing our own happiness.

The gratitude letter strategy, which was developed by Dr. Martin Seligman at the University of Pennsylvania, asks people to think about someone who was important in changing or shaping their lives for the better.[28] Perhaps you're thinking of a teacher, or first boss, or neighbor—it doesn't matter who the person is, or the specific way in which that person shaped your life. All that matters is that it's someone you feel grateful for having known.

After you've imagined such a person, you then are asked to write a letter of gratitude to this individual, stating specifically what he or she did for you and how it shaped your life.

Then, and this is perhaps the most important part, go visit that person and read the letter aloud. As you can probably imagine, the feeling of happiness—in both the person reading the letter and the person hearing the letter—that results from this experience can be truly profound.

When I think about the person I'm most grateful to in shaping my life, I think of my seventh- and eighth-grade English teacher, Eugene Dougherty. Mr. Dougherty served in World War II and lost his right arm in the battle of Iwo Jima. He walked around the classroom with a scary-looking silver hook (this was in the early

1980s, and prosthetics were not really what they are now)—it was literally like Captain Hook's hook. Mr. Dougherty would write on the blackboard with the chalk in his hook, and regularly smoked cigarettes (again, times have changed!) while teaching with the cigarette clutched in this hook. So, overall, he was pretty scary.

But every single paper I ever wrote for his class was returned with tons and tons of feedback—"expand," "unpack," "nice use of detail," "tell me more here," and so on. I went on to study at Stanford and Princeton, but I learned how to write from Mr. Dougherty. And this feedback on my writing was how I first came to understand the value of revising as the key strategy to improving my writing and has clearly shaped and changed my career: I write now for a living (articles, chapters, books).

But unfortunately, I learned about the value of gratitude letters too late. I wrote Mr. Dougherty's widow my letter of gratitude only after hearing of his death.

So, here's a really important takeaway from this happiness-inducing strategy: don't save your kind words for the person's eulogy, which is too often the only time when we express what someone has meant to us.

Chapter 12

Build Relationships: All You Need Is Love

n 1974, twenty-one-year-old Laura Carstensen was being
driven home late at night from a concert when the driver, who
had been drinking, rolled the car over an embankment. She
suffered a serious head injury, multiple broken bones, and internal
bleeding, and spent months recovering in the hospital.

As she lay in that bed and realized how close she had come
to dying, Laura became aware that all the things that she had
thought were important to her—what was she going to do with
her life, would she be successful, and so on—all of a sudden didn't
matter. As she describes, "What mattered were other people in my
life."[1]

That realization was the start of what would become her life's
work. After recovering from her accident, she started taking college classes, and then went on to a graduate degree in psychology. Today she is a professor of psychology at Stanford University.

As you'll read about later in this chapter, Professor Carstensen's research examines how our beliefs about how much time we have left to live influence how we spend our time.

So, what do people prioritize when they believe time is running out? Relationships. Throughout this book I've described factors that increase our happiness. And although these factors—spending money on experiences, giving gifts, exercising, and so on—do make us happier, the single biggest predictor of our life satisfaction is the quality of our relationships. As Harvard University professor Daniel Gilbert describes, "We are happy when we have family, we are happy when we have friends, and almost all the other things we think make us happy are actually just ways of getting more family and friends."[2]

One of the first studies to demonstrate the importance of having close personal relationships examined factors predicting men's well-being from adolescence through the end of their lives.[3] The findings were clear: the only real and consistent predictor of happiness was relationships. As Dr. George Valliant, the lead researcher on this study, wrote, there are two pillars of happiness: "One is love. The other is finding a way of coping with life that doesn't push love away." And subsequent research bears out this finding again and again.

In this chapter, I'll describe why investing time and energy in building and maintaining close relationships is the single best way to live a longer, happier life. Now, having good relationships doesn't in and of itself make us happy; it is possible to have good relationships and still, for whatever reason, feel unhappy. But if we lack good relationships, no matter what else we have, we won't feel happy.

THE VALUE OF MEANINGFUL CONVERSATIONS

I have a good friend whom I don't see so often, but every few months we have lunch. And every time we get together, our conversations are intimate and intense—a marital separation, a child's academic struggle, a cancer diagnosis, and so on. Every time we get together, even for just an hour or two, I feel connected, close, and extremely happy. Our close relationships with others provide opportunities to have this type of in-depth, real conversation about things that matter. And these interactions are a strong predictor of happiness.

Researchers in one study examined conversation patterns of seventy-nine college-aged men and women over a four-day period.[4] Study participants carried an unobtrusive recording device in a pocket or purse, and the researchers taped thirty seconds of sound every twelve and a half minutes, amassing more than twenty thousand audio snippets of sound from the participants' daily lives.

Researchers then listened to the recordings and coded the number of conversations each participant had. They also measured whether each conversation was substantive ("She fell in love with your dad? So, did they get divorced soon after?") or small talk ("What do you have there? Popcorn?"). Each participant's overall level of happiness level was also measured.

These findings revealed substantial differences in both the quantity and quality of people's interactions. First, those who were rated as happiest spent about 25 percent less time alone and 70 percent more time talking to others, compared with the unhappiest people. Moreover, the happiest participants had twice as many substantive conversations, and about one-third as much small talk. So, happy people do spend more time talking with others, but this time isn't just spent on idle chitchat. Instead, they spend more time having meaningful and substantive conversations—precisely the type of interactions that we know help build strong relationships.

This finding that the happiest people engaged more often in meaningful conversations is an especially important one in today's world, given the heavy reliance on technology as a form of communication. Many people "communicate" only in brief snippets via texts and tweets. Have you ever had a conversation with someone who was simultaneously sending a text or checking email? This type of a conversation is not a meaningful one. And, as I'll describe later in this chapter, even the presence of a cell phone reduces the quality of our conversations.

Why do meaningful conversations feel so good? They provide social approval—it feels good when we believe someone likes and respects us.[5] They also allow us to be our real selves, to be authentic. As I described in chapter 6, "'Comparison Is the Thief of Joy': Environment Matters," many more casual interactions feel less authentic, as we often present an idealized version of ourselves, sharing only the positive things in our lives. But interacting with close people, who approve of us and allow us to be who we really are, feels especially good.

Although research provides strong support for the value of meaningful conversations, even brief personal interactions with strangers can increase positive feelings. Similarly, people who report having more casual interactions with others—greeting a clerk at a store, casual conversations with coworkers or neighbors, and so on—on a given day report greater feelings of belonging and happiness.[6]

In one study, researchers bribed people on public transportation—with five-dollar gift cards to Starbucks—to initiate a conversation with a stranger.[7] These bus and train riders were initially pretty hesitant to participate, in part because they assumed that strangers would not be very receptive to their approach. However, most people were pleased to have a casual conversation with a stranger. Moreover, people who had such conversations then reported higher levels of happiness than those who had simply sat alone.

Apparently any type of human connection—including casual contact with a stranger—can provide a sense of personal contact that increases positive feelings. A simple way of increasing happiness—our own and others'—is therefore to make an effort to have such interactions. So, make a point of smiling at strangers, making small talk while waiting in line, and exchanging greetings with neighbors and coworkers. Even these little moments of interaction can make us—and them—feel better.

SHARING FEELS GOOD

Relationships allow us to share our positive life experiences, which in turn makes these good events feel even better. We call people we care about—and who care about us—to share news of job offers, college admissions, engagements, and new babies. And this sharing increases the happiness we feel.

To test this link between sharing and happiness, researchers first asked people to report on their overall tendency to share positive experiences with others.[8] Some people reported having a general tendency to share such experiences, describing themselves as "the type of person that loves to share it with others when something good happens to me." Other people reported having less of a tendency to share, reporting, "I usually keep good feelings bottled up and don't share them very often."

Next, all people in this study kept a journal for four weeks. This journal included ratings over time of mood as well as life satisfaction, so that researchers could see how these measures changed over time. As it turns out, people who reported a higher tendency to share good things with other people also showed increases in positive mood and overall life satisfaction over time.

Relationships also provide opportunities for us to share experiences—and doing something with someone we care about makes us happier than the same experience alone. So, you might enjoy seeing a great movie sitting alone in a theater or in your living room. But watching the same movie with a friend will probably enhance your enjoyment of the experience. As author Charlotte Brontë wrote, "Happiness quite unshared can scarcely be called happiness; it has no taste."[9]

In a simple demonstration of the impact of sharing experiences, researchers asked people to engage in a really fun activity: tasting and rating chocolate.[10] Half of the people in this study completed this activity alone. The other half also tasted and rated chocolate, but they did so at the same time as another person (a stranger). These people didn't have to agree on ratings with the other person, but they both tasted the different types of chocolate at the same time, and then both completed separate ratings of this chocolate (how intense, how flavorful, how much did you like it). Even in this very simple design, people who had the opportunity to share the chocolate-rating experience with a partner showed greater liking for the chocolate than those who rated it alone.

Now, one problem with the studies described thus far is that they don't necessarily test whether sharing specifically helps improve mood, or whether just thinking about positive things—even if those things aren't shared—improves mood. So to test this important question, researchers in yet another study asked people to keep a journal over the course of several weeks in which they thought about and recorded "things they were grateful for" at the end of each evening.[11] Half these people simply kept this journal; the others were asked to keep the journal and to share these experiences with a friend at least twice a week.

Their findings provided strong evidence that sharing in fact makes us feel better: people who shared the things they were grateful for with a friend reported more happiness and more satisfaction with life than those who simply recorded these things but didn't share them.

WITH AGE COMES HAPPINESS

This finding about the importance of high-quality relationships helps explain some fascinating research on how happiness changes across the life span. For many years, it was assumed that happiness would decrease with age. After all, older people have experienced more loss—deaths of love ones, difficult personal circumstances. But studies repeatedly show this belief is wrong, as I described in chapter 7, "Embrace Adversity: Trauma Matters."

Instead, happiness across the life span shows a U-shaped curve, meaning happiness is high in teenagers and young adults, then falls in the middle-aged period, and then rises again for people in their sixties, seventies, and eighties.[12]

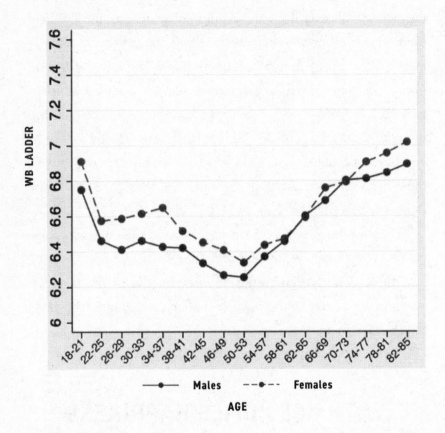

Figure 12.1: For both men (the solid line) and women (the dotted line), well-being shows a U-shaped curve, with well-being increasing after age 50.

Stone, A. A., Schwartz, J. E., Broderick, J. E., & Deaton, A. (2010). A snapshot of the age distribution of psychological well-being in the United States. *Proceedings of the National Academy of Sciences of the United States of America, 107*(22), 9985–9990.

On a certain level, this data isn't so surprising. After all, what's not to feel happy about during the college and young-adult years, during which time most people live pretty relaxed and easy lives? It also isn't so surprising that happiness is harder to come by during middle age, which corresponds with what we describe as the "mid-life crisis" period. What is so hard about the midlife period? As I write this book, I've just turned forty-nine, so am feeling acutely aware of some of the threats to happiness during this life period. Many people in this age are struggling over perhaps the most difficult child-raising time: the teenage years. Like many people in this life period, my husband and I are simultaneously navigating the surly adolescent period, which seems to consist largely of requests for money and the car, while feeling the financial pressure of paying for college (it is not a good combination).

Other aspects of midlife may also make it harder to find happiness. Many people in this age period are dealing with challenging situations with their own parents, such as Alzheimer's disease and physical health problems. And these years are often ones in which work pressures are intense. People in their forties and fifties may be at the pinnacle of their careers, having made partner or achieved tenure, but are now working long hours.

But the really good—and perhaps surprising—news is that there is light at the end of the midlife tunnel. After this midlife low point, happiness increases steadily throughout the life span, meaning those who survive the difficult forties and fifties can look forward to increased happiness as they enter their sixties, seventies, eighties, and even nineties. In fact, people in their seventies and eighties report higher levels of happiness than people in their late teenage years!

What is particularly remarkable is that U-shaped curve describing the link between age and happiness is seen across cultures—in all the seventy-two different countries that have been studied so far. Now, the specific age at which people experience the lowest level of happiness varies across culture, from a high of sixty-two (in the Ukraine) to a low of thirty-five (Switzerland). But the overall shape of the curve is quite consistent across countries. And in most of these countries, unhappiest is highest in the forties and fifties (with a mean age of forty-six).

EXPLAINING THE AGE-HAPPINESS LINK

What explains this increase in happiness during older adulthood? To examine this question, Laura Carstensen, whom I mentioned at the start of this chapter, professor of psychology and director of the Stanford Center on Longevity, has examined how the quantity and quality of people's social relationships change across their life spans. And her research shows substantial differences in these relationships with age.

Young people tend to have lots of casual friends and acquaintances. They are focused on expanding their social networks and meeting new people, and thus tend to have large social circles. As Carstensen describes, "Young people will go to cocktail parties because they might meet somebody who will be useful to them in the future, even though nobody I know actually likes going to cocktail parties."[13]

Older people, in contrast, know what really matters. People up to about age fifty keep adding more and more people to their social networks. But after age fifty, people evince the opposite pattern: they eliminate their more casual, less close relationships and instead concentrate their time and energy on relationships with people they really value.[14] In other words, they tend to get rid of the chaff and prioritize cultivating deeper, more intimate relationships, but with fewer people. This choice about spending time with people we feel close and connected to is a strong predictor of greater happiness.

A caption in a *Peanuts* cartoon captures this finding perfectly: "As we grow up, we realize it is less important to have lots of friends and more important to have real ones."

Here's an example of how our preferences change with age: Carstensen and her colleagues conducted a study that asked people to rate how interested they would be in spending thirty minutes with one of the following:[15]

- the author of a book they had just read;
- an acquaintance with whom they could see a
  friendship potentially developing; or
- a family member or close friend.

The researchers found that younger people's preferences were pretty evenly divided across these three choices. However, older people consistently preferred to spend time with a family member or close friend.

Now, a very important question about this finding is what leads older people to choose to structure their relationships in this way, and, in particular, whether you only learn about how to spend time with age. In other words, do you have to live sixty or seventy years in order to realize the importance of choosing quality over quantity in relationships?

To test this question, researchers conducted a study with a unique sample: HIV-positive gay men in their forties and fifties living in San Francisco in the early 1990s.[16] Now, in the 1990s, being HIV-positive was truly a death sentence; we didn't have the ways of managing this disease then that we do now, so these men were facing what was almost certainly a shortened life expectancy. The researchers therefore examined how these men structured their lives and relationships, knowing that their time was limited.

These men—who were far younger than the seventy- and eighty-year-old people described in the previous study—structured their relationships in precisely the same way. They stopped spending time with people who they didn't feel close to, and they focused instead on spending time on high-quality relationships. In other words, when time is running out (either because of advanced age or a terminal illness), people make a conscious choice about how to spend their remaining time, and they do so in ways that maximize happiness.

These findings illustrate that we don't have to be seventy or eighty years old to make a choice about how we spend time in our close relationships. We can make the choice at any age to spend more time with the people who matter most to us in the world, which in turn brings us greater happiness.

WE GET BY WITH A LOT OF HELP FROM OUR FRIENDS

Having high-quality relationships doesn't just make us happier— they also make us healthier. Across their life spans, people with more social relationships have better physical health, including lower blood pressure, lower BMI, and stronger immune systems.[17] They engage in healthier behaviors, recover from surgery faster, and are less likely to develop chronic diseases, such as cardio-vascular disease.[18]

Most important, people with strong social relationships have longer life expectancies.[19] One of the earliest studies showing the impact of our interpersonal relationships on health examined social connections in nearly seven thousand men and women living in Alameda County, California, in 1965.[20] Overall, people who lacked social ties—with family members, friends, or social groups—were two to three times more likely to die during the seven-year follow-up period than those with such connections. More recently, a study of adults ages seventy and older compared the impact of different types of social relationships—friends, chil-dren, and family members other than spouses and children—on survival over a ten-year period.[21] People with a stronger network of friends—particularly ones they felt close to and kept in regular contact with—were 22 percent less likely to die during follow-up than those with fewer friends.

Good relationships are especially important for those with serious, even life-threatening, health conditions. For example, a study of women with breast cancer found that those without close friends were four times more likely to die from the disease as those with ten or more friends.[22] Close relationships also increase life expectancy among those who've experienced a heart attack.[23] For example, people with coronary heart disease who lack close rela-tionships are more than twice as likely to die from this condition as those with such contacts.[24]

Why do close relationships have such a strong impact on health? Our relationships help us cope with minor and major daily life stressors, and thereby reduce the negative physiological effects of such events.[25] Good support networks help us in real ways—from recovering following a natural disaster to borrowing a cup of sugar to getting a ride to the airport.

Close relationships also have powerful influences on our physiological responses to stressful situations. For example, simply holding a spouse's hand in anticipation of a stressful experience calms the brain in the same way that pain-relieving drugs work.[26] These findings about the benefits of close relationships on our physiological response to stress help explain why people who get more frequent hugs—a specific demonstration of the availability of such support—are less susceptible to infection and experience less severe illness symptoms.[27]

Chronic loneliness, on the other hand, leads to increases in cortisol, a stress hormone, which can raise blood pressure and disrupt the immune system.[28] These findings help explain why people who lack strong relationships are more likely to develop heart disease, more likely to have a stroke, and have shorter life expectancies.[29] As Vivek Murthy, a former United States surgeon general, notes, "Loneliness and weak social connections are associated with a reduction in life span similar to that caused by smoking 15 cigarettes a day and even greater than that associated with obesity."[30]

ALL RELATIONSHIPS
ARE NOT CREATED EQUAL

But it's not having just any close relationships that make us feel better; only high-quality relationships increase happiness, improve health outcomes, and extend life expectancy.

In fact, people in unhappy marriages are more likely to develop depression than those who have satisfying relationships or than those who are single.[31] Those with the least satisfying marriages are more than twice as likely to develop depression than those with the most satisfying relationships. In practical terms, this means that one in seven adults with the lowest-quality relationships will become depressed, compared to just one in fifteen adults who have the highest-quality relationships.

Bad relationships don't just hurt our psychological well-being. Married people who feel ambivalent toward their spouse—meaning they have both positive and negative feelings about their partner on a daily basis—experience worse physical health, including high blood pressure.[32] Similarly, although in general people who are married show better health outcomes than those who are unmarried, the quality of the marriage also matters; patients who undergo heart surgery and are high in marital satisfaction are three times as likely to be alive fifteen years later as those with low marital satisfaction.[33]

As Julianne Holt-Lunstad, a professor of psychology at the University of Utah, says, "Just being married per se isn't helpful, because you can potentially be worse off in an unhappy marriage."[34] These findings point to the importance of choosing relationship partners well and working to improve the quality of these relationships.

WHAT'S THE TAKE-HOME POINT?

Close relationships play an essential role in improving the quality and length of our lives. Yet a 2017 survey by the Bureau of Labor

Statistics found that the average American spends on average only thirty-nine minutes a day socializing with other people, including talking with friends and going to parties.[35] In contrast, people spend about 2.7 hours watching TV. So, the bad news is that most of us clearly aren't placing a priority on spending quality time with people we care about.

But the good news is that once we recognize the fundamental benefits that relationships provide, we can all make a choice to devote time and energy to building and maintaining these relationships. If you don't feel satisfied with your current social network, find ways to meet new people—volunteer, take a class, join a book club or religious organization, invite a coworker or casual friend to lunch. And make sure to spend time, energy, and effort on maintaining and deepening current close relationships. Here are some strategies you can try to develop strong and lasting relationships.

Put Away the Cell Phone

Close relationships increase our happiness in part because they provide opportunities for us to have substantive, meaningful conversations. But we can only have this type of quality interaction by putting away our cell phones. After all, spending time with a spouse or friend while each of you scrolls through your phones isn't exactly quality time.

In one very clever study, researchers asked college students to have a ten-minute "get to know you conversation" with a stranger.[36] Half these students had this conversation with a nondescript phone placed on a table outside their direct view. This phone was turned off, so it didn't ring or vibrate during the conversation. The other half of the students had this conversation without the presence of a phone. After the conversation, the researchers asked both groups of students to rate how close they felt to their conversation partner, and whether they thought they could become friends.

The findings in this study were clear—and depressing. Students who had a conversation in the presence of a phone reported feeling less close to their conversation partner and felt it was less likely they could become friends. Remember, in this study the phone didn't even belong to either of the students and didn't ring or vibrate during the conversation. But its mere presence led to a lower quality of interaction.

Now, the study just described, having taken place in a research laboratory, was quite artificial. This means it may or may not really tell us how the presence of cell phones can affect people's conversations in more naturalistic settings.

To examine this important question, researchers in another study asked students to have a ten-minute conversation in a coffee shop in Washington, DC.[37] (Some of these students were strangers, whereas others were friends.) A researcher sat nearby and measured whether either person put a mobile device on the table, or held it in a hand, at any point during the conversation.

After the couple was finished talking, each person was asked to rate the quality of their conversation. For example, they were asked to rate how much they really trusted their conversation partner, and whether they felt their partner made an effort to understand their thoughts and feelings.

Once again, this data provided powerful evidence that the presence of cell phones does not benefit relationships: Conversations in which either person put a device on the table or in the hand were rated as less fulfilling. Moreover, the negative effects of cell phone use were even stronger among people who were already friends.

So, this is a simple yet effective strategy. When spending time with friends, family members, and romantic partners, put away the phone and focus entirely on the conversation at hand. This is the best way to have precisely those meaningful conversations that strengthen our close relationships.

Get a Pet (Ideally a Dog)

Although you read earlier about the benefits of close relationships on happiness, these relationships don't have to be with people. In fact, strong evidence suggests that pets can also lead to greater physical and psychological well-being. Studies comparing pet owners to non–pet owners reveal that those with pets feel less lonely. They also have higher levels of self-esteem and extroversion, which are both associated with greater happiness.

One recent study even found that dog owners live longer.[38] In fact, dog owners had a 20 percent lower risk of dying over the course of this twelve-year study, and were 23 percent less likely to die of cardiovascular disease.

What factors cause pet owners to experience these benefits? Many people report that pets fulfill valuable roles in their lives— such as increasing self-esteem, sense of belonging, and feeling of meaning. These beliefs, in turn, lead to greater well-being.

Pets may also help buffer the negative effects of stressful life experiences, such as coping with a chronic or terminal disease.[39] During stressful situations, the presence of a pet decreases our body's natural physiological reaction and lowers both blood pressure and heart rate.

Although pet owners in general experience greater happiness, dogs may be especially beneficial in providing valuable emotional support. Dogs have a particular ability to make connections with humans (so, no, that connection you feel with your dog isn't just in your mind). In fact, dogs can distinguish different types of emotional expressions on people's faces and are particularly sensitive to human voices.[40]

Perhaps most important, dogs may help reduce loneliness by providing absolute and unconditional love; they are *always* happy to see us. As an illustration of this unconditional love, consider this joke about the differences between dogs and spouses. Imagine you come home from work one day, put your dog and your spouse in the trunk of your car, and then drive around for an hour. When you open the trunk, which one is still happy to see you?

Expend Time, Energy, and Effort

As I write this book, my husband and I have just celebrated twenty-five years of marriage. He is a great man: He supports me, he believes in me, and he loves me. But our marriage is not perfect, and frankly it's not easy. We struggle over balancing two careers and three children, unloading the dishwasher and folding the laundry, and making sure the kids have finished their homework and practiced the piano and maybe even showered.

But that's the reality of close relationships. They are the single most important predictor of our happiness, but good relationships don't happen by magic. Instead, they involve struggle, conflict, and compromise.

One of my favorite quotes, which speaks to the value of relationships, yet also the work they take to maintain, comes from Leo Tolstoy's character Levin in *Anna Karenina*:

> But on entering upon family life he saw at every step that it was utterly different from what he had imagined. At every step he experienced what a man would experience who, after admiring the smooth, happy course of a little boat on a lake, should get himself into that little boat. He saw that it was not all sitting still, floating smoothly; that one had to think too, not for an instant to forget where one was floating; and that there was water under one, and that one must row; and that his unaccustomed hands would be sore; and that it was only to look at it that was easy; but that doing it, though very delightful, was very difficult.[41]

These words perfectly illustrate the difference between what having good relationships looks like from a distance—easy and effortless—and the reality of what having these relationships involves—time, energy, effort, conflict, and compromise.

In 2013 my in-laws celebrated fifty years of marriage—which in this day and age is quite an accomplishment. My gift to them was a small plaque that read, "The first fifty years of marriage are the hardest." Because marriage, like all relationships, is indeed hard. But having high-quality relationships—with a spouse or other romantic partner, family members, and friends—is the best route to living a happy, healthy, and long life.

Conclusion

For most of us, it's tempting to think of happiness as some quirk of fate or luck. Do we have the right genes? Are we blessed with good health? Did we win the lottery?

But what I hope you've gotten from reading this book is that greater happiness—and better health—is within our own control. Some people have a head start, but no matter your genes or life circumstances, we can all do things to improve the quality and increase the longevity of our lives. And another hope I have is that, if you've read this far, you are now motivated to spend time, energy, and effort to find the happiness you deserve by pursuing the specific strategies that work for you. Just keep in mind that the strategies for achieving happiness are very much not "one size fits all."

There's a scale in psychology called the Sensation Seeking Scale that basically measures how much people like—or don't like—feeling high levels of physiological arousal, such as a fast heartbeat, tense muscles, and rapid breathing.[1] Some people like this feeling; others don't. (And, no, this isn't a scale like IQ where high numbers are good—people just differ in what types of situations they find most desirable.)

Let me give you a few examples so you can figure out where you fall. I'm going to give you two choices, and you have to pick whichever one best describes you:

- Some people would like to parachute out of an airplane; other people would like to never parachute out of an airplane.
- Some people get into a pool by diving or jumping right in; other people get in gradually—toe, ankle, knee, thigh.
- Some people like the excitement and adventure of camping outside; other people prefer the warmth and comfort of a luxury hotel.

As you can probably tell, the first choice in each of the three pairs describes the high-sensation seekers, whereas the second choice describes the low-sensation seekers. (Count me solidly in the low group; as I say to my husband, "Your 'camping wife' is your second wife.)

And what scores on this scale tell is that the route to happiness is different for different people. For some people, that may mean shifting how they think about the world—developing more positive expectations about aging, reframing the minor (and major) stressors of daily life, recognizing the rosy images people present on social media don't reflect the reality of their lives.

For other people, that may mean changing their behavior—starting and sticking with an exercise program, choosing to spend money on experiences instead of belongings, spending more time with close friends.

So, figure out what strategies I described for changing your mindset work best for you and adopt those—and ignore the others!

And here's perhaps the most important point: by choosing to take steps to increase your own happiness, you'll inevitably increase the happiness of those around you. As you learned in chapter 5, "Are You Tigger or Eeyore: Personality Matters," happiness is contagious. Therefore, if you take steps to increase your own happiness, your new and improved mood will rub off on those around you, and increase their own happiness.

We've all had the experience of smiling at a stranger, and then seeing that person reciprocate our smile. Happiness works in precisely the same way; people who are happy help others around them see the world in a more positive light, take small daily life stresses in stride, and stop and smell the roses. And these steps happy people take transfer to others, who in turn pass them on again. As English theologian Frederick William Faber said, "The single act of kindness throws out roots in all directions, and the roots spring up and make new trees."[2]

So, take what you've learned in this book and work as hard as you can to take steps to live a happier, healthier life . . . and to pass on that happiness to those around you.

Acknowledgments

First, I want to thank Glenn Yeffeth, publisher of BenBella Books, for taking a chance on publishing *The Positive Shift*. From our very first call in July 2017, I was convinced BenBella was a perfect fit for my book, and I feel lucky to have landed with this publisher. I also owe much gratitude toward so many people at BenBella who helped make this project a reality, including Adrienne Lang, Jennifer Canzoneri, Sarah Avinger, Susan Welte, Alicia Kania, and Jessika Rieck. I especially appreciate the considerable efforts Vy Tran, my editor, took to improve virtually every aspect of this book, from organization to clarity to tone.

Many people contributed to making this book a reality at some stage along the way. Thanks go out to Steven Schragis (who encouraged me to develop a talk on happiness), my brother Matt Sanderson (who first told me I should write this book), and Isabel Margolin (who read early drafts and urged me to keep going). PJ Dempsey was extremely helpful in reading my proposal and sample chapters, pushing me to move beyond an academic style and providing the unusual but effective advice to have a glass of wine before writing.

Finally, I want to thank my husband, Bart, who continued to tell me that, yes, this really was a book, and my children—Andrew, Robert, and Caroline—who at times gave me some peace and quiet for writing.

Notes

INTRODUCTION

[1] Kross, E., Verduyn, P., Demiralp, E., Park, J., Lee, D. S., Lin, N., . . . Ybarra, O. (2013). Facebook use predicts declines in subjective well-being in young adults. *PLOS One, 8*(8), e69841.

[2] Faasse, K., Martin, L. R., Grey, A., Gamble, G., & Petrie, K. J. (2016). Impact of brand or generic labeling on medication effectiveness and side effects. *Health Psychology, 35*(2), 187–190.

[3] Przybylski, A. K., & Weinstein, N. (2012). Can you connect with me now? How the presence of mobile communication technology influences face-to-face conversation quality. *Journal of Social and Personal Relationships, 30*(3), 237–246.

[4] Ulrich, R. S. (1984). View through a window may influence recovery from surgery. *Science, 224*(4647), 420–421.

[5] Levy, B. R., Slade, M. D., Kunkel, S. R., & Kasl, S. V. (2002). Longevity increased by positive self-perceptions of aging. *Journal of Personality and Social Psychology, 83*(2), 261–270.

CHAPTER 1—MINDSET MATTERS

[1] Plassmann, H., O'Doherty, J., Shiv, B., & Rangel, A. (2008). Marketing actions can modulate neural representations of experienced pleasantness. *Proceedings of the National Academy of Sciences of the United States of America, 105*(3), 1050–1054.

[2] Estill, A., Mock, S. E., Schryer, E., & Eibach, R. P. (2018). The effects of subjective age and aging attitudes on mid- to late-life sexuality. *Journal of Sex Research, 55*(2), 146–151.

[3] Damisch, L., Stoberock, B., & Mussweiler, T. (2010). Keep your fingers crossed!: How superstition improves performance. *Psychological Science, 21*(7), 1014–1020.

[4] Steele, C. M., & Aronson, J. (1995). Stereotype threat and the intellectual test performance of African Americans. *Journal of Personality and Social Psychology, 69*(5), 797–811.

[5] Steele, C. M. (2010). *Issues of our time. Whistling Vivaldi: How stereotypes affect us and what we can do.* New York: W. W. Norton.

[6] Sherman, A. M., & Zurbriggen, E. L. (2014). "Boys can be anything": Effect of Barbie play on girls' career cognitions. *Sex Roles, 70*, 195–208.

[7] Cheryan, S., Plaut, V. C., Davies, P. G., & Steele, C. M. (2009). Ambient belonging: How stereotypical cues impact gender participation in computer science. *Journal of Personality and Social Psychology, 97*(6), 1045–1060.

[8] Bargh, J. A., Chen, M., & Burrows, L. (1996). Automaticity of social behavior: Direct effects of trait construct and stereotype activation on action. *Journal of Personality and Social Psychology, 71*(2), 230–244.

[9] Dweck, C. S. (2008) *Mindset: The new psychology of success.* New York: Ballantine Books.

[10] Krakovsky, M. (2007, March/April). The effort effect. *Stanford Magazine.* Retrieved from https://alumni.stanford.edu/get/page/magazine/article/?article_id=32124.

[11] Blackwell, L. S., Trzesniewski, K. H., & Dweck, C. S. (2007). Implicit theories of intelligence predict achievement across an adolescent transition: A longitudinal study and an intervention. *Child Development, 78*, 246–263.

[12] Schleider, J., & Weisz, J. (2018). A single-session growth mindset intervention for adolescent anxiety and depression: 9-month outcomes of a randomized trial. *Journal of Child Psychology and Psychiatry, 59*, 160–170.

[13] Schroder, H. S., Dawood, S., Yalch, M. M., Donnellan, M. B., & Moser, J. S. (2016). Evaluating the domain specificity of mental health–related mind-sets. *Social Psychological and Personality Science, 7*(6), 508–520.

[14] Weiss, D. (2016). On the inevitability of aging: Essentialist beliefs moderate the impact of negative age stereotypes on older adults' memory performance and physiological reactivity. *Journals of Gerontology, Series B: Psychological Sciences and Social Sciences*, gbw08.

[15] Schumann, K., Zaki, J., & Dweck, C. S. (2014). Addressing the empathy deficit: Beliefs about the malleability of empathy predict effortful responses when empathy is challenging. *Journal of Personality and Social Psychology, 107*(3), 475–493.

[16] Franiuk, R., Cohen, D., & Pomerantz, E. M. (2002). Implicit theories of relationships: Implications for relationship satisfaction and longevity. *Personal Relationships, 9*, 345–367; Knee, C. R. (1998). Implicit theories of relationships: Assessment and prediction of romantic relationship initiation, coping, and longevity. *Journal of Personality and Social Psychology, 74*(2), 360–370.

[17] Maxwell, J. A., Muise, A., MacDonald, G., Day, L. C., Rosen, N. O., & Impett, E. A. (2017). How implicit theories of sexuality shape sexual and relationship well-being. *Journal of Personality and Social Psychology, 112*(2), 238–279.

[18] Neff, K. D. (2003). Development and validation of a scale to measure self-compassion. *Self and Identity, 2*, 223–250.

[19] Gunnell, K. E., Mosewich, A. D., McEwen, C. E., Eklund, R. C., & Crocker, P. R. E. (2017). Don't be so hard on yourself! Changes in self-compassion during the first year of university are associated with changes in well-being. *Personality and Individual Differences, 107*, 43–48.

[20] Neff, K. D. (2003). Development and validation of a scale to measure self-compassion. *Self and Identity, 2*, 223–250.

[21] Dougherty, K. (2015). Reframing test day. *Teaching/Learning Matters*, 11–12.

[22] Gilovich, T., & Medvec, V. H. (1995). The experience of regret: What, when, and why. *Psychological Review, 102*(2), 379–395.

[23] Brown, H. J., Jr. (1999). *P.S. I love you* (p. 13). Nashville, TN: Rutledge Hill.

[24] Paunesku, D., Walton, G. M., Romero, C. L., Smith, E. N., Yeager, D. S., & Dweck, C. S. (2015). Mindset interventions are a scalable treatment for academic underachievement. *Psychological Science, 26*(6), 784–93; Yeager, D. S., Johnson, R., Spitzer, B. J., Trzesniewski, K. H., Powers, J., & Dweck, C. S. (2014). The far-reaching effects of believing people can change: Implicit theories of personality shape stress, health, and achievement during adolescence. *Journal of Personality and Social Psychology, 106*(6), 867–884.

[25] Schumann, K., Zaki, J., & Dweck, C. S. (2014). Addressing the empathy deficit: Beliefs about the malleability of empathy predict effortful responses when empathy is challenging. *Journal of Personality and Social Psychology, 107*(3), 475–493.

CHAPTER 2—WHY ZEBRAS DON'T GET ULCERS: MINDSET AFFECTS HEALTH

[1] Sapolsky, R. M. (1998). *Why zebras don't get ulcers: An updated guide to stress, stress-related diseases, and coping.* New York: W. H. Freeman.

2 Faasse, K., Martin, L. R., Grey, A., Gamble, G., & Petrie, K. J. (2016). Impact of brand or generic labeling on medication effectiveness and side effects. *Health Psychology, 35*(2), 187–190.

3 Waber, R. L., Shiv, B., Carmon, Z., & Ariely, D. (2008). Commercial features of placebo and therapeutic efficacy. *Journal of the American Medical Association, 299*(9), 1016–1017.

4 Espay, A. J., Norris, M. M., Eliassen, J. C., Dwivedi, A., Smith, M. S., Banks, C., . . . Szaflarski, J. P. (2015). Placebo effect of medication cost in Parkinson's disease: A randomized double-blind study. *Neurology, 84*(8), 794–802.

5 Moseley, J. B., O'Malley, K., Petersen, N. J., Menke, T. J., Brody, B. A., Kuykendall, D. H., . . . Wray, N. P. (2002). A controlled trial of arthroscopic surgery for osteoarthritis of the knee. *New England Journal of Medicine, 347*, 81–88.

6 Buchbinder, R., Osborne, R. H., Ebeling, P. R., Wark, J. D., Mitchell, P., Wriedt, C., . . . Murphy, B. (2009). A randomized trial of vertebroplasty for painful osteoporotic vertebral fractures. *The New England Journal of Medicine, 361*, 557–568; Kallmes, D. F., Comstock, B. A., Heagerty, P. J., Turner, J. A., Wilson, D. J., Diamond, T. H., . . . Jarvik, J. G. (2009). A randomized trial of vertebroplasty for osteoporotic spinal fractures. *New England Journal of Medicine, 361*(6), 569–579; Goetz, C. G., Wuu, J., McDermott, M. P., Adler, C. H., Fahn, S., Freed, C. R., . . . Leurgans, S. (2008). Placebo response in Parkinson's disease: Comparisons among 11 trials covering medical and surgical interventions. *Movement Disorders, 23*, 690–699.

7 Wager, T. D., Rilling, J. K., Smith, E. E., Sokolik, A., Casey, K. L., Davidson, R. J., . . . Cohen, J. D. (2004). Placebo-induced changes in fMRI in the anticipation and experience of pain. *Science, 303*(5661), 1162–1167.

8 Tinnermann, A., Geuter, S., Sprenger, C., Finsterbusch, J., & Büchel, C. (2017). Interactions between brain and spinal cord mediate value effects in nocebo hyperalgesia. *Science, 358*(6359), 105–108.

9 Crum, A. J., Corbin, W. R., Brownell, K. D., & Salovey, P. (2011). Mind over milkshakes: Mindsets, not just nutrients, determine ghrelin response. *Health Psychology, 30*(4), 424–429.

10 Crum, A. J., & Langer, E. J. (2007). Mind-set matters: Exercise and the placebo effect. *Psychological Science, 18*(2), 165–171.

11 Keller, A., Litzelman, K., Wisk, L. E., Maddox, T., Cheng, E. R., Creswell, P. D., & Witt, W. P. (2012). Does the perception that stress affects health matter? The association with health and mortality. *Health Psychology, 31*(5), 677–684.

12 Nabi, H., Kivimäki, M., Batty, G. D., Shipley, M. J., Britton, A., Brunner, E. J., . . . Singh-Manoux, A. (2013). Increased risk of coronary heart

disease among individuals reporting adverse impact of stress on their health: The Whitehall II prospective cohort study. *European Heart Journal, 34*, 2697–2705.

[13] Scheier, M. E., & Carver, C. S. (1987). Dispositional optimism and physical well-being: The influence of generalized outcome expectancies on health. *Journal of Personality, 55*, 169–210; Scheier, M. F., & Carver, C. S. (1992). Effects of optimism on psychological and physical well-being: Theoretical overview and empirical update. *Cognitive Therapy and Research, 16*(2), 201–228.

[14] De Moor, J. S., De Moor, C. A., Basen-Engquist, K., Kudelka, A., Bevers, M. W., & Cohen, L. (2006). Optimism, distress, health-related quality of life, and change in cancer antigen 125 among patients with ovarian cancer undergoing chemotherapy. *Psychosomatic Medicine, 68*(4), 555–562.

[15] Segerstrom, S. C., Taylor, S. E., Kemeny, M. E., & Fahey, J. L. (1998). Optimism is associated with mood, coping, and immune change in response to stress. *Journal of Personality and Social Psychology, 74*(6), 1646–1655; Taylor, S. E., Burklund, L. J., Eisenberger, N. I., Lehman, B. J., Hilmert, C. J., & Lieberman, M. D. (2008). Neural bases of moderation of cortisol stress responses by psychosocial resources. *Journal of Personality and Social Psychology, 95*(1), 197–211; Tugade, M. M., & Fredrickson, B. L. (2004). Resilient individuals use positive emotions to bounce back from negative emotional experiences. *Journal of Personality and Social Psychology, 86*(2), 320–333.

[16] Cohen, S., Alper, C. M., Doyle, W. J., Treanor, J. J., & Turner, R. B. (2006). Positive emotional style predicts resistance to illness after experimental exposure to rhinovirus or influenza A virus. *Psychosomatic Medicine, 68*(6), 809–815.

[17] Crum, A. J., Salovey, P., & Achor, S. (2013). Rethinking stress: The role of mindsets in determining the stress response. *Journal of personality and social psychology, 104*(4), 716-733.

[18] Ewart, C. K., Harris, W. L., Iwata, M. M., Coates, T. J., Bullock, R., & Simon, B. (1987). Feasibility and effectiveness of school-based relaxation in lowering blood pressure. *Health Psychology, 6*(5), 399–416.

[19] Seppälä, E. M., Nitschke, J. B., Tudorascu, D. L., Hayes, A., Goldstein, M. R., Nguyen, D. T. H., . . . Davidson, R. J. (2014). Breathing-based meditation decreases posttraumatic stress disorder symptoms in U.S. military veterans: A randomized controlled longitudinal study. *Journal of Traumatic Stress, 27*, 397–405.

[20] Blumenthal, J. A., Sherwood, A., Smith, P. J., Watkins, L., Mabe, S., Kraus, W. E., . . . Hinderliter, A. (2016). Enhancing cardiac rehabilitation with stress management training: A randomized clinical efficacy trial. *Circulation, 133*(14), 1341–1350; Stagl, J. M., Bouchard, L. C., Lechner,

262 THE POSITIVE SHIFT

S. C., Blomberg, B. B., Gudenkauf, L. M., Jutagir, D. R., . . . Antoni, M. H. (2015). Long-term psychological benefits of cognitive-behavioral stress management for women with breast cancer: 11-year follow-up of a randomized controlled trial. *Cancer, 121*(11), 1873–1881.

[21] Hemenover, S. H. (2001). Self-reported processing bias and naturally occurring mood: Mediators between personality and stress appraisals. *Personality and Social Psychology Bulletin, 27*(4), 387–394.

[22] Troy, A. S., Wilhelm, F. H., Shallcross, A. J., & Mauss, I. B. (2010). Seeing the silver lining: Cognitive reappraisal ability moderates the relationship between stress and depressive symptoms. *Emotion, 10*(6), 783–795.

[23] Jamieson, J. P., Peters, B. J., Greenwood, E. J., & Altose, A. (2016). Reappraising stress arousal improves performance and reduces evaluation anxiety in classroom exam situations. *Social Psychological and Personality Science, 7*(6), 579–587.

[24] Crum, A. J., Salovey, P., & Achor, S. (2013). Rethinking stress: The role of mindsets in determining the stress response. *Journal of Personality and Social Psychology, 104*(4), 716–733.

[25] Allen, A. B., & Leary, M. R. (2010). Self-compassion, stress, and coping. *Social and Personality Psychology Compass, 4*(2), 107–118.

[26] Breines, J. G., Thoma, M. V., Gianferante, D., Hanlin, L., Chen, X., & Rohleder, N. (2014). Self-compassion as a predictor of interleukin-6 response to acute psychosocial stress. *Brain, Behavior, and Immunity, 37*, 109–114.

CHAPTER 3—OLDER ADULTS ARE WISE, NOT FORGETFUL: MINDSET AFFECTS MEMORY

[1] Kennedy, P. (2017, April 7). To be a genius, think like a 94-year-old. *New York Times*. Retrieved from https://www.nytimes.com/2017/04/07/opinion/sunday/to-be-a-genius-think-like-a-94-year-old.html

[2] Hartshorne, J. K., & Germine, L. T. (2015). When does cognitive functioning peak? The asynchronous rise and fall of different cognitive abilities across the lifespan. *Psychological Science, 26*(4), 433–443.

[3] Li, Y., Baldassi, M., Johnson, E. J., & Weber, E. U. (2013). Complementary cognitive capabilities, economic decision-making, and aging. *Psychology and Aging, 28*(3), 595–613.

[4] Hess, T. M., Auman, C., Colcombe, S. J., & Rahhal, T. A. (2003). The impact of stereotype threat on age differences in memory performance.

Journals of Gerontology, Series B: Psychological Sciences and Social Sciences, 58(1), P3–P11.

5 Rahhal, T. A., Hasher, L., & Colcombe, S. J. (2001). Instructional manipulations and age differences in memory: Now you see them, now you don't. *Psychology and Aging, 16*(4), 697–706.

6 Haslam, C., Morton, T. A., Haslam, S. A., Varnes, L., Graham, R., & Gamaz, L. (2012). "When the age is in, the wit is out": Age-related self-categorization and deficit expectations reduce performance on clinical tests used in dementia assessment. *Psychology and Aging, 27*(3), 778–784.

7 Wu, S. (2013, July 1). Aging stereotypes can hurt older adults' memory. *USC News*. Retrieved from https://news.usc.edu/52707/aging-stereotypes-can-hurt-older-adults-memory/

8 Levy, B. (1996). Improving memory in old age through implicit self-stereotyping. *Journal of Personality and Social Psychology, 71*(6), 1092–1107.

9 Hughes, M. L., Geraci, L., & De Forrest, R. L. (2013). Aging 5 years in 5 minutes: The effect of taking a memory test on older adults' subjective age. *Psychological Science, 24*(12), 2481–2488.

10 Levy, B. R., Zonderman, A. B., Slade, M. D., & Ferrucci, L. (2012). Memory shaped by age stereotypes over time. *Journals of Gerontology, Series B: Psychological Sciences and Social Sciences, 67*(4), 432–436.

11 Levy, B., & Langer, E. (1994). Aging free from negative stereotypes: Successful memory in China among the American deaf. *Journal of Personality and Social Psychology, 66*(6), 989–997.

12 Goodwin, J. (2010, April 5). With age comes wisdom: Study. HealingWell.com. Retrieved from http://news.healingwell.com/index.php?p=news1&id=637723

13 Burzynska, A. Z., Jiao, Y., Knecht, A. M., Fanning, J., Awick, E. A., Chen, T., . . . Kramer, A. F. (2017). White matter integrity declined over 6-months, but dance intervention improved integrity of the fornix of older adults. *Frontiers in Aging Neuroscience, 9*, 59.

14 Park, D. C., Lodi-Smith, J., Drew, L., Haber, S., Hebrank, A., Bischof, G. N., & Aamodt, W. (2014). The impact of sustained engagement on cognitive function in older adults: The Synapse Project. *Psychological Science, 25*(1), 103–112.

15 Barber, S. J., & Mather, M. (2013). Stereotype threat can enhance, as well as impair, older adults' memory. *Psychological Science, 24*(12), 2522–2529.

16 Robertson, D. A., & Weiss, D. (2017). In the eye of the beholder: Can counter-stereotypes change perceptions of older adults' social status? *Psychology and Aging, 32*(6), 531–542.

[17] Whitbourne, S. K. (2012, January 28). 15 wise and inspiring quotes about aging. *Psychology Today*. Retrieved from https://www.psychologytoday.com/us/blog/fulfillment-any-age/201201/15-wise-and-inspiring-quotes-about-aging

CHAPTER 4—SECRETS OF CENTENARIANS: MINDSET AFFECTS LONGEVITY

[1] Frankl, V. E. (1984). *Man's search for meaning: An introduction to logotherapy*. New York: Simon & Schuster.

[2] Hill, P. L., & Turiano, N. A. (2014). Purpose in life as a predictor of mortality across adulthood. *Psychological Science, 25*(7), 1482–1486.

[3] Buettner, D. (2012, October 24). The island where people forget to die. *New York Times*. Retrieved from https://www.nytimes.com/2012/10/28/magazine/the-island-where-people-forget-to-die.html

[4] Cavallini, E., Bottiroli, S., Fastame, M. C., & Hertzog, C. (2013). Age and subcultural differences on personal and general beliefs about memory. *Journal of Aging Studies, 27*(1), 71–81.

[5] Buettner, D. (2008). *Blue zones* (p. 180). Washington, DC: National Geographic Society.

[6] Levy, B. R., Zonderman, A. B., Slade, M. D., & Ferrucci, L. (2009). Age stereotypes held earlier in life predict cardiovascular events in later life. *Psychological Science, 20*(3), 296–298.

[7] Levy, B. R., Slade, M. D., Murphy, T. E., & Gill, T. M. (2012). Association between positive age stereotypes and recovery from disability in older persons. *Journal of the American Medical Association, 308*(19), 1972–1973; Segel-Karpas, D., Palgi, Y., & Shrira, A. (2017). The reciprocal relationship between depression and physical morbidity: The role of subjective age. *Health Psychology, 36*(9), 848–851.

[8] Bellingtier, J. A., & Neupert, S. D. (2016). Negative aging attitudes predict greater reactivity to daily stressors in older adults. *Journals of Gerontology, Series B: Psychological Sciences and Social Sciences*, gbw086.

[9] Levy, B. R., & Bavishi, A. (2016). Survival advantage mechanism: Inflammation as a mediator of positive self-perceptions of aging on longevity. *Journals of Gerontology, Series B: Psychological Sciences and Social Sciences*, gbw035.

[10] Levy, B. R., Slade, M. D., Kunkel, S. R., & Kasl, S. V. (2002). Longevity increased by positive self-perceptions of aging. *Journal of Personality and Social Psychology, 83*(2), 261–270.

[11] Stephan, Y., Sutin, A. R., & Terracciano, A. (2016). Feeling older and risk of hospitalization: Evidence from three longitudinal cohorts. *Health Psychology, 35*(6), 634–637.

[12] Zahrt, O. H., & Crum, A. J. (2017). Perceived physical activity and mortality: Evidence from three nationally representative U.S. samples. *Health Psychology, 36*(11), 1017–1025.

[13] Frey, B. S. (2011). Happy people live longer. *Science, 4, Feb*, 542–543; Kim, E. S., Hagan, K. A., Grodstein, F., DeMeo, D. L., De Vivo, I., & Kubzansky, L. D. (2017). Optimism and cause-specific mortality: A prospective cohort study. *American Journal of Epidemiology, 185*(1), 21–29; Terracciano, A., Löckenhoff, C. E., Zonderman, A. B., Ferrucci, L., & Costa, P. T., Jr. (2008). Personality predictors of longevity: Activity, emotional stability, and conscientiousness. *Psychosomatic Medicine, 70*(6), 621–627.

[14] Danner, D. D., Snowdon, D. A., & Friesen, W. V. (2001). Positive emotions in early life and longevity: Findings from the nun study. *Journal of Personality and Social Psychology, 80*(5), 804–813; Pressman, S. D., & Cohen, S. (2012). Positive emotion word use and longevity in famous deceased psychologists. *Health Psychology, 31*(3), 297–305.

[15] Giltay, E. J., Geleijnse, J. M., Zitman, F. G., Hoekstra, T., & Schouten, E. G. (2004). Dispositional optimism and all-cause and cardiovascular mortality in a prospective cohort of elderly Dutch men and women. *Archives of General Psychiatry, 61*(11), 1126–1135.

[16] Maruta, T., Colligan, R. C., Malinchoc, M., & Offord, K. P. (2000). Optimists vs. pessimists: Survival rate among medical patients over a 30-year period. *Mayo Clinic Proceedings, 75*(2), 140–143.

[17] Reece, T. (2015, December 24). 10 habits of people who've lived to be 100. *Prevention.* Retrieved from https://www.prevention.com/life/a20492770/z-redirected-10-habits-of-people-whove-lived-to-be-100/

[18] Novotny, P., Colligan, R. C., Szydlo, D. W., Clark, M. M., Rausch, S., Wampfler, J., . . . Yang, P. (2010). A pessimistic explanatory style is prognostic for poor lung cancer survival. *Journal of Thoracic Oncology, 5*(3), 326–332.

[19] Abel, E. L., & Kruger, M. L. (2010). Smile intensity in photographs predicts longevity. *Psychological Science, 21*(4), 542–544.

[20] Kraft, T. L., & Pressman, S. D. (2012). Grin and bear it: The influence of manipulated facial expression on the stress response. *Psychological Science, 23*(11), 1372–1378.

[21] Goldstein, E. (2009, September 21). Living without joy? Thich Nhat Hanh shares a secret. *PsychCentral* (blog). Retrieved from https://blogs.

psychcentral.com/mindfulness/2009/09/living-without-joy-thich-nhat-hanh-shares-a-secret/

[22] Sarkisian, C. A., Prohaska, T. R., Davis, C., & Weiner, B. (2007). Pilot test of an attribution retraining intervention to raise walking levels in sedentary older adults. *Journal of the American Geriatrics Society, 55,* 1842–1846.

[23] Jakubiak, B. K., & Feeney, B. C. (2016). Daily goal progress is facilitated by spousal support and promotes psychological, physical, and relational well-being throughout adulthood. *Journal of Personality and Social Psychology, 111*(3), 317–340.

[24] Sagi-Schwartz, A., Bakermans-Kranenburg, M. J., Linn, S., & van IJzendoorn, M. H. (2013). Against all odds: Genocidal trauma is associated with longer life-expectancy of the survivors. *PLOS One 8*(7): e69179.

CHAPTER 5—ARE YOU TIGGER OR EEYORE: PERSONALITY MATTERS

[1] Freud, S. (2013). *The interpretation of dreams* (A. A. Brill, Trans.). New York: Macmillan. (Original work published 1899)

[2] Carver, C. S., Pozo, C., Harris, S. D., Noriega, V., Scheier, M. F., Robinson, D. S., . . . Clark, K. C. (1993). How coping mediates the effect of optimism on distress: A study of women with early stage breast cancer. *Journal of Personality and Social Psychology, 65*(2), 375–390; Ong, A. D., Bergeman, C. S., Bisconti, T. L., & Wallace, K. A. (2006). Psychological resilience, positive emotions, and successful adaptation to stress in later life. *Journal of Personality and Social Psychology, 91*(4), 730–749; Tugade, M. M., & Fredrickson, B. L. (2004). Resilient individuals use positive emotions to bounce back from negative emotional experiences. *Journal of Personality and Social Psychology, 86*(2), 320–333.

[3] Vieselmeyer, J., Holguin, J., & Mezulis, A. (2017). The role of resilience and gratitude in posttraumatic stress and growth following a campus shooting. *Psychological Trauma: Theory, Research, Practice, and Policy, 9*(1), 62–69.

[4] Jackson, L. (n.d.). Your health and emotions. *Mountain Express Magazine.* http://mountainexpressmagazine.com/your-health-and-emotions/

[5] Scheier, M. F., Matthews, K. A., Owens, J. F., Magovern, G. J., Lefebvre, R. C., Abbott, R. A., & Carver, C. S. (1989). Dispositional optimism and recovery from coronary artery bypass surgery: The beneficial effects on physical and psychological well-being. *Journal of Personality and Social Psychology, 57*(6), 1024–1040.

[6] Mandela, N. (1994). *Long walk to freedom: The autobiography of Nelson Mandela.* Boston: Little, Brown.

[7] Brissette, I., Scheier, M. F., & Carver, C. S. (2002). The role of optimism in social network development, coping, and psychological adjustment during a life transition. *Journal of Personality and Social Psychology, 82*(1), 102–111.

[8] Chan, C. S., Lowe, S. R., Weber, E., & Rhodes, J. E. (2015). The contribution of pre- and postdisaster social support to short and long term mental health after Hurricanes Katrina: A longitudinal study of low-income survivors. *Social Science & Medicine, 138*, 38–43; McDonough, M. H., Sabiston, C. M., & Wrosch, C. (2014). Predicting changes in posttraumatic growth and subjective well-being among breast cancer survivors: The role of social support and stress. *Psycho-Oncology, 23*(1), 114–120; Paul, L. A., Felton, J. W., Adams, Z. W., Welsh, K., Miller, S., & Ruggiero, K. J. (2015). Mental health among adolescents exposed to a tornado: The influence of social support and its interactions with sociodemographic characteristics and disaster exposure. *Journal of Traumatic Stress, 28*(3), 232–239.

[9] Murray, S. L., Rose, P., Bellavia, G. M., Holmes, J. G., & Kusche, A. G. (2002). When rejection stings: How self-esteem constrains relationship-enhancement processes. *Journal of Personality and Social Psychology, 83*(3), 556–573.

[10] Pausch, R., & Zaslow, J. (2008). *The last lecture.* New York: Hyperion.

[11] Nolen-Hoeksema, S., & Morrow, J. (1991). A prospective study of depression and posttraumatic stress symptoms after a natural disaster: The 1989 Loma Prieta earthquake. *Journal of Personality and Social Psychology, 61*(1), 115–121.

[12] Nolen-Hoeksema, S., Parker, L. E., & Larson, J. (1994). Ruminative coping with depressed mood following loss. *Journal of Personality and Social Psychology, 67*(1), 92–104.

[13] Nolen-Hoeksema, S. (1991). Responses to depression and their effects on the duration of depressive episodes. *Journal of Abnormal Psychology, 100*(4), 569–582.

[14] Dupont, A., Bower, J. E., Stanton, A. L., & Ganz, P. A. (2014). Cancer-related intrusive thoughts predict behavioral symptoms following breast cancer treatment. *Health Psychology, 33*(2), 155–163.

[15] Joormann, J. (2011, June 2). Depression and negative thoughts. *Association for Psychological Science.* Retrieved from https://www.psychologicalscience.org/news/releases/depression-and-negative-thoughts.html

[16] Archontaki, D., Lewis, G. J., & Bates, T. C. (2013). Genetic influences on psychological well-being: A nationally representative twin study. *Journal of Personality, 81*, 221–230.

[17] Caspi, A., Sugden, K., Moffitt, T. E., Taylor, A., Craig, I. W., Harrington, H., . . . Poulton, R. (2003). Influence of life stress on depression: Moderation by a polymorphism in the 5-HTT gene. *Science,* 18 Jul, 386–389.

[18] Brooks, A. C. (2015, July 25). We need optimists. *New York Times*. Retrieved from https://www.nytimes.com/2015/07/26/opinion/sunday/arthur-c-brooks-we-need-optimists.html

[19] Fritz, H. L., Russek, L. N., & Dillon, M. M. (2017). Humor use moderates the relation of stressful life events with psychological distress. *Personality and Social Psychology Bulletin, 43*(6), 845–859.

[20] Ford, B. Q., Lam, P., John, O. P., & Mauss, I. B. (2018). The psychological health benefits of accepting negative emotions and thoughts: Laboratory, diary, and longitudinal evidence. *Journal of Personality and Social Psychology*. Advance online publication. doi: 10.1037/pspp0000157.

[21] Baer, R. A., Smith, G. T., Hopkins, J., Krietemeyer, J., & Toney, L. (2006). Using self-report assessment methods to explore facets of mindfulness. *Assessment, 13*(1), 27–45.

[22] Anwar, Y. (2017, August 10). Feeling bad about feeling bad can make you feel worse. *Berkeley News*. Retrieved from http://news.berkeley.edu/2017/08/10/emotionalacceptance/

[23] Fowler, J. H., & Christakis, N. A. (2008). Dynamic spread of happiness in a large social network: Longitudinal analysis over 20 years in the Framingham Heart Study. *The BMJ, 337*, a2338.

[24] Coviello, L., Sohn, Y., Kramer, A. D. I., Marlow, C., Franceschetti, M., Christakis, N. A., & Fowler, J. H. (2014). Detecting emotional contagion in massive social networks. *PLOS One 9*(3): e90315.

CHAPTER 6–"COMPARISON IS THE THIEF OF JOY": ENVIRONMENT MATTERS

[1] Card, D., Mas, A., Moretti, E., & Saez, E (2012). Inequality at work: The effect of peer salaries on job satisfaction. *American Economic Review, 102*(6), 2981–3003.

[2] Dachis, A. (2013, May 10). Comparison is the thief of joy. *Lifehacker* (blog). Retrieved from https://lifehacker.com/comparison-is-the-thief-of-joy-499152017

[3] Solnick, S. J., & Hemenway, D. (1998). Is more always better?: A survey on positional concerns. *Journal of Economic Behavior & Organization, 37*(3), 373–383.

[4] Zhang, J. W., Howell, R. T., & Howell, C. J. (2014). Living in wealthy neighborhoods increases material desires and maladaptive consumption. *Journal of Consumer Culture, 16*(1), 297–316.

5 Tay, L., Morrison, M., & Diener, E. (2014). Living among the affluent: Boon or bane? *Psychological Science, 25*, 1235–1241.

6 Stephens-Davidowitz, S. (2017, May 6). Don't let Facebook make you miserable. *New York Times.* Retrieved from https://www.nytimes.com/2017/05/06/opinion/sunday/dont-let-facebook-make-you-miserable.html

7 Chekhov, A. (1979). Gooseberries. In R. E. Matlaw (ed.). *Anton Chekhov's short stories* (pp. 185–193). New York: W. W. Norton. (Original work published 1898)

8 Jordan, A. H., Monin, B., Dweck, C. S., Lovett, B. J., John, O. P., & Gross, J. J. (2011). Misery has more company than people think: Underestimating the prevalence of others' negative emotions. *Personality & Social Psychology Bulletin, 37*(1), 120–135.

9 Haushofer, J. (2016). CV of failures. Retrieved from https://www.princeton.edu/~joha/Johannes_Haushofer_CV_of_Failures.pdf

10 Lamott, A. (2017, June 9). 12 truths I learned from life and writing [Transcript of video file]. TED Talks. Retrieved from https://www.ted.com/talks/anne_lamott_12_truths_i_learned_from_life_and_writing/transcript?language=en

11 Kraut, R., Patterson, M., Lundmark, V., Kiesler, S., Mukophadhyay, T., & Scherlis, W. (1998). Internet paradox: A social technology that reduces social involvement and psychological well-being? *American Psychologist, 53*(9), 1017–1031.

12 Huang, C. (2010). Internet use and psychological well-being: A meta-analysis. *Cyberpsychology, Behavior, and Social Networking, 13*(3), 241–249.

13 Song, H., Zmyslinski-Seelig, A., Kim, J., Drent, A., Victor, A., Omori, K., & Allen, M. (2014). Does Facebook make you lonely?: A meta analysis. *Computers in Human Behavior, 36*, 446–452.

14 Kross, E., Verduyn, P., Demiralp, E., Park, J., Lee, D. S., Lin, N., . . . Ybarra, O. (2013). Facebook use predicts declines in subjective well-being in young adults. *PLOS One, 8*(8), e69841.

15 Twenge, J. M., Joiner, T. E., Rogers, M. L., & Martin, G. N. (2017). Increases in depressive symptoms, suicide-related outcomes, and suicide rates among U.S. adolescents after 2010 and links to increased new media screen time. *Clinical Psychological Science, 6*(1), 3–17.

16 Shakya, H. B., & Christakis, N. A. (2017). Association of Facebook use with compromised well-being: A longitudinal study. *American Journal of Epidemiology, 185*(3), 203–211.

[17] Schwartz, B., Ward, A., Monterosso, J., Lyubomirsky, S., White, K., & Lehman, D. R. (2002). Maximizing versus satisficing: Happiness is a matter of choice. *Journal of Personality and Social Psychology, 83*(5), 1178–1197.

[18] Gibbons, F. X., & Buunk, B. P. (1999). Individual differences in social comparison: Development of a scale of social comparison orientation. *Journal of Personality and Social Psychology, 76*(1), 129–142.

[19] Borgonovi, F. (2008). Doing well by doing good. The relationship between formal volunteering and self-reported health and happiness. *Social Science & Medicine, 66*(11), 2321–2334.

[20] Epictetus (1865). *The Works of Epictetus. Consisting of His Discourses, in Four Books, The Enchiridion, and Fragments* (T. W. Higginson, Ed., & E. Carter, Trans.). Boston: Little, Brown.

[21] Emmons, R. A., & McCullough, M. E. (2003). Counting blessings versus burdens: An experimental investigation of gratitude and subjective well-being in daily life. *Journal of Personality and Social Psychology, 84*(2), 377–389.

[22] Otto, A. K., Szczesny, E. C., Soriano, E. C., Laurenceau, J.-P., & Siegel, S. D. (2016). Effects of a randomized gratitude intervention on death-related fear of recurrence in breast cancer survivors. *Health Psychology, 35*(12), 1320–1328.

[23] Krieger, L. S., & Sheldon, K. M. (2015). What makes lawyers happy?: A data-driven prescription to redefine professional success. *George Washington Law Review, 83*(2), 554–627.

CHAPTER 7—EMBRACE
ADVERSITY: TRAUMA MATTERS

[1] Rigoglioso, M. (2014, February 5). BJ Miller '93: Wounded healer. *Princeton Alumni Weekly*. Retrieved from https://paw.princeton.edu/article/bj-miller-%E2%80%9993-wounded-healer

[2] Galanes, P. (2017, May 13). Sheryl Sandberg and Elizabeth Alexander on love, loss and what comes next. *New York Times*. Retrieved from https://www.nytimes.com/2017/05/13/fashion/sheryl-sandberg-and-elizabeth-alexander-on-love-loss-and-what-comes-next.html

[3] Cann, A., Calhoun, L. G., Tedeschi, R. G., Taku, K., Vishnevsky, T., Triplett, K. N., & Danhauer, S. C. (2010). A short form of the posttraumatic growth inventory. *Anxiety, Stress & Coping, 23*(2), 127–137.

[4] Carver, C. S., & Antoni, M. H. (2004). Finding benefit in breast cancer during the year after diagnosis predicts better adjustment 5 to 8 years after diagnosis. *Health Psychology, 23*(6), 595–598; Rinaldis, M., Pakenham, K. I., & Lynch, B. M. (2010). Relationships between quality of life and finding

benefits in a diagnosis of colorectal cancer. *British Journal of Psychology, 101,* 259–275; Wang, A. W.-T., Chang, C.-S., Chen, S.-T., Chen, D.-R., Fan, F., Carver, C. S., & Hsu, W.-Y. (2017). Buffering and direct effect of posttraumatic growth in predicting distress following cancer. *Health Psychology, 36*(6), 549–559.

5 Rassart, J., Luyckx, K., Berg, C. A., Oris, L., & Wiebe, D. J. (2017). Longitudinal trajectories of benefit finding in adolescents with type 1 diabetes. *Health Psychology, 36*(10), 977–986.

6 Lieber, R. (2017, March 19). Basing life on what you can afford. *New York Times.* Retrieved from https://www.nytimes.com/2017/03/19/your-money/budget-what-you-can-afford.html

7 Levitt, S. (2014, February 24). The science of post-traumatic growth. *Live Happy.* Retrieved from https://www.livehappy.com/science/positive-psychology/science-post-traumatic-growth

8 Croft, A., Dunn, E.W., & Quoidbach, J. (2014). From tribulations to appreciation: Experiencing adversity in the past predicts greater savoring in the present. *Social Psychological and Personality Science, 5,* 511–516.

9 Carstensen, L. L., Turan, B., Scheibe, S., Ram, N., Ersner-Hershfield, H., Samanez-Larkin, G. R., . . . Nesselroade, J. R. (2011). Emotional experience improves with age: Evidence based on over 10 years of experience sampling. *Psychology and Aging, 26*(1), 21–33.

10 Thomas, M. L., Kaufmann, C. N., Palmer, B. W., Depp, C. A., Martin, A. S., Glorioso, D. K., . . . Jeste, D. V. (2016). Paradoxical trend for improvement in mental health with aging: A community-based study of 1,546 adults aged 21–100 years. *Journal of Clinical Psychiatry, 77*(8), e1019–e1025.

11 LaFee, S. (2016, August 24). Graying but grinning: Despite physical ailments, older adults happier. UC San Diego News Center. Retrieved from https://ucsdnews.ucsd.edu/pressrelease/graying_but_grinning_despite_physical_ailments_older_adults_happier

12 Mather, M., & Carstensen, L. L. (2005). Aging and motivated cognition: The positivity effect in attention and memory. *Trends in Cognitive Sciences, 9,* 496–502.

13 Williams, L. M., Brown, K. J., Palmer, D., Liddell, B. J., Kemp, A. H., Olivieri, G., . . . Gordon, E. (2006). The mellow years?: Neural basis of improving emotional stability over age. *Journal of Neuroscience, 26*(24), 6422–6430.

14 Addis, D. R., Leclerc, C. M., Muscatell, K. A., & Kensinger, E. A. (2010). There are age-related changes in neural connectivity during the encoding of positive, but not negative, information. *Cortex, 46*(4), 425–433.

[15] Mallozzi, V. M. (2017, August 11). She's 98. He's 94. They met at the gym. *New York Times*. Retrieved from https://www.nytimes.com/2017/08/11/fashion/weddings/senior-citizen-older-couple-wedding.html

[16] Hoerger, M., Chapman, B. P., Prigerson, H. G., Fagerlin, A., Mohile, S. G., Epstein, R. M., . . . Duberstein, P. R. (2014). Personality change pre- to post-loss in spousal caregivers of patients with terminal lung cancer. *Social Psychological and Personality Science, 5*(6), 722–729.

[17] Lim, D., & DeSteno, D. (2016). Suffering and compassion: The links among adverse life experiences, empathy, compassion, and prosocial behavior. *Emotion, 16*(2), 175–182.

[18] Hayhurst, J., Hunter, J. A., Kafka, S., & Boyes, M. (2015). Enhancing resilience in youth through a 10-day developmental voyage. *Journal of Adventure Education and Outdoor Learning, 15*(1), 40–52.

[19] Seery, M. D., Holman, E. A., & Silver, R. C. (2010). Whatever does not kill us: Cumulative lifetime adversity, vulnerability, and resilience. *Journal of Personality and Social Psychology, 99*(6), 1025–1041.

[20] Wade, J. B., Hart, R. P., Wade, J. H., Bekenstein, J., Ham, C., & Bajaj, J. S. (2016). Does the death of a spouse increase subjective well-being: An assessment in a population of adults with neurological illness. *Healthy Aging Research, 5*(1), 1–9.

[21] Carey, B. (2011, January 3). On road to recovery, past adversity provides a map. *New York Times*. Retrieved from https://www.nytimes.com/2011/01/04/health/04mind.html

[22] Talbot, M. (2013, October 21). Gone girl. *New Yorker*. Retrieved from https://www.newyorker.com/magazine/2013/10/21/gone-girl-2

[23] Rilke, R. M. (2005). *Rilke's book of hours: Love poems to God* (A. Barrows & J. Macy, Eds.). New York: Riverhead Books.

[24] Diener, E., & Diener, C. (1996). Most people are happy. *Psychological Science, 7*(3), 181–184.

[25] Sheryl Sandberg's 2016 commencement address at University of California, Berkeley. (2016, May 14). *Los Angeles Times*. Retrieved from http://www.latimes.com/local/california/la-sheryl-sandberg-commencement-address-transcript-20160514-story.html

[26] Sikkema, K. J., Hansen, N. B., Ghebremichael, M., Kochman, A., Tarakeshwar, N., Meade, C. S., & Zhang, H. (2006). A randomized controlled trial of a coping group intervention for adults with HIV who are AIDS bereaved: Longitudinal effects on grief. *Health Psychology, 25*(5), 563–570.

[27] Mancini, A. D., Littleton, H. L., & Grills, A. E. (2016). Can people benefit from acute stress? Social support, psychological improvement, and

resilience after the Virginia Tech campus shootings. *Clinical Psychological Science, 4*(3), 401–417.

[28] Becker, H. A. (n.d.). This grieving mom donated 92 gallons of breastmilk in her stillborn's honor. *Parents*. Retrieved from https://www.parents.com/baby/all-about-babies/this-grieving-mom-donated-92-gallons-of-breastmilk-in-her-stillborns-honor/

[29] Egan, N. W. (2018, April 19). How the Krims found love and healing after their children were murdered. *People*. Retrieved from https://people.com/crime/how-the-krims-found-love-and-healing-after-their-children-were-murdered/

CHAPTER 8—CHANGE YOUR BEHAVIOR AND YOUR MINDSET WILL FOLLOW

[1] Pergament, K. I. (1997). *The psychology of religion and coping: Theory, research, practice.* London: Guilford.

[2] McCarthy, J., & Brown, A. (2015, March 2). Getting more sleep linked to higher well-being. Gallup. Retrieved from http://news.gallup.com/poll/181583/getting-sleep-linked-higher.aspx

[3] Tang, N. K. Y., Fiecas, M., Afolalu, E. F., & Wolke, D. (2017). Changes in sleep duration, quality, and medication use are prospectively associated with health and well-being: Analysis of the UK household longitudinal study. *Sleep, 40*(3).

[4] Steptoe, A., O'Donnell, K., Marmot, M., & Wardle, J. (2008). Positive affect, psychological well-being, and good sleep. *Journal of Psychosomatic Research, 64*(4), 409–415.

[5] Nota, J. A., & Coles, M. E. (2018). Shorter sleep duration and longer sleep onset latency are related to difficulty disengaging attention from negative emotional images in individuals with elevated transdiagnostic repetitive negative thinking. *Journal of Behavior Therapy and Experimental Psychiatry, 58*, 114–122; Nota, J. A., & Coles, M. E. (2015). Duration and timing of sleep are associated with repetitive negative thinking. *Cognitive Therapy and Research, 39*(2), 253–256; Vargas, I., Drake, C. L., & Lopez-Duran, N. L. (2017). Insomnia symptom severity modulates the impact of sleep deprivation on attentional biases to emotional information. *Cognitive Therapy and Research, 41*(6), 842–852.

[6] Jike, M., Itani, O., Watanabe, N., Buysse, D. J., & Kaneita, Y. (2018). Long sleep duration and health outcomes: A systematic review, meta-analysis and meta-regression. *Sleep Medicine Reviews, 39*, 25–36; Redeker, N. S., Ruggiero, J. S., & Hedges, C. (2004). Sleep is related to physical function and emotional well-being after cardiac surgery. *Nursing Research, 53*(3), 154–162.

[7] Prather, A. A., Janicki-Deverts, D., Hall, M. H., & Cohen, S. (2015). Behaviorally assessed sleep and susceptibility to the common cold. *Sleep*, *38*(9), 1353–1359.

[8] Potter, L. M., & Weiler, N. (2015, August 31). Sleep deprived? Expect to get sick too. *University of California News*. Retrieved from https://www.universityofcalifornia.edu/news/sleep-deprived-get-sick-more-often

[9] Gabriel, S., & Young, A. F. (2011). Becoming a vampire without being bitten: The narrative collective-assimilation hypothesis. *Psychological Science*, *22*(8), 990–994.

[10] Kidd, D. C., & Castano, E. (2013, October 18). Reading literary fiction improves theory of mind. *Science*, 377–380.

[11] Vezzali, L., Stathi, S., Giovannini, D., Capozza, D., & Trifiletti, E. (2015). The greatest magic of Harry Potter: Reducing prejudice. *Journal of Applied Social Psychology*, *45*(2), 105–121.

[12] Johnson, D. (2016, July 21). Reading fictional novels can make you more empathetic. *Science World Report*. Retrieved from https://www.scienceworldreport.com/articles/44162/20160721/reading-fictional-novels-can-make-you-more-empathetic.htm

[13] Bavishi, A., Slade, M. D., & Levy, B. R. (2016). A chapter a day— Association of book reading with longevity. *Social Science & Medicine*, *164*, 44–48.

[14] Forcier, K., Stroud, L. R., Papandonatos, G. D., Hitsman, B., Reiches, M., Krishnamoorthy, J., & Niaura, R. (2006). Links between physical fitness and cardiovascular reactivity and recovery to psychological stressors: A meta-analysis. *Health Psychology*, *25*(6), 723–739; Zschucke, E., Renneberg, B., Dimeo, F., Wüstenberg, T., & Ströhle, A. (2015). The stress-buffering effect of acute exercise: Evidence for HPA axis negative feedback. *Psychoneuroendocrinology*, *51*, 414–425.

[15] Bherer, L., Erickson, K. I., & Liu-Ambrose, T. (2013). A review of the effects of physical activity and exercise on cognitive and brain functions in older adults. *Journal of Aging Research*, *2013*, 657508.

[16] Hsu, C. L., Best, J. R., Davis, J. C., Nagamatsu, L. S., Wang, S., Boyd, L. A., . . . Liu-Ambrose, T. (2018). Aerobic exercise promotes executive functions and impacts functional neural activity among older adults with vascular cognitive impairment. *British Journal of Sports Medicine*, *52*(3), 184–191.

[17] McCann, I. L., & Holmes, D. S. (1984). Influence of aerobic exercise on depression. *Journal of Personality and Social Psychology*, *46*(5), 1142–1147; Mammen, G., & Faulkner, G. (2013). Physical activity and the prevention of depression. *American Journal of Preventive Medicine*, *45*(5), 649–657.

[18] Puterman, E., Weiss, J., Beauchamp, M. R., Mogle, J., & Almeida, D. M. (2017). Physical activity and negative affective reactivity in daily life. *Health Psychology, 36*(12), 1186–1194.

[19] Craft, L. L., & Perna, F. M. (2004). The benefits of exercise for the clinically depressed. *Primary Care Companion to the Journal of Clinical Psychiatry, 6*(3), 104–111; Schuch, F. B., Vancampfort, D., Richards, J., Rosenbaum, S., Ward, P. B., & Stubbs, B. (2016). Exercise as a treatment for depression: A meta-analysis adjusting for publication bias. *Journal of Psychiatric Research, 77*, 42–51.

[20] Blumenthal, J. A., Babyak, M. A., Moore, K. A., Craighead, W. E., Herman, S., Khatri, P., . . . Krishnan, K. R. (1999). Effects of exercise training on older patients with major depression. *Archives of Internal Medicine, 159*(19), 2349–2356.

[21] Diaz, K. M., Howard, V. J., Hutto, B., Colabianchi, N., Vena, J. E., Safford, M. M., . . . Hooker, S. P. (2017). Patterns of sedentary behavior and mortality in U.S. middle-aged and older adults: A national cohort study. *Annals of Internal Medicine, 167*, 465–475.

[22] Blanchflower, D. G., & Oswald, A. J. (2004). Money, sex and happiness: An empirical study. *Scandinavian Journal of Economics, 106*, 393–415.

[23] Loewenstein, G., Krishnamurti, T., Kopsic, J., & McDonald, D. (2015). Does increased sexual frequency enhance happiness? *Journal of Economic Behavior & Organization, 116*, 206–218.

[24] Koenig, H. G., McCullough, M. E., & Larson, D. B. (2001). *Religion and health.* New York: Oxford University Press; VanderWeele, T. J. (2017). Religious communities and human flourishing. *Current Directions in Psychological Science, 26*(5), 476–481.

[25] McCullough, M., Hoyt, W. T., Larson, D. B., Koenig, H. G., & Thoresen, C. (2000). Religious involvement and mortality. *Health Psychology, 19*(3), 211–222.

[26] Contrada, R. J., Goyal, T. M., Cather, C., Rafalson, L., Idler, E. L., & Krause, T. J. (2004). Psychosocial factors in outcomes of heart surgery: The impact of religious involvement and depressive symptoms. *Health Psychology, 23*(3), 227–238.

[27] Li, S., Stampfer, M. J., Williams, D. R., & VanderWeele, T. J. (2016). Association of religious service attendance with mortality among women. *JAMA Internal Medicine, 176*(6), 777–785.

[28] Ai, A. L., Park, C. L., Huang, B., Rodgers, W., & Tice, T. N. (2007). Religious coping styles: A study of short-term psychological distress following cardiac surgery. *Personality and Social Psychology Bulletin, 33*(6), 867–882.

[29] Leeson, L. A., Nelson, A. M., Rathouz, P. J., Juckett, M. B., Coe, C. L., Caes, E. W., & Costanzo, E. S. (2015). Spirituality and the recovery of quality of life following hematopoietic stem cell transplantation. *Health Psychology, 34*(9), 920–928.

[30] Park, C. L., George, L., Aldwin, C. M., Choun, S., Suresh, D. P., & Bliss, D. (2016). Spiritual peace predicts 5-year mortality in congestive heart failure patients. *Health Psychology, 35*(3), 203–210.

[31] Oishi, S., & Diener, E. (2014). Residents of poor nations have a greater sense of meaning in life than residents of wealthy nations. *Psychological Science, 25*(2), 422 –430.

[32] Gu, J., Strauss, C., Bond, R., & Cavanagh, K. (2015). How do mindfulness-based cognitive therapy and mindfulness-based stress reduction improve mental health and wellbeing? A systematic review and meta-analysis of mediation studies. *Clinical Psychology Review, 37*, 1–12; Khoury, B., Sharma, M., Rush, S. E., & Fournier, C. (2015). Mindfulness-based stress reduction for healthy individuals: A meta-analysis. *Journal of Psychosomatic Research, 78*(6), 519–528.

[33] Fredrickson, B. L., Cohn, M. A., Coffey, K. A., Pek, J., & Finkel, S. M. (2008). Open hearts build lives: Positive emotions, induced through loving-kindness meditation, build consequential personal resources. *Journal of Personality and Social Psychology, 95*(5), 1045–1062; Kok, B. E., Coffey, K. A., Cohn, M. A., Catalino, L. I., Vacharkulksemsuk, T., Algoe, S. B., . . . Fredrickson, B. L. (2013). How positive emotions build physical health: Perceived positive social connections account for the upward spiral between positive emotions and vagal tone. *Psychological Science, 24*(7), 1123–1132.

[34] Braden, B. B., Pipe, T. B., Smith, R., Glaspy, T. K., Deatherage, B. R., & Baxter, L. C. (2016). Brain and behavior changes associated with an abbreviated 4-week mindfulness-based stress reduction course in back pain patients. *Brain and Behavior, 6*(3), e00443; Feuille, M., & Pargament, K. (2015). Pain, mindfulness, and spirituality: A randomized controlled trial comparing effects of mindfulness and relaxation on pain-related outcomes in migraineurs. *Journal of Health Psychology, 20*(8), 1090–1106.

[35] Johns, S. A., Brown, L. F., Beck-Coon, K., Monahan, P. O., Tong, Y., & Kroenke, K. (2015). Randomized controlled pilot study of mindfulness-based stress reduction for persistently fatigued cancer survivors. *Psycho-Oncology, 24*(8), 885–893; Lengacher, C. A., Shelton, M. M., Reich, R. R., Barta, M. K., Johnson-Mallard, V., Moscoso, M. S., . . . Lucas, J. (2014). Mindfulness based stress reduction (MBSR(BC)) in breast cancer: Evaluating fear of recurrence (FOR) as a mediator of psychological and physical symptoms in a randomized control trial (RCT). *Journal of Behavioral Medicine, 37*(2), 185–195; Witek-Janusek, L., Albuquerque, K., Chroniak,

K. R., Chroniak, C., Durazo-Arvizu, R., & Mathews, H. L. (2008). Effect of mindfulness based stress reduction on immune function, quality of life and coping in women newly diagnosed with early stage breast cancer. *Brain, Behavior, and Immunity, 22*(6), 969–981.

[36] Barnes, V. A., Kapuku, G. K., & Treiber, F. A. (2012). Impact of transcendental meditation on left ventricular mass in African American adolescents. *Evidence-Based Complementary and Alternative Medicine*, 923153.

[37] Ornish, D., Scherwitz, L. W., Billings, J. H., Gould, K. L., Merritt, T. A., Sparler, S., . . . Brand, R. J. (1998). Intensive lifestyle changes for reversal of coronary heart disease. *Journal of the American Medical Association, 280*(23), 2001–2007.

[38] Jazaieri, H., Lee, I. A., McGonigal, K., Jinpa, T., Doty, J. R., Gross, J. J., & Goldin, P. R. (2016). A wandering mind is a less caring mind: Daily experience sampling during compassion meditation training. *Journal of Positive Psychology, 11*(1), 37–50.

[39] Sweeny, K., & Howell, J. L. (2017). Bracing later and coping better: Benefits of mindfulness during a stressful waiting period. *Personality and Social Psychology Bulletin, 43*(10), 1399–1414.

[40] Hölzel, B. K., Carmody, J., Vangel, M., Congleton, C., Yerramsetti, S. M., Gard, T., & Lazar, S. W. (2011). Mindfulness practice leads to increases in regional brain gray matter density. *Psychiatry Research, 191*(1), 36–43.

[41] Luders, E., Cherbuin, N., & Kurth, F. (2015). Forever young(er): potential age-defying effects of long-term meditation on gray matter atrophy. *Frontiers in Psychology, 5.*

[42] Hoge, E. A., Chen, M. M., Orr, E., Metcalf, C. A., Fischer, L. E., Pollack, M. H., . . . Simon, N. M. (2013). Loving-kindness meditation practice associated with longer telomeres in women. *Brain, Behavior, and Immunity, 32,* 159–163.

[43] Eyre, H. A., Acevedo, B., Yang, H., Siddarth, P., Van Dyk, K., Ercoli, L., . . . Lavretsky, H. (2016). Changes in neural connectivity and memory following a yoga intervention for older adults: A pilot study. *Journal of Alzheimer's Disease, 52*(2), 673–684.

[44] Schulte, B. (2015, May 26). Harvard neuroscientist: Meditation not only reduces stress, here's how it changes your brain. *Washington Post.* Retrieved from https://www.washingtonpost.com/news/inspired-life/wp/2015/05/26/harvard-neuroscientist-meditation-not-only-reduces-stress-it-literally-changes-your-brain/

[45] Patrick, V. M., & Hagtvedt, H. (2012). "I don't" versus "I can't": When empowered refusal motivates goal-directed behavior. *Journal of Consumer Research, 39*(2), 371–381.

[46] Kushlev, K., & Dunn, E. W. (2015). Checking email less frequently reduces stress. *Computers in Human Behavior, 43*, 220–228.

CHAPTER 9—NATURE DOES THE MIND AND BODY GOOD

[1] Ryan, R. M., Weinstein, N., Bernstein, J., Brown, K. W., Mistretta, L., & Gagné, M. (2010). Vitalizing effects of being outdoors and in nature. *Journal of Environmental Psychology, 30*(2), 159–168.

[2] White, M. P., Alcock, I., Wheeler, B. W., & Depledge, M. H. (2013). Would you be happier living in a greener urban area? A fixed-effects analysis of panel data. *Psychological Science, 24*(6), 920–928.

[3] Beyer, K. M. M., Kaltenbach, A., Szabo, A., Bogar, S., Nieto, F. J., & Malecki, K. M. (2014). Exposure to neighborhood green space and mental health: Evidence from the survey of the health of Wisconsin. *International Journal of Environmental Research and Public Health, 11*(3), 3453–3472.

[4] Bertrand, K. Z., Bialik, M., Virdee, K., Gros, A., & Bar-Yam, Y. (2013, August 20). *Sentiment in New York City: A high resolution spatial and temporal view.* Cambridge, MA: New England Complex Systems Institute. arXiv:1308.5010.

[5] Dravigne, A., Waliczek, T. M., Lineberger, R. D., & Zajicek, J. M. (2008). The effect of live plants and window views of green spaces on employee perceptions of job satisfaction. *HortScience, 43*, 183–187.

[6] Nieuwenhuis, M., Knight, C., Postmes, T., & Haslam, S. A. (2014). The relative benefits of green versus lean office space: Three field experiments. *Journal of Experimental Psychology: Applied, 20*(3), 199–214.

[7] Berman, M. G., Jonides, J., & Kaplan, S. (2008). The cognitive benefits of interacting with nature. *Psychological Science, 19*(12), 1207–1212.

[8] Berman, M. G., Kross, E., Krpan, K. M., Askren, M. K., Burson, A., Deldin, P. J., . . . Jonides, J. (2012). Interacting with nature improves cognition and affect for individuals with depression. *Journal of Affective Disorders, 140*(3), 300–305.

[9] Li, D., & Sullivan, W. C. (2016). Impact of views to school landscapes on recovery from stress and mental fatigue. *Landscape and Urban Planning, 148*, 149–158.

[10] Lee, K. E., Williams, K. J. H., Sargent, L. D., Williams, N. S. G., & Johnson, K. A. (2015). 40-second green roof views sustain attention: The role of micro-breaks in attention restoration. *Journal of Environmental Psychology, 42*, 182.

[11] Aspinall, P., Mavros, P., Coyne, R., & Roe, J. (2015). The urban brain: Analysing outdoor physical activity with mobile EEG. *British Journal of Sports Medicine, 49*, 272–276.

[12] Bratman, G. N., Daily, G. C., Levy, B. J., & Gross, J. J. (2015). The benefits of nature experience: Improved affect and cognition. *Landscape and Urban Planning, 138*, 41–50.

[13] Bratman, G. N., Hamilton, J. P., Hahn, K. S., Daily, G. C., & Gross, J. J. (2015). Nature experience reduces rumination and subgenual prefrontal cortex activation. *Proceedings of the National Academy of Sciences of the United States of America, 112*(28), 8567–8572. doi: 10.1073/pnas.1510459112.

[14] Li, Q. (2010). Effect of forest bathing trips on human immune function. *Environmental Health and Preventive Medicine, 15*(1), 9–17; Park, B. J., Tsunetsugu, Y., Kasetani, T., Kagawa, T., & Miyazaki, Y. (2010). The physiological effects of *shinrin-yoku* (taking in the forest atmosphere or forest bathing): Evidence from field experiments in 24 forests across Japan. *Environmental Health and Preventive Medicine, 15*(1), 18–26.

[15] Grahn, P., & Stigsdotter, U. A. (2003). Landscape planning and stress. *Urban Forestry & Urban Greening, 2*(1), 1–18.

[16] Bhatt, V. (2014, August 12). People living in green neighborhoods are happy: Study. *MDnewsdaily*. Retrieved from https://www.mdnewsdaily.com/articles/1135/20140412/living-around-greenery-makes-you-happy.htm

[17] Van den Berg, M. M. H. E., Maas, J., Muller, R., Braun, A., Kaandorp, W., van Lien, R., . . . van den Berg, A. E. (2015). Autonomic nervous system responses to viewing green and built settings: Differentiating between sympathetic and parasympathetic activity. *International Journal of Environmental Research and Public Health, 12*(12), 15860–15874.

[18] Kim, G.-W., Jeong, G.-W., Kim, T.-H., Baek, H.-S., Oh, S.-K., Kang, H.-K., . . . Song, J.-K. (2010). Functional neuroanatomy associated with natural and urban scenic views in the human brain: 3.0T functional MR imaging. *Korean Journal of Radiology, 11*(5), 507–513.

[19] Ulrich, R. S. (1984). View through a window may influence recovery from surgery. *Science, 224*(4647), 420–421.

[20] Park, S-.H., & Mattson, R. H. (2009). Ornamental indoor plants in hospital rooms enhanced health outcomes of patients recovering from surgery. *Journal of Alternative and Complementary Medicine, 15*(9), 975–980.

[21] Park, S.-H., & Mattson, R. H. (2008). Effects of flowering and foliage plants in hospital rooms on patients recovering from abdominal surgery. *HortTechnology, 18*, 563–568.

[22] Ulrich R. S., Lundén O., & Eltinge J. L. (1993). Effects of exposure to nature and abstract pictures on patients recovering from heart surgery. *Psychophysiology, 30*, 7.

[23] De Vries, S., Verheij, R. A., Groenewegen, P. P., & Spreeuwenberg, P. (2003). Natural environments—healthy environments? An exploratory analysis of the relationship between greenspace and health. *Environment and Planning, 35*(10), 1717–1731.

[24] Brown, S. C., Lombard, J., Wang, K., Byrne, M. M., Toro, M., Plater-Zyberk, E., . . . Szapocznik, J. (2016). Neighborhood greenness and chronic health conditions in Medicare beneficiaries. *American Journal of Preventive Medicine, 51*(1), 78–89.

[25] Shanahan, D. F., Bush, R., Gaston, K. J., Lin, B. B., Dean, J., Barber, E., & Fuller, R. A. (2016). Health benefits from nature experiences depend on dose. *Scientific Reports, 6*, 28551.

[26] James, P., Hart, J. E., Banay, R. F., & Laden, F. (2016). Exposure to greenness and mortality in a nationwide prospective cohort study of women. *Environmental Health Perspectives, 124*, 1344–1352.

[27] Franklin, D. (2012, March 1). How hospital gardens help patients heal. *Scientific American.* Retrieved from https://www.scientificamerican.com/article/nature-that-nurtures/

[28] Nisbet, E. K., & Zelenski, J. M. (2011). Underestimating nearby nature: Affective forecasting errors obscure the happy path to sustainability. *Psychological Science, 22*(9), 1101–1106.

[29] Largo-Wight, E., Chen, W. W., Dodd, V., & Weiler, R. (2011). Healthy workplaces: The effects of nature contact at work on employee stress and health. *Public Health Reports, 126*(Suppl. 1), 124–130.

[30] Passmore, H.-A., & Holder, M. D. (2017). Noticing nature: Individual and social benefits of a two-week intervention. *Journal of Positive Psychology, 12*(6), 537–546.

[31] Van den Berg, A. E., & Custers, M. H. (2011). Gardening promotes neuroendocrine and affective restoration from stress. *Journal of Health Psychology, 16*(1), 3–11.

[32] Soga, M., Gaston, K. J., & Yamaura, Y. (2017). Gardening is beneficial for health: A meta-analysis. *Preventive Medicine Reports, 5*, 92–99.

[33] Ulrich, R. S. (1983). Natural versus urban scenes: Some psychophysiological effects. *Environment and Behavior, 13*, 523–556; White, M., Smith, A., Humphryes, K., Pahl, S., Cracknell, D., & Depledge, M. (2010). Blue space: The importance of water for preferences, affect and restorativeness ratings of natural and built scenes. *Journal of Environmental Psychology, 30*, 482–493.

CHAPTER 10—SPEND MONEY WISELY:
TAKE A TRIP, SEE A PLAY, GO TO A GAME

[1] Böll, H. (2011). *The collected stories*. Brooklyn, NJ: Melville House Books

[2] Brickman, P., Coates, D., & Janoff-Bulman, R. (1978). Lottery winners and accident victims: Is happiness relative? *Journal of Personality and Social Psychology, 36*(8), 917–927.

[3] Graham, C. (2012). *Happiness around the world: The paradox of happy peasants and miserable millionaires*. New York: Oxford University Press, 214.

[4] Brooks, D. (2011). *The social animal: The hidden sources of love, character, and achievement*. New York: Random House.

[5] Kahneman, D., & Deaton, A. (2010). High income improves evaluation of life but not emotional well-being. *Proceedings of the National Academy of Sciences of the United States of America, 107*(38), 16489–16493.

[6] Kahneman, D., Krueger, A. B., Schkade, D., Schwarz, N., & Stone, A. A. (2006, June 30). Would you be happier if you were richer? A focusing illusion. *Science*, 1908–1910.

[7] Haushofer, J., & Shapiro, J. (2016). The short-term impact of unconditional cash transfers to the poor: Experimental evidence from Kenya. *Quarterly Journal of Economics, 131*(4), 1973–2042.

[8] Dittmar, H., Bond, R., Hurst, M., & Kasser, T. (2014). The relationship between materialism and personal well-being: A meta-analysis. *Journal of Personality and Social Psychology*, 107(5), 879–924; Kasser, T. (2002). *The high price of materialism*. Boston: MIT Press.

[9] Carroll, J. S., Dean, L. R., Call, L. L., & Busby, D. M. (2011). Materialism and marriage: Couple profiles of congruent and incongruent spouses. *Journal of Couple & Relationship Therapy, 10*(4), 287–308.

[10] Bauer, M. A., Wilkie, J. E. B., Kim, J. K., & Bodenhausen, G. V. (2012). Cuing Consumerism: Situational materialism undermines personal and social well-being. *Psychological Science, 23*(5), 517–523.

[11] Corless, R. (1989). *The vision of Buddhism: The space under the tree*. New York: Paragon House.

[12] Franklin, B. (1998). *Benjamin Franklin: Wit and wisdom*. White Plains, NY: Peter Pauper Press.

[13] Kahneman, D., Krueger, A. B., Schkade, D. A., Schwarz, N., & Stone, A. A. (2004, December 3). A survey method for characterizing daily life experience: The day reconstruction method. *Science*, 1776–1780.

[14] Bianchi, E. C., & Vohs, K. D. (2016). Social class and social worlds: Income predicts the frequency and nature of social contact. *Social Psychological and Personality Science, 7*(5), 479–486.

[15] Piff, P. K., & Moskowitz, J. (2018). Wealth, poverty, and happiness: Social class is differentially associated with positive emotions. *Emotion, 18*, 902–905.

[16] Sliwa, J. (2017, December 18). How much people earn is associated with how they experience happiness. *American Psychological Association.* Retrieved from http://www.apa.org/news/press/releases/2017/12/earn-happiness.aspx

[17] Van Boven, L., & Gilovich, T. (2003). To do or to have? That is the question. *Journal of Personality and Social Psychology, 85*(6), 1193–1202.

[18] Weed, J. (2016, December 12). Gifts that Santa, the world traveler, would love. *New York Times.* Retrieved from https://www.nytimes.com/2016/12/12/business/gifts-that-santa-the-world-traveler-would-love.html

[19] Pchelin, P., & Howell, R. T. (2014). The hidden cost of value-seeking: People do not accurately forecast the economic benefits of experiential purchases. *Journal of Positive Psychology, 9*(4), 332–334.

[20] Nowlis, S. M., Mandel, N., & McCabe, D. B. (2004). The effect of a delay between choice and consumption on consumption enjoyment. *Journal of Consumer Research, 31*(3), 502–510.

[21] Kumar, A., Killingsworth, M. A. & Gilovich, T. (2014). Waiting for Merlot: Anticipatory consumption of experiential and material purchases. *Psychological Science, 25*(10), 1924–1931.

[22] Krakauer, J. (1997). *Into the wild.* New York: Anchor Books.

[23] Caprariello, P. A., & Reis, H. T. (2013). To do, to have, or to share? Valuing experiences over material possessions depends on the involvement of others. *Journal of Personality and Social Psychology, 104*(2), 199–215.

[24] Kumar, A. & Gilovich, T. (2015). Some "thing" to talk about? Differential story utility from experiential and material purchases. *Personality and Social Psychology Bulletin, 41*(10), 1320–1331.

[25] Hershfield, H. E., Mogilner, C., & Barnea, U. (2016). People who choose time over money are happier. *Social Psychological and Personality Science, 7*(7), 697–706; Whillans, A. V., Dunn, E. W., Smeets, P., Bekkers, R., & Norton, M. I. (2017). Buying time promotes happiness. *Proceedings of the National Academy of Sciences of the United States of America, 114*(32), 8523–8527.

[26] Whillans, A. V., Weidman, A. C., & Dunn, E. W. (2016). Valuing time over money is associated with greater happiness. *Social Psychological and Personality Science, 7*, 213–222.

27 Diehl, K., Zauberman, G., & Barasch, A. (2016). How taking photos increases enjoyment of experiences. *Journal of Personality and Social Psychology, 111*(2), 119–140.

28 Nawijn, J., Marchand, M. A., Veenhoven, R., & Vingerhoets, A. J. (2010). Vacationers happier, but most not happier after a holiday. *Applied Research in Quality of Life, 5*(1), 35–47.

29 Van Boven, L., & Ashworth, L. (2007). Looking forward, looking back: Anticipation is more evocative than retrospection. *Journal of Experimental Psychology: General, 136*(2), 289–300.

CHAPTER 11—GIVE A GIFT—TO ANYONE

1 Santi, J. (2015, December 1). The science behind the power of giving (op-ed). *LiveScience*. Retrieved from https://www.livescience.com/52936-need-to-give-boosted-by-brain-science-and-evolution.html

2 Dunn, E. W., Aknin, B. B., & Norton, M. I. (2008). Spending money on others promotes happiness. *Science, 21*, 1687–1688.

3 Aknin, L. B., Barrington-Leigh, C. P., Dunn, E. W., Helliwell, J. F., Burns, J., Biswas-Diener, R., . . . Norton, M. I. (2013). Prosocial spending and well-being: Cross-cultural evidence for a psychological universal. *Journal of Personality and Social Psychology, 104*(4), 635–652.

4 Dunn, E. W., Aknin, L. B., & Norton, M. I. (2008, March 21). Spending money on others promotes happiness. *Science, 21*, 1687–1688.

5 Deaton, A. (2008). Income, health, well-being around the world: Evidence from the Gallup World Poll. *Journal of Economic Perspectives, 22*, 53–72.

6 Aknin, L. B., Dunn, E. W., Sandstrom, G. M., & Norton, M. I. (2013). Does social connection turn good deeds into good feelings? On the value of putting the 'social' in prosocial spending. *International Journal of Happiness and Development, 1*(2), 155–171.

7 Dulin, P. L., Gavala, J., Stephens, C., Kostick, M., & McDonald, J. (2012). Volunteering predicts happiness among older Māori and non-Māori in the New Zealand health, work, and retirement longitudinal study. *Aging & Mental Health, 16*(5), 617–624.

8 Borgonovi, F. (2008). Doing well by doing good. The relationship between formal volunteering and self-reported health and happiness. *Social Science & Medicine, 66*(11), 2321–2334.

9 McCann, S. J. H. (2017). Higher USA state resident neuroticism is associated with lower state volunteering rates. *Personality and Social Psychology Bulletin, 43*(12), 1659–1674.

[10] Twain, M. (1935). *Mark Twain's notebook*. New York: Harper & Brothers.

[11] Cunningham, M. R., Steinberg, J., & Grev, R. (1980). Wanting to and having to help: Separate motivations for positive mood and guilt-induced helping. *Journal of Personality and Social Psychology, 38*, 181–192.

[12] Aknin, L. B., Hamlin, J. K., & Dunn, E. W. (2012). Giving leads to happiness in young children. *PLOS One, 7*(6): e39211.

[13] Moll, J., Krueger, F., Zahn, R., Pardini, M., de Oliveira-Souza, R., & Grafman, J. (2006). Human fronto-mesolimbic networks guide decisions about charitable donation. *Proceedings of the National Academy of Sciences of the United States of America, 103*(42), 15623–15628.

[14] Harbaugh, W. T., Mayr, U., & Burghart, D. R. (2007, June 15). Neural responses to taxation and voluntary giving reveal motives for charitable donations. *Science*, 1622–1625.

[15] Sullivan, G. B., & Sullivan, M. J. (1997). Promoting wellness in cardiac rehabilitation: Exploring the role of altruism. *Journal of Cardiovascular Nursing, 11*(3), 43–52; Ironson, G., Solomon, G. F., Balbin, E. G., O'Cleirigh, C., George, A., Kumar, M., . . . Woods, T. E. (2002). The Ironson-Woods Spirituality/Religiousness Index is associated with long survival, health behaviors, less distress, and low cortisol in people with HIV/AIDS. *Annals of Behavioral Medicine, 24*(1), 34–48.

[16] Whillans, A. V., Dunn, E. W., Sandstrom, G. M., Dickerson, S. S., & Madden, K. M. (2016). Is spending money on others good for your heart? *Health Psychology, 35*(6), 574–583.

[17] Piferi, R. L., & Lawler, K. A. (2006). Social support and ambulatory blood pressure: An examination of both receiving and giving. *International Journal of Psychophysiology, 62*(2), 328–336.

[18] Raposa, E. B., Laws, H. B., & Ansell, E. B. (2016). Prosocial behavior mitigates the negative effects of stress in everyday life. *Clinical Psychological Science, 4*(4), 691–698.

[19] Inagaki, T. K., & Eisenberger, N. I. (2016). Giving support to others reduces sympathetic nervous system-related responses to stress. *Psychophysiology, 53*(4), 427–435; Brown, S. L., Fredrickson, B. L., Wirth, M. M., Poulin, M. J., Meier, E. A., Heaphy, E. D., . . . Schultheiss, O. C. (2009). Social closeness increases salivary progesterone in humans. *Hormones and Behavior, 56*(1), 108–111.

[20] Brown, S. L., Nesse, R. M., Vinokur, A. D., & Smith, D. M. (2003). Providing social support may be more beneficial than receiving it: Results from a prospective study of mortality. *Psychological Science, 14*(4), 320–327.

[21] Oman, D., Thoresen, C. E., & McMahon, K. (1999). Volunteerism and mortality among the community-dwelling elderly. *Journal of Health Psychology, 4*(3), 301–316.

[22] Poulin, M. J., Brown, S. L., Dillard, A. J., & Smith, D. M. (2013). Giving to others and the association between stress and mortality. *American Journal of Public Health, 103*(9), 1649–1655.

[23] Weinstein, N., & Ryan, R. M. (2010). When helping helps: Autonomous motivation for prosocial behavior and its influence on well-being for the helper and recipient. *Journal of Personality and Social Psychology, 98*(2), 222–244.

[24] Poulin, M. J. (2014). Volunteering predicts health among those who value others: Two national studies. *Health Psychology, 33*(2), 120–129.

[25] Konrath, S., Fuhrel-Forbis, A., Lou, A., & Brown, S. (2012). Motives for volunteering are associated with mortality risk in older adults. *Health Psychology, 31*(1), 87–96.

[26] Buchanan, K. E., & Bardi, A. (2010). Acts of kindness and acts of novelty affect life satisfaction. *Journal of Social Psychology, 150*(3), 235–237.

[27] Aknin, L, B., Dunn, E. W., Whillans, A. V., Grant, A. M., & Norton, M. I. (2013). Making a difference matters: Impact unlocks the emotional benefits of prosocial spending. *Journal of Economic Behavior & Organization, 88*, 90–95.

[28] Seligman, M. E. P., Steen, T. T., Park, N., & Peterson, C. (2005). Positive psychology progress: Empirical validation of interventions. *American Psychologist, 60*, 410–421.

CHAPTER 12—BUILD RELATIONSHIPS: ALL YOU NEED IS LOVE

[1] Gawande, A. (2014). *Being mortal: Medicine and what matters in the end*. New York: Metropolitan Books.

[2] Gilbert, D. (2007, June 12). What is happiness? *Big Think*. Retrieved from https://bigthink.com/videos/what-is-happiness

[3] Vaillant, G. E. (2002). *Aging well: Surprising guideposts to a happier life from the landmark Harvard study of adult development*. Boston: Little, Brown.

[4] Mehl, M. R., Vazire, S., Holleran, S. E., & Clark, C. S. (2010). Eavesdropping on happiness: Well-being is related to having less small talk and more substantive conversations. *Psychological Science, 21*(4), 539–541.

[5] Venaglia, R. B., & Lemay, E. P., Jr. (2017). Hedonic benefits of close and distant interaction partners: The mediating roles of social approval and authenticity. *Personality and Social Psychology Bulletin, 43*(9), 1255–1267.

[6] Sandstrom, G. M., & Dunn, E. W. (2014). Social interactions and well-being: The surprising power of weak ties. *Personality and Social Psychology Bulletin, 40*(7), 910–922.

[7] Epley, N., & Schroeder, J. (2014). Mistakenly seeking solitude. *Journal of Experimental Psychology: General, 143*(5), 1980–1999.

[8] Lambert, N. M., Gwinn, A. M., Baumeister, R. F., Strachman, A., Washburn, I. J., Gable, S. L., & Fincham, F. D. (2013). A boost of positive affect: The perks of sharing positive experiences. *Journal of Social and Personal Relationships, 30*, 24–43.

[9] Smith, M. (2000). *The letters of Charlotte Brontë: With a selection of letters by family and friends* (Vol. 2, 1848–1851). Oxford: Oxford University Press.

[10] Boothby, E., Clark, M. S., & Bargh, J. A. (2014). Shared experiences are amplified. *Psychological Science, 25*(12), 2209–2216.

[11] Lambert, N. M., Gwinn, A. M., Baumeister, R. F., Strachman, A., Washburn, I. J., Gable, S. L., & Fincham, F. D. (2013). A boost of positive affect: The perks of sharing positive experiences. *Journal of Social and Personal Relationships, 30*, 24–43.

[12] Stone, A. A., Schwartz, J. E., Broderick, J. E., & Deaton, A. (2010). A snapshot of the age distribution of psychological well-being in the United States. *Proceedings of the National Academy of Sciences of the United States of America, 107*(22), 9985–9990.

[13] U-bend of life, the. (2010, December 16). *Economist*. Retrieved from https://www.economist.com/christmas-specials/2010/12/16/the-u-bend-of-life

[14] English, T., & Carstensen, L. L. (2014). Selective narrowing of social networks across adulthood is associated with improved emotional experience in daily life. *International Journal of Behavioral Development, 38*(2), 195–202.

[15] Fredrickson, B. L., & Carstensen, L. L. (1990). Choosing social partners: How old age and anticipated endings make people more selective. *Psychology and Aging, 5*(3), 335–347.

[16] Carstensen, L. L., & Fredrickson, B. L. (1998). Influence of HIV status and age on cognitive representations of others. *Health Psychology, 17*(6), 494–503.

[17] Yang, Y. C., Boen, C., Gerken, K., Li, T., Schorpp, K., & Harris, K. M. (2016). Social relationships and physiological determinants of longevity across the human life span. *Proceedings of the National Academy of Sciences of the United States of America, 113*(3), 578–583.

[18] Orth-Gomér, K., Rosengren, A., & Wilhelmsen, L. (1993). Lack of social support and incidence of coronary heart disease in middle-aged Swedish men. *Psychosomatic Medicine, 55*(1), 37–43.

[19] Holt-Lunstad, J., Smith, T. B., & Layton, J. B. (2010). Social relationships and mortality risk: A meta-analytic review. *PLOS Medicine, 7*(7), e1000316.

[20] Berkman, L. F., & Syme, S. L. (1979). Social networks, host resistance, and mortality: A nine-year follow-up study of Alameda County residents. *American Journal of Epidemiology, 109*(2), 186–204.

[21] Giles, L., Glonek, G., Luszcz, M., & Andrews, G. (2005). Effect of social networks on 10 year survival in very old Australians: The Australian longitudinal study of aging. *Journal of Epidemiology and Community Health, 59*(7), 574–579.

[22] Kroenke, C. H., Kubzansky, L. D., Schernhammer, E. S., Holmes, M. D., & Kawachi, I. (2006). Social networks, social support, and survival after breast cancer diagnosis. *Journal of Clinical Oncology, 24*(7), 1105–1111.

[23] Ruberman, W., Weinblatt, E., Goldberg, J. D., & Chaudhary, B. S. (1984). Psychosocial influences on mortality after myocardial infarction. *New England Journal of Medicine, 311*(9), 552–559.

[24] Brummett, B. H., Barefoot, J. C., Siegler, I. C., Clapp-Channing, N. E., Lytle, B. L., Bosworth, H. B., . . . Mark, D. B. (2001). Characteristics of socially isolated patients with coronary artery disease who are at elevated risk for mortality. *Psychosomatic Medicine, 63*(2), 267–272.

[25] Rosengren, A., Orth-Gomér, K., Wedel, H., & Wilhelmsen, L. (1993). Stressful life events, social support, and mortality in men born in 1933. *BMJ: British Medical Journal, 307*(6912), 1102–1105.

[26] Coan, J. A., Schaefer, H. S., & Davidson, R. J. (2006). Lending a hand: Social regulation of the neural response to threat. *Psychological Science, 17*(12), 1032–1039.

[27] Cohen, S., Janicki-Deverts, D., Turner, R. B., & Doyle, W. J. (2015). Does hugging provide stress-buffering social support? A study of susceptibility to upper respiratory infection and illness. *Psychological Science, 26*(2), 135–147.

[28] Hawkley, L. C., & Cacioppo, J. T. (2010). Loneliness matters: A theoretical and empirical review of consequences and mechanisms. *Annals of Behavioral Medicine, 40*(2), 218–227.

[29] Perissinotto, C. M., Cenzer, I. S., & Covinsky, K. E. (2012). Loneliness in older persons: A predictor of functional decline and death. *Archives of Internal Medicine, 172*(14), 1078–1083; Valtorta, N. K., Kanaan, M., Gilbody, S., Ronzi, S., & Hanratty, B. (2016). Loneliness and social isolation as risk factors for coronary heart disease and stroke: Systematic review and meta-analysis of longitudinal observational studies. *Heart, 102*, 1009–1016.

[30] Murthy, V. (2017, September 27). Work and the loneliness epidemic. *Harvard Business Review*. Retrieved from https://hbr.org/cover-story/2017/09/work-and-the-loneliness-epidemic

[31] Teo, A. R., Choi, H., & Valenstein, M. (2013). Social relationships and depression: Ten-year follow-up from a nationally representative study. *PLOS One, 8*(4), e62396.

[32] Birmingham, W. C., Uchino, B. N., Smith, T. W., Light, K. C., & Butner, J. (2015). It's complicated: Marital ambivalence on ambulatory blood pressure and daily interpersonal functioning. *Annals of Behavioral Medicine, 49*(5), 743–753.

[33] King, K. B., & Reis, H. T. (2012). Marriage and long-term survival after coronary artery bypass grafting. *Health Psychology, 31*(1), 55–62; King, K. B., Reis, H. T., Porter, L. A., & Norsen, L. H. (1993). Social support and long-term recovery from coronary artery surgery: Effects on patients and spouses. *Health Psychology, 12*(1), 56–63.

[35] Bakalar, N. (2008, April 1). Patterns: Another reason to choose a mate wisely. *New York Times.* Retrieved from https://www.nytimes.com/2008/04/01/health/research/01patt.html

[35] American Time Use Survey Summary. (2018, June 28). Bureau of Labor Statistics. Retrieved from https://www.bls.gov/news.release/atus.nr0.htm/

[36] Przybylski, A. K., & Weinstein, N. (2012). Can you connect with me now? How the presence of mobile communication technology influences face-to-face conversation quality. *Journal of Social and Personal Relationships, 30*(3), 237–246.

[37] Misra, S., Cheng, L., Genevie, J., & Yuan, M. (2014). The iPhone effect: The quality of in-person social interactions in the presence of mobile devices. *Environment and Behavior, 48*(2), 275–298.

[38] Mubanga, M., Byberg, L., Nowak, C., Egenvall, A., Magnusson, P. K., Ingelsson, E., & Fall, T. (2017). Dog ownership and the risk of cardiovascular disease and death—a nationwide cohort study. *Scientific Reports, 7*(1), 15821.

[39] Siegel, J. M. (1990). Stressful life events and use of physician services among the elderly: The moderating role of pet ownership. *Journal of Personality and Social Psychology, 58*(6), 1081–1086.

[40] Müller, C. A., Schmitt, K., Barber, A. L. A., & Huber L. (2015). Dogs can discriminate emotional expressions of human faces. *Current Biology, 25*(5), 601–605.

[41] Tolstoy, L. (2003). *Anna Karenina: A novel in eight parts* (R. Pevear & L. Volokhonsky, Trans.). London: Penguin.

CONCLUSION

[1] Zuckerman, M., Kolin, E. A., Price, L., & Zoob, I. (1964). Development of a sensation-seeking scale. *Journal of Consulting Psychology, 28*(6), 477–482.

[2] Faber, F. W. (1860). *Spiritual conferences.* London: Thomas Richardson and Son.

Index

I

J

K

L

S

About the Author

CATHERINE A. SANDERSON is the Manwell Family Professor of Life Sciences (Psychology) at Amherst College in Amherst, Massachusetts. She received a bachelor's degree with honors in psychology and a specialization in health and development from Stanford University, and received both master's and doctoral degrees in psychology from Princeton University.

Photo by Jo Chattman

Professor Sanderson's research examines how personality and social variables influence health-related behaviors, the development of persuasive messages and interventions to prevent unhealthy behavior, and the predictors of relationship satisfaction. This research has received grant funding from the National Science Foundation and the National Institute of Health.

She has served on multiple editorial boards, as a member of the GRE psychology committee with the Educational Testing Service (ETS), and as a consultant for the American Medical College. In 2012 she was named one of the country's top three hundred professors by the Princeton Review. Professor Sanderson has published more than twenty-five journal articles and book chapters in addition to four college textbooks, middle school and high school health textbooks, and a book on parenting.

Professor Sanderson speaks regularly for public and corporate audiences on topics such as the science of happiness, the power of emotional intelligence, the mind-body connection, and the psychology of good and evil; more information about these presentations can be found on her website, SandersonSpeaking.com. These talks have been featured in numerous mainstream media outlets, including the *Washington Post*, the *Boston Globe*, the *Atlantic*, and *CBS Sunday Morning with Jane Pauley*.

She lives with her husband, Bart Hollander, and their three children—Andrew, Robert, and Caroline—in Hadley, Massachusetts.